MUSIC LUST

MUSIC
LUST

NIC HARCOURT

RECOMMENDED LISTENING FOR EVERY
MOOD, MOMENT, AND REASON

SASQUATCH BOOKS
SEATTLE

Printed in the United States of America
Published by Sasquatch Books
Distributed by Publishers Group West
10 09 08 07 06 05   10 9 8 7 6 5 4 3 2 1

Cover photograph: Elke Van De Velde/elkevandevelde.com
Series and interior design: Rowen Moore
Cover design and interior composition: William Quinby
Back cover photo: Larry Hirshowitz

Library of Congress Cataloging-in-Publication Data
Harcourt, Nic.
    Music lust : recommended listening for every mood, moment, and reason / Nic Harcourt.
        p. cm.
    Includes index.
    ISBN 1-57061-437-7
    1. Sound recordings—Reviews. 2. Sound recordings—
Discography. 3. Popular music—Reviews. 4. Popular music—
Discography. I. Title.

ML156.9.H23 2005
016.78164'0266—dc22
                                                    2005042591

Sasquatch Books
119 South Main Street, Suite 400
Seattle, WA 98104
(206) 467-4300
www.sasquatchbooks.com
custserv@sasquatchbooks.com

For Sam and Luna
(How'd I get so lucky to be your dad?)

Contents

INTRODUCTION

My first memory of music was the fuss my mum and dad made about the Beatles. It must have been 1963 and I was five years old. My parents, whose own childhood had been interrupted by World War II, were young adults when rock and roll happened in the 1950s, and as the black-and-white world of postwar England suddenly burst into color, they were caught up in the moment, like most young people. My dad was an on-camera journalist working for ATV, the independent television company that covered the British Midlands from Birmingham. This was back in the day when there were just two channels, the other channel being the BBC (in black and white, I might add); at that time, it actually meant something to be on TV. My dad would bring home promo 7-inch 45s by the hot bands of the day, which included the Beatles, Gerry and the Pacemakers, Petula Clark, the Rolling Stones, and others. But it was the Beatles' songs that got me. In fact, when my parents separated when I was about seven, after my mum told me that my dad was going to live somewhere else, my initial reaction was "Did he leave the Beatles records?"

My mum bought me my first album on my eighth birthday: the Beatles' **Help!**. A year later when their next album, **Sgt. Pepper's Lonely Hearts Club Band**, was released, I emptied out my money box and found fifteen shillings; the album cost thirty shillings though, so my mum came up with the other half, and we split the cost of that groundbreaking album. (This was before the UK decimalized its currency, but either way that'd be about $2.50 U.S. today.)

I had been given a portable transistor radio around this time, and I would listen under the covers at night to two stations, Radio Luxembourg (which broadcast from that small country in Europe) and Radio Caroline (a pirate station operating from a ship in the international waters of the North Sea). Funny thing is, I don't remember the music, just commercials for a record by comedian Freddy "Parrot Face" Davies, but unbeknownst to me, a seed had been planted. At that time the BBC didn't have a station devoted purely to pop music; there was no commercial radio in Britain until 1972.

My next musical memory was seeing Jimi Hendrix on the weekly television chart show *Top of the Pops* and being mesmerized—and, I think, a little scared. I'd never seen anybody like him before, a wild-looking black man wailing on his guitar and singing the blues. By the time I was thirteen glam was happening. T. Rex, David Bowie, the Sweet, Elton John, and Slade were among the bands and performers I fell in love with. With my limited pocket money I could afford one single a week, and so off I'd head to the local record store at WH Smith on Saturday mornings to pick up something that was on the charts. My first live show was around this time as well: I'm not ashamed of admitting it was Gary Glitter at the Birmingham Town Hall. It was also around this time that I began listening to BBC Radio for live Saturday-night concert broadcasts (some of which I would tape on reel to reel) and the weekly chart countdown on BBC on Sunday nights; Thursday nights at 7:30 I'd watch *Top of the Pops* on TV.

One afternoon, an older kid at school said that he wanted to play me some music. We went down into the school's basement, where there were a couple of recreation rooms, table tennis, and a record player. He told me to close my eyes and listen, then he put on side 1 of **Led Zeppelin IV**. It was one of those moments that can never be fully described with words, but suffice it to say that the way I heard music was changed forever. My mind was blown and my teenybopper days were over. Within a short period of time I owned albums by Black Sabbath, Pink Floyd, Genesis, Uriah Heep, and more. I remember trading all my toy Matchbox and Hot Wheels cars to buy **Machine Head** by Deep Purple on the day it was released, something I kind of regret doing now! And so at fifteen I wore my ripped, flared jeans with their smiley patches and hung out in cafes like all generations of young people do, trying desperately to figure out how to get a girlfriend and deal with all the wonder and awkwardness of being a teenager.

I dropped out of school at sixteen and began living in a town about twenty miles north of Birmingham called Lichfield, working in a factory making concrete blocks. With hindsight it's clear that I was stagnating in many ways—including being stuck in that musical place called progressive rock—and then the Sex Pistols and punk rock exploded. I have to admit that I didn't really get it at first until another of those "moments" happened. It was 1979 and I was twenty-one, when a friend I'd been to school with, Dicky Bannister, played me the Clash's **London Calling**, and right there, once again, my third eye got a squeegee!

Around the same time, myself, Dicky, and another school friend Martin Johnson, both of whom played guitar, were sitting around with a few other friends one night in the local pub when Dick and Martin decided that it was time they put a group together. Naturally, as a failed guitar player myself, I volunteered to sing. We recruited another friend Steve Thompson to play bass, and voilà! We had a group we called Bloop! (The drummer's seat changed several times throughout the band's two-year history, eventually settling with a younger guy, Jacko.) We rehearsed once a week in a small cold barn on a farm just outside of town, playing mostly the Who, Stones, and Eddie Cochran covers to start with, before we started working on our own material. We played our first few gigs for beer money, changed the name to Red Cassette, recorded some demos (which are today safely under lock and key), and did what bands do—rehearse, fight, drink too much, chase girls, and break up. It was a crazy time.

I formed another group a few months later, around the time of the New Romantic movement, called Decadance, which was followed by an experimental band (we smoked a lot of pot, had TVs going on stage, and basically made up our songs as we went along) called the Kissing Frogs. But my personal life was in something of a crisis and I couldn't really get it together. I decided to leave England and go to Europe. You can make those kinds of decisions when you're twenty-four.

After bumming around Greece and Turkey for a summer, I met an Australian girl called Sue who I married and followed down under to Brisbane, where I pretty much quit being involved with music (apart from making mix tapes . . . does that count?) and spent a mostly miserable five and a half years. I did, however, listen to a lot of radio, two radio stations in particular: FM 104, the big rock station in town, and 4ZZZ, the college station on the University of Queensland campus. I discovered some great music, bands like the Riptides, the Warumpi Band, and the Go-Betweens, as well as groups like Midnight Oil, INXS, and Crowded House before they broke internationally. I did try to put a band together with a couple of guys that I worked with, but we were never quite able to get the party out of the garage.

When my marriage ended, and with my tail between my legs, I wasn't quite ready to head back to England. So I came to the States to visit a friend who'd been in the Kissing Frogs and who was now living and working on his music in Woodstock in upstate

New York. And that's where this story now settles into some kind of order. There was (and still is) a very cool independently owned radio station in Woodstock called WDST, and when I arrived in town in the fall of 1988 the station's format was a mix of progressive free-form music, jazz, and classical shows. As I'd arrived with everything I owned, including my record collection—which at this point was mainly Australian bands—my friend suggested that I approach the station and ask them if they'd let me do an Australian show. To my great surprise the program director then, Richard Fusco, was interested, and although I never got to do the Australian show, I did eventually get hired as a part-time DJ. I realized pretty quickly that I'd finally found something I loved.

I worked at WDST for about eight years. It was during an amazingly creative and exciting time in American radio when "alternative" music was breaking into the mainstream. My own musical palette also expanded during these years, as I discovered not only new music but also classic American artists like Bob Dylan and the Band. During my time there I learned my trade, and after a few years I became the morning show host, then music director, and finally the program director. WDST has always been regarded as a station that takes chances when it comes to spotting trends and playing new music, and I consider myself very fortunate to have cut my radio teeth there. I guess I developed a reputation myself, as well, after giving early play to artists like Alanis Morrisette, Semisonic, and Moby.

In the spring of 1998 I was a comfortable medium-size fish living in a small pond, when quite unexpectedly the opportunity to move to Los Angeles to become music director and host of the daily show *Morning Becomes Eclectic* at public radio station KCRW came up. My girlfriend, who is a wonderfully gifted songwriter and performer in her own right (see for yourself at www.abbaroland.com), and I agonized over the move. But ultimately we realized that we were at one of those crossroads in life where you just have to jump and trust that the universe will take care of you, and it has.

KCRW has a huge reputation as a taste-making station. Being in Los Angeles, the station has a fair amount of movers and shakers in its audience who use the music programming as a resource. Consequently, music played on KCRW finds its way into the mainstream. It took a year or so for me to settle in at the station and for Abba and myself to find the right place to call home. Los Angeles can be a harsh place to live; we now live in the hills of Topanga Canyon. Since I've been in LA, I've had the good fortune to help expose some amazing talents to the world through my radio programs. I've helped put music into commercials, TV shows, and movies, and now I've written this book. It's all a long way from Birmingham.

So, what is *Music Lust*? It's a book of recommendations. I've put together some essays and some lists of albums that I think are worth your attention. Chances are you won't like everything, and chances are that you'll already know some of the musicians and albums in a few of the categories—however, I'm sure you'll make at least a few discoveries along the way. As with any personal recommendations, the lineup is, well, personal. We start with a brief history of Afro-beat and end with an introduction to Frank Zappa. Along the way we look at brothers who've made music together, naughty girls, nice girls, artists named after cats and dogs, music to make out to, and much more.

What *Music Lust* is not: It's not a guide. If you're looking for the history of jazz, for example, it's not here. There are hundreds of books that cover jazz in great detail. I do, though, have a few essays that give a little background on some of the jazz giants and recommend an album by each artist. Or, if you're looking for the history of sixties music, again, it's not here, but I have a list of what I think are the top 20 albums from that decade.

All entries show original release dates and the record label the album is currently available on. (Note: While I believe that the label information is accurate, it is possible that with reissues I may have missed something.) To the best of my knowledge almost every album in *Music Lust* is available on CD; at least they were at the time of writing. Exceptions are noted in the text.

At the end of the day, whether music makes you think, throw your body around in wild abandon, or just tap your toes, I think you'll find something new to lust for here. The book is at times random, but then so is life. I hope you enjoy it.

ACKNOWLEDGMENTS

Music has enriched my life in so many ways that to be asked to write a book recommending some of my favorite albums was an honor. In compiling the various categories and lists, in an attempt to be as accurate as possible with record label and release dates, I referred to a number of publications and Web sites, most notably Allmusic.com, a wonderful online resource, and *The Rolling Stone Album Guide.* I also referred to the *New Grove Dictionary of Jazz*, the Internet Movie Database (IMDB. com), and Amazon.com, as well as numerous artist and record label Web sites.

I am extremely grateful to all of the staff at Sasquatch Books, in particular to Terence Maikels, who asked me if I would like to write the book and ever so gently helped this first-time writer through the process; Kurt Stephan, who provided enthusiasm and guidance; Diane Sepanski, my copy editor, who challenged me to think about what I was saying; William Quinby, who designed the book; Laura Gronewold, who proofread it; and Michael Ferreira, who indexed it. I'd also like to thank Gina Johnston, Sarah Franklin, and Sarah Hanson for their help in getting the word out about the book.

Thank you also to all of the staff and volunteers at KCRW who make me look good every day and especially to Ruth Seymour, who gave me the opportunity of a lifetime; Ariana Morgenstern, the producer of *Morning Becomes Eclectic*; and Debbie Adler, the station's music publicist. On a personal note this book would not exist had I not received support and guidance at key moments in my life from the following people: Eddie Eccles, Geoff Hurley and Tony Deller (I miss you TD), Angela and Stephanie Clarke, Julie Spence, Steve Thompson and Ian Lowe in Lichfield, Ike Phillips, Richard Fusco, Gary Chetkof and Mark Zip from my WDST days, Susan Barnes, Crystal Kingston, and Delcy Steffy for love along the road. Thanks to Michael Blankshen and Rob Sanducci for their ears. Thanks also to Karen Glauber and Robert Urband for mentoring me without my asking and to David and Leah Roland for their support.

For many years my mum Olive has said to me "Tell them your mother thinks you're wonderful"; my thanks to her for unconditional love and support. Thanks to my dad Reg for his help with "Livin' Large: The Big Band Boom!" Thanks also to Anne and Jennifer Harcourt. Special thanks and gratitude to my girlfriend and partner Abba for arriving in my life right on time in 1992 and challenging me to be a better man every day, and to our wonderful twins Sam and Luna for showing up in 2003 and enriching my life in ways I could never have imagined.

Finally, my sincere thanks to all of the songwriters and musicians whose words and music have touched my life.

AFRO-BEAT: THE POLITICAL DANCE

In the 1960s African musicians began incorporating Western jazz and pop styles into their traditional percussion-heavy music. From Nigeria came "Afro-beat," a musical style that fused guitar and horn–based grooves into long, winding jams. It has inspired people to not only dance but also, through its overtly political lyrics, to be aware of their social circumstances and responsibilities.

The originator of Afro-beat was **FELA ANIKULAPO KUTI**, born in Nigeria of well-to-do parents whose political beliefs were firmly against the colonial domination of the continent. In the late 1950s he was sent to school in England, where he enrolled in music school and formed a band, Koola Lobitos, that played around London in the early sixties with Fela on saxophone and vocals. When he returned home in 1963, he formed another band with the same name that he brought to the United States in 1970 to perform and record. During that time he became aware of the American Black Nationalist movement and the teachings of activists such as Malcolm X. As a result, Fela incorporated his rediscovered political awareness into the music of the band, which he renamed **NIGERIA 70**.

On the band's return to West Africa, he became a voice for the poor and a champion of the less privileged. This led through the years to various arrests and exiles as the military government in Nigeria sought to keep him quiet. At one point his home was raided by soldiers, he and his family were beaten (his elderly mother eventually died from injuries sustained in the attack), and his studio burned down. He nonetheless continued throughout the eighties to be politically active and a thorn in the side of successive Nigerian governments.

While the impact on his countrymen is probably his most important legacy, he also left a major imprint on the musical landscape, with bands like Talking Heads and the Red Hot Chili Peppers citing him as an influence. Fela Kuti passed away in 1997. I would recommend readers learn more about both his life and music, as I think his influence will be felt for years to come. (For a start, read the biography *Fela: The Life & Times of an African Musical Icon* by Michael E. Veal.) A good portion of his back catalog has been remastered and reissued in recent years by MCA/Universal, and a good place to start would be **Confusion**, originally released in 1975 on Polydor. The album showcases the band (with original drummer and key collaborator Tony Allen) at their best, with long jamlike arrangements and lyrics that question the leadership of Fela's homeland. (The album was repackaged with the 1973 album **Gentleman** in 2000 as a double CD on MCA.)

Afro-beat's torch has been picked up and carried by a number of musicians, most notably Fela's son Femi. **FEMI KUTI** played in his father's group for a number of years before forming his own band, Positive Force, in 1986. After Fela's death, Femi came into his own with a somewhat more commercial take on Afro-beat and several album releases that were successful in Europe. His 2001 MCA release **Fight to Win** included collaborations with several American hip-hop artists, including the high profile Mos Def.

TONY ALLEN was the master percussionist who laid down the backbeat for Fela Kuti. He has continued to tour and record and has expanded his own musical vision by including hip-hop, electronic, and dub music in his recent recordings. His 2002 release **Home Cooking**, on the Narada label, showcases his musical evolution.

Of the several Afro-beat bands that continue to celebrate Fela Kuti's legacy, the Brooklyn-based **ANTIBALAS AFROBEAT ORCHESTRA** are perhaps the best known in America. A collective of 14 members, the band explores the roots of the music and gives it a little New York twist by adding Latin dance grooves. Their 2004 release **Who Is This America**, on Ropeadope records, holds true to Fela's political manifesto with lyrics that confront and question the America of today.

AIN'T NOTHIN' LIKE THE BLUES

The blues has its roots in Africa and the various ethnic groups that were enslaved and forcefully brought to the New World during the seventeenth century to work on white-owned plantations in the North Mississippi Delta. Several things united these people in their persecution, but the most profound were Christianity and music. The original field songs incorporated whatever percussive instruments could be found, such as pots and spoons, with the telling of tales of woe. Originally the songs were passed on through oral tradition; when the tales began to incorporate songs of praise, the spiritual aspect of the music was born and the seeds of gospel music were sown.

After the Civil War and with the addition of real musical instruments, most notably the banjo and guitar, blues music began to find an audience in cities like Memphis and St. Louis, and then later on in Houston, Chicago, and Detroit. By the turn of the twentieth century, recording techniques had allowed some of the more popular musicians to make records, and as word got out, the music began to find a white audience. Over the years the music (which later gave birth to jazz) has evolved and mutated to include country music and rock and roll, with lead instruments as diverse as piano, harmonica, and electric guitar giving it a dimension that has appealed to a wide audience and led to most of the music we hear today.

The following are 20 recommended albums sure to kick-start any blues collection. Keep in mind that some of the older recordings don't have the clarity or production values of contemporary recordings.

MEMPHIS SLIM: *The Gate of the Horn* (Collectables, 1959)

SONNY BOY WILLIAMSON: *Down and Out Blues* (MCA, 1959)

MUDDY WATERS: *At Newport* (Chess, 1960)

JOHN LEE HOOKER: *Plays and Sings the Blues* (Chess, 1961)

FREDDIE KING: *Let's Hideaway and Dance Away with Freddie King* (King, 1961)

HOWLIN' WOLF: *Moanin' in the Moonlight* (Chess, 1962)

PAUL BUTTERFIELD: *The Paul Butterfield Blues Band* (Elektra, 1965)

JUNIOR WELLS: *Hoodoo Man Blues* (Delmark, 1965)

ROBERT JOHNSON: *King of the Delta Blues Singers* (Columbia, 1966)

JOHN MAYALL: *Bluesbreakers with Eric Clapton* (Polygram, 1966)

ALBERT KING: *Born Under a Bad Sign* (Stax, 1967)

MAGIC SAM: *West Side Soul* (Delmark, 1967)

BUDDY GUY: *A Man and the Blues* (Vanguard, 1968)

JIMMY DAWKINS: *Fast Fingers* (Delmark, 1969)

B.B. KING: *Completely Well* (MCA, 1969)

WILLIE DIXON: *I Am the Blues* (Columbia, 1970)

JIMMY ROGERS: *Chicago Bound* (MCA, 1976)

OTIS RUSH: *Right Place Wrong Time* (Hightone, 1976)
STEVIE RAY VAUGHAN: *Texas Flood* (Epic, 1983)
MISSISSIPPI JOHN HURT: *Avalon Blues: The Complete 1928 Okeh Recordings* (Columbia, 1996)

ANARCHY IN THE UK

While there's no doubt that the seeds of the punk rock revolution were sown in New York City in the mid-seventies, London and Manchester, England, were where punk exploded and changed the fashion and music industries. The mainstream press and the British establishment treated the rise of punk as if it threatened the foundations of society, with bands being refused airplay on the BBC's pop music outlets and questions being asked in the Houses of Parliament. The following are some of the most influential and important punk bands that emerged from that first wave and the albums they recorded that mattered.

THE SEX PISTOLS (Johnny Rotten, Steve Jones, Paul Cook, and Glen Matlock, who was replaced early on by Sid Vicious) turned punk from a marginal musical movement into a full-fledged phenomenon. They burst onto the scene in England as a result of a now-legendary interview on the live television program "Today" hosted by Bill Grundy. Grundy, who clearly wasn't happy to be talking with a band he perceived as untalented, baited the group to be controversial, and they replied with a string of expletives.

They made the front page of almost every daily newspaper the following morning.

Managed by Malcolm McLaren, who'd seen the potential of punk rock music when he briefly managed the New York Dolls, the Pistols' confrontational stance got them the attention McLaren was looking for. Johnny Rotten's lyrics, addressing such non–dinner table topics as abortion, fascism, and violence, and song titles like **Anarchy in the UK** and **God Save the Queen** got them fired from two record labels, and their notoriety soon got them banned from many live venues and radio airplay. Nonetheless, when Richard Branson's Virgin Records signed them and released their debut album, it went straight into the charts.

But the cracks were beginning to open: When the band headed to the United States in 1977, Rotten, realizing that it was all a sham, quit the band after a show in San Francisco. Bassist Sid Vicious died of a heroin overdose a few months later in New York while on bail for the alleged murder of his girlfriend Nancy Spungen, and that was pretty much it. Their one studio album, **Never Mind the Bollocks Here's the Sex Pistols**, released on Virgin in 1977, stands up extremely well almost thirty years later. To be perfectly honest, I wonder if today's kids would under-stand what the fuss was about.

THE CLASH were the first punk band to take the amped-up garage rock that was the basis of punk rock music and mix it with other musical styles, most notably reggae and dub. They also pursued a left-wing political agenda through their lyrics and were intent on spreading a message of personal accountability through the songs written by the two front men Mick Jones and Joe Strummer. Their third album, 1979's **London Calling** on Columbia, is one of my favorite albums of all time. It was a double album that added R&B and rockabilly to their already potent mix and cemented the Clash's popularity on both sides of the Atlantic.

The band toured relentlessly for the next few years, but by 1982, at the height of their popularity, Strummer took off for several months to Europe without telling anybody; he was effectively missing. It seems that he realized the band was about to enter into supergroup status, and it was something that he wasn't comfortable with. In 1983, with tensions between the two songwriters rising, the band pretty much fell apart. Unlike many of their peers, they resisted many lucrative opportunities to get back together. Joe Strummer's untimely death of a heart attack at just fifty years of age in 2002 put to rest any hopes that they would reconsider.

THE BUZZCOCKS are from Manchester in the north of England. Although inspired by London bands, the Sex Pistols in particular, the group (led by Pete Shelley), instead of taking raging political positions in their music, turned their youthful energy into writing fast and furious pop songs. Their singles **What Do I Get?** and **Ever Fallen in Love?** are classic punk pop songs. The group's second full-length album, **Love Bites**, released on United Artists in 1978 and reissued on CD by Nettwerk, is a great example of punk rock as pop music. The band originally called it quits in 1981 but have since reunited to tour and record a number of times.

SIOUXSIE & THE BANSHEES were originally a group formed by Sex Pistols fans, led by Sue Dallion (who called herself Siouxsie Sue) and bass player Steve Severin. Early members of the band included drummer Simon Ritchie, who later changed his name to Sid Vicious and joined the Sex Pistols, and guitarist Marco Perroni, who later joined up with Adam & the Ants. Siouxsie & the Banshees are covered more extensively in the "Unknown Pleasures: Goth Music" and "Queens of Punk" essays in this book.

THE DAMNED took the idea of punk rock as a movement that could change the way music was made and then put their own spin on it—humor! As their London peers the Sex Pistols and the Clash were taking anarchy and rebellion as their jumping-off point, the

Damned, led by Ray Burns and Chris Millar (aka Captain Sensible and Rat Scabies), decided it was an opportunity to have some fun. The first incarnation of the band actually split in 1978 after just two albums, but after a few lineup changes, they returned a year later to record the album **Machine Gun Etiquette**, later reissued on Roadrunner. The band has gone through so many lineup changes and fallings-out in the subsequent years that it's hard to keep up with who's in the group. But the Damned do still exist as an entity and are touring to this very day.

THE JAM were probably the most successful band to emerge from the British punk movement, at least at home in the UK. The trio, led by Paul Weller, were largely influenced by the mod bands of the sixties, such as the Who and Small Faces. In fact, the group inadvertently led a revival of parka-wearing Lambretta riders in England as the seventies made way for the eighties. From their inception in 1977 and throughout their career, they had a string of singles that consistently hit the UK Top 10. In 1982 Weller abruptly left the band, effectively causing its breakup. Through his work with his next project, the Style Council, and later his solo career, Weller has been considered one of the most important UK artists of the last twenty-five years. The Jam's 1980 album **Sound Affects**, on Polydor, is as good a place to start as any and finds Weller's songwriting skills maturing. It also includes the song **Start**, which was the very first song I played as host of KCRW's *Morning Becomes Eclectic.*

THE ADVERTS were only together for four years and recorded just two albums. Their claim to punk rock immortality lies in the single **Gary Gilmore's Eyes**, a song inspired by a U.S. death row inmate (Gary Gilmore) who had requested that after his execution his eyes be donated for transplant. The band's first album, **Crossing the Red Sea with the Adverts**, is packed with energetic punk pop songs that recall UK punk's breakthrough summer of 1977. The original album was reissued in 2002 on CD by Fire Records, with bonus tracks including "Gary Gilmore's Eyes."

X-RAY SPEX got together in 1976 and were led by the wonderfully named Poly Styrene (UK English for Styrofoam), playing their punk rock with a feminist twist. Their debut album, **Germ Free Adolescents**, typified the alienation expressed by most other punk bands in Margaret Thatcher's Britain, but interestingly the lyrics were pointed more toward the culture than the government. The album was reissued by Caroline Records in 1993 on CD with additional tracks, including their classic first single, **Oh Bondage, Up Yours!** It's worth buying this album just for that track.

THE ART OF THE COVER: ROGER DEAN

As the music business has evolved over the years, we've gone from an industry built on the sale of piano sheet music to the sales of 78s and 45s in paper sleeves to 12-inch albums in elaborately designed cardboard packaging to small 5-inch compact discs—and now downloadable files that don't come with any packaging, which is good for the planet, but bad for artists and designers. Back in the mid-1960s, the 12-inch LP cover became an opportunity for a band to make an artistic statement with their cover art, and it was a wonderful time for the many artists and photographers who made a living designing albums.

ROGER DEAN is a British illustrator who became famous as a designer of some of the most iconic LP covers and logos, including the original Virgin Records logo. His work featured stylized desert arches and canyons, strange oceans, and jungles, as well as the occasional dragon. Fittingly enough, as the progressive rock movement took hold in the 1970s, he seemed to be the artist of choice for many of those bands, most notably Yes. In fact, it's reasonable to say in many ways Dean's artwork helped define the genre of album-cover art. Here's a list of just some of the classic albums that featured his distinctive covers.

GUN were a hard rock band out of the UK who gave Dean his first album-cover commission, in which he featured a dragon and some very strange devil-like creatures. Their self-titled album from 1968 is available on import from SPM Records.

OSIBISA were one of the first African pop bands to achieve international success. Dean designed several of their album covers, including the 1971 release **Woyaya**, which had a cool flying elephant on the front. It's available on CD from Aim Records.

LIGHTHOUSE were a Canadian jazz-rock band; their 1971 album **One Fine Morning** on Evolution featured an image I can only describe as a building similar to Seattle's Space Needle reaching out of a frothy ocean with skulls on top. At this time the album is out of print, but you can find the artwork online (see the Web address at end of this essay).

The band **YES** defined Roger Dean's early career as an illustrator and artist, probably because they were the biggest prog rock band out there and because he designed their iconic logo. He's worked with them throughout their career and because his work is so identified with the band, he's created most of the art for the various members' solo projects as well. His first cover for them was for the 1971 Atlantic Records release **Fragile**, which featured a blue-and-green planet that looked like earth, with trees sprouting from it.

GREENSLADE was a progressive band that featured two keyboards, bass, and drums, led by one of the keyboard players, Dave Greenslade. Dean designed the first two of their four album sleeves. Their self-titled first album, released in 1973, features a wizardly looking character bathed in green shafts of light with three arms pointing somewhere off to the left. The album was reissued in 2001 on CD by WEA International.

URIAH HEEP took progressive rock and mixed it with heavy metal; they recorded several albums in the early 1970s that were hugely successful. A number of their albums featured Dean's illustrations, the best known being **Demons & Wizards**, which had an image of a demonlike wizard heading toward some kind of white liquid falls emanating from a tree. The album was released in 1972 and is available on CD from Polygram.

BADGER was formed by ex-Yes keyboard player Tony Kaye. The 1973 album **One Live Badger** was recorded live in the studio, and the artwork featured a pair of the cute woodland creatures that gave the band their name in a bleak winter setting, complete with one of Dean's trademarks: ghostly stretching trees. A CD reissue was made available in 2003 by Wounded Bird Records.

ASIA were a supergroup of sorts that included former members of Yes, King Crimson, and Emerson, Lake & Palmer. As the seventies gave way to the eighties, Asia found a receptive audience. Dean created an angular pyramid logo for them that was something of a departure from his trademark flowing lines. The logo was featured on all of their artwork, and he also created a series of album covers for them, including a sea serpent rising from the ocean on their 1982 debut **Asia** on Geffen, which became one of the biggest-selling albums of that year.

Roger Dean's Web site at www.rogerdean.com includes some of the images from these albums, as well as a lot of his other work. You can also visit rateyourmusic.com/lists/list_view/list_id_is_ 8881, where you can see a fairly comprehensive list of Dean's album illustrations.

BANDS OF BROTHERS

Brothers can often make good or at least handy bandmates. Throughout music history there have been a number of brothers who've teamed up to make music. It's not always easy to work with someone you know so well; inevitably sibling rivalry will rear its ugly head. But whatever the creative spark may be, the music written and performed by the guys included in this category is what counts.

Hailing from Piqua, Ohio, **THE MILLS BROTHERS**—John, Herbert, Harry, and Donald—teamed up in the late 1920s and became the most important vocal group in musical history. However, it wasn't just their harmonies that entertained; they did vocal imitations of wind instruments, such as trumpet and trombone, as well, accompanied only by a guitar. They took their act to a Cincinnati radio station and eventually to New York City, where in the early part of the 1930s they became a big success and had a string of hit songs to their name. In 1936 John died unexpectedly, so the boy's father, John, Sr., stepped in, and the group continued. In the 1940s they began appearing in movies and continued recording into the 1950s, by now performing with orchestras. They in fact continued performing into the 1980s. There is a box set, **The Mills Brothers Anthology 1931–1968**, available from MCA.

Starting off in the early part of the 1950s as a gospel group, **THE ISLEY BROTHERS**—Ronald, Rudolph, O'Kelly, and Vernon—began singing in their hometown of Cincinnati, Ohio. After Vernon was killed in a road accident, the boys became a trio with Ronald taking the role of leader. In their early years they wrote and recorded songs that never quite made it for the group but did well for other artists such as the Beatles and the Yardbirds. In the mid-sixties, however, they began to see some chart success both in the United States and also in England, and **This Old Heart of Mine (Is Weak for You)** on Tamla Motown put them on the map.

It was around this time that they also hired a guitarist called Jimmy James, who just a couple of years later as Jimi Hendrix would take the music world by storm. By 1970 two younger brothers, Ernie and Marvin, had joined, and the group's music started to shift away from the Motown sound to a more rock- and funk-infused groove with songs like **Who's That Lady** and **Fight the Power (Part One)**. The Isley Brothers went on to become one of the most important funk bands of the decade. They continued with various lineups through the eighties and into the nineties, but in the seventies they were at their most vital. 1973's **3+3** on Epic was the album where the younger brothers and their brother-in-law Chris Jasper joined the group (hence the title); it was also the album that first brought them to a much wider audience.

There is a more detailed history of **RAY AND DAVE DAVIES** and **THE KINKS** in another segment in the essay "The British Invasion, Part One." But this chapter cannot be written without a nod to these two brothers who were at the heart of one of the most significant British bands of the sixties. Ray was the leader and chief songwriter of the group, but Dave gave them their trademark guitar sound. **Something Else**, released by Reprise in 1967, is considered to be one of the Kinks' finest collections of songs and includes a couple tunes penned by Dave.

GREG AND DUANE ALLMAN were in a couple of bands together before forming **THE ALLMAN BROTHERS BAND** with a bunch of friends in 1969. They were to become within just a few short years one of the most important American rock groups of their generation. Their Southern blend of blues and rock evolved through their first few albums, and their live shows became legendary for their extended jams. (Now you know who to blame for all the jam bands out there today!) The band suffered an early tragedy with the death of Duane in a motorcycle accident toward the end of 1971, but they kept going with second guitarist Dicky Betts taking over all the guitar playing.

The history of this band deserves more space than I can give it here. (I suggest reading *Midnight Riders: The Story of the Allman Brothers Band* by Scott Freeman to learn more about the band.) Let's just say that they became something of a soap opera of drug, alcohol, and legal problems (mainly Greg's), two breakups, and bankruptcy, before coming back together at the end of the 1980s and managing to reinvigorate their career as one of the most popular touring bands out there. **Eat a Peach** from 1972 on Polydor was in the process of being recorded when Duane died. The double album ended up as a tribute to him, featuring songs recorded before and after his death, as well as live cuts such as the 33-minute track **Mountain Jam**.

Hailing from New Zealand, **TIM AND NEIL FINN** have played music together on and off for 30 years. In the early seventies Tim founded the seminal New Wave band **SPLIT ENZ**, which went through a lot of lineup, record label, and musical changes in the early years before Neil joined the band in 1977. The band finally broke through in New Zealand and Australia in 1979 with the album **True Colours**, which also saw them garner overseas recognition in the UK, Canada, and the United States.

After another couple of albums, Tim recorded a solo album, **Escapade**, that was well received. Although he was still a member of Split Enz, his solo career was distracting him, so he effectively ceded leadership of the band to Neil, who wrote most of the songs on what was to be Tim's last album with Split Enz, **Conflicting Emotions**, in 1983. After Tim's departure, Neil and the rest of the band carried on for another year or so, releasing one final album before calling it quits.

While Tim continued with his solo career, Neil, along with Paul Hester, the Enz drummer, in 1985 formed **CROWDED HOUSE**, a band who achieved worldwide success with their first two albums, **Crowded House** and **Temple of Low Men**. In 1991, after the brothers had spent time working on material for an expected Finn Brothers album, Tim joined Crowded House. Most of the material they had been working on ended up on the third Crowded House album, **Woodface**. Tim, however, soon left the band during the *Woodface* promotional tour. The final Crowded House album, **Together Alone**, was released in 1993, and the brothers did eventually release a **FINN BROTHERS** album, **Finn**, in 1995 on Discovery records. In the intervening years both brothers have continued with solo careers but got back together for another Finn Brothers record in 2004, **Everyone Is Here**, on Nettwerk records. The songwriting legacy of these brothers continues.

CHRIS AND RICH ROBINSON formed **THE BLACK CROWES** in Atlanta in the mid-1980s, developing their mix of Southern rock and Rolling Stones/Faces–style British blues rock into a sound that was an immediate hit on their 1990 debut release **Shake Your Money Maker**. With Chris (the older brother by two and a half years) on vocals and Rich on lead guitar, the group recorded and toured throughout the nineties and staked a pretty good claim as the best band of their generation to play in the "classic rock" mold. Their second album, **The Southern Harmony and Musical Companion,** released in 1992 on Def American, catches them at their swaggering best. The band called it quits in 2001, but had just reunited for some live dates at this writing.

In the mid-1990s British rock music reinvented itself with a whole slew of new and exciting bands. At a time when the UK economy was picking up and British art, fashion, and pop music were experiencing a rebirth, along came the brothers **NOEL AND LIAM GALLAGHER** with their Manchester band **OASIS**. Noel wrote the songs and Liam sang them. Noel had a knack with words and a love of the Beatles, whom he borrowed heavily from, and for a brief moment Oasis were the biggest band in the world—even cracking America, the first English band to have broken through in the States for a decade. There was a certain attitude that went along with the music, not unlike that of bands like the Who and the Sex Pistols, which helped create a cool rock-and-roll image as well.

Problem was, the brothers fought like crazy, and it was compounded by their excessive use of booze and drugs. There were times when Liam wouldn't show up for gigs and Noel would have to sing, and on other occasions Noel wouldn't want to play; in fact he once flew home in the middle of a U.S. tour and left everyone—fans, promoters, and bandmates—in the lurch. Despite the madness, though, they made several exceptional albums, my favorite of which is the 1995 release **(What's the Story) Morning Glory?** on Epic, which includes one of the best singles of that decade, **Wonderwall**.

BEATLES TOP 10

There's been so much written about the Beatles: who they were, what they did, and what they meant. For me they were the catalyst for getting interested in music and ultimately to a music-related career. I can remember as a young kid my dad bringing home the 7-inch 45s in the early sixties, and both he and my mum excitedly putting on the new records for the first time. The first album I ever owned was **Help!**, which my mum bought for my eighth birthday in 1965, and my second album was **Sgt. Pepper**, bought with my piggy bank savings—my mum and I split the price of thirty shillings.

One of the truly amazing things about the Beatles is how much they evolved as both performers and songwriters in just a few short years. Some of the early material sounds so different from the later albums that it could almost have been recorded by a different band, and in a way, it was. The band were barely out of their teens when they made their first records; by the time they split up they were world-weary millionaires. But the early recordings are just as important as the classic later releases, as they were the albums that created the phenomenon known as Beatlemania, which in turn allowed them the luxury to experiment in the studio and make the records that they wanted to.

Here's my top-10 Beatles records. It wasn't easy but I've listed them in order of preference, with my favorite first:

Sgt. Pepper's Lonely Hearts Club Band (1967)
Abbey Road (1969)
Rubber Soul (1965)
Help! (1965)
The White Album (1968)
A Hard Day's Night (1964)
Revolver (1966)
With the Beatles (1963)
Please Please Me (1963)
Beatles for Sale (1964)
Let It Be (1970)

Okay, so I picked eleven, but remember this: they made all these records and a couple of EPs and additional singles (all on Capitol) over a period of just eight years, so it hardly seems fair to leave any of them out!

BIRMINGHAM, MY HOMETOWN

The city of my birth and alleged nurture, Birmingham is England's second largest city outside of London and has produced its fair share of legendary musicians and bands. My favorite is Black Sabbath, whose first album hit me over the head like a mallet as I was entering my teens, although I have to confess a soft spot for Duran Duran as well. Here's a list of some of Birmingham's finest artists and their best albums.

THE MOODY BLUES formed in 1964 and were one of the first Birmingham bands to break internationally, with the single **Go Now** becoming a Top-10 hit in the United States as well as hitting No. 1 in Britain. Its success was hard to replicate, though, and by the end of 1966 original members Clint Warwick and Denny Laine left and were replaced by John Lodge and Justin Hayward. With the new members in place and keyboardist Mike Pinder adding Mellotron (incidentally, an instrument made by Streetly Electronics in Birmingham, where Pinder worked at the factory) to the band's sound, the group refashioned itself. Their next album, **Days of Future Passed**, on Decca subsidiary Deram in 1967, was one of the world's first "concept" albums, in which the band explored more progressive music by recording with an orchestra; they scored a major hit with the single **Nights in White Satin**. The Moody Blues continued to be successful on both sides of the Atlantic throughout the seventies and eighties.

The **SPENCER DAVIS GROUP** were formed around guitarist Spencer Davis. Other members of the band were Pete York and the Winwood brothers, Muff and young singer Steve, who would go on to front Traffic. They started off as an R&B band and had the reputation of being one of the best live bands in the city. Their big break came when their single **Keep on Running** pushed the Beatles out of the No. 1 slot in the UK charts in 1965. The 1967 album **I'm a Man**, on United Artists, was the last release with Steve Winwood and is probably their best collection. It was reissued on CD with bonus tracks via Sundazed records.

Steve Winwood left the Spencer Davis Group to form **TRAFFIC**, along with Jim Capaldi, Dave Mason, and Chris Wood. The band mixed Winwood's experimental jazz–influenced material with Mason's more tuneful compositions; major clashes of musical ideology caused Mason to leave the band several times. By 1970 the band was pretty much done, and when Winwood went into the studio to work on what was originally intended as a solo album, he ended up calling Capaldi and Wood in to help with the new material. The result was **John Barleycorn Must Die**; released as a Traffic album on Island in 1970, it cracked the U.S. market, where the band achieved great success until they called it a day in 1974. Steve Winwood went on to become a major solo artist in the eigthties. His album **Back in the Highlife**, released in 1986 on Island, won a Grammy for album of the year.

THE MOVE were one of the most successful Birmingham bands from the sixties. The original lineup formed in 1967 and was led by Carl Wayne and Roy Wood. The band's music was hard to pigeonhole, as they mixed up psychedelic rock with harder rock and more standard rock and roll. They had a number of hit singles at the end of the decade, including **Flowers in the Rain**, which had the distinction of being the first song played on the BBC's new pop station, Radio 1, in 1967. When Wayne left in 1970, he was replaced by Jeff Lynne. Lynne and Wood, together with drummer Bev Bevan, formed another group, Electric Light Orchestra, which ultimately led to the demise of the Move. The Move's second album, 1970's **Shazam**, is hard to find these days but worth seeking out as an import.

With **ELECTRIC LIGHT ORCHESTRA**, Roy Wood and Jeff Lynne imagined a group that would meld rock and classical music. Their self-titled debut album in 1971 showed great promise. Wood, however, left shortly after its release to form glam band Wizzard, leaving Lynne to hone the sound that he was looking for. With the addition of an orchestra, the 1974 album **Eldorado** on Jet records was the one where it all came together, setting the stage for ELO to have a hugely successful decade, especially in the United States. The albums's 2001 CD reissue on Epic/Legacy includes a couple of previously unreleased bonus tracks.

In the Birmingham suburb of Aston in 1969, when Ozzy Osbourne joined up with "Geezer" Butler, Bill Ward, and Tony Iommi, no one could have predicted that their group **BLACK SABBATH** (originally called Earth, they renamed themselves after a Boris Karloff movie) would pretty much invent heavy metal. Their first album was recorded in just one day, and the band broke out of Birmingham pretty quickly as their brand of heavy blues rock connected with audiences in both the UK and the United States. Ozzy, of course, would end up becoming a solo star in his own right and an outsized entertainment personality. Despite clocking in at a brief 34 minutes, **Master of Reality**, their third album, released on Warner Brothers in 1971, is a perfect example of their early work.

DEXY'S MIDNIGHT RUNNERS formed out of the punk band the Killjoys. Led by Kevin Rowland and Al Archer, the band effectively melded together elements of Irish folk music and soul, and featured a large group of musicians, including various horn and string players. They had an early hit single with a song called **Geno**, and their first album also sold well, but it was the second release that assured their status in pop history. Archer had departed the band by the time **Too-Rye-Ay** was released by Mercury in 1982, and driven by the single **Come on Eileen**, it became the soundtrack to that summer in England and the United States.

DURAN DURAN are probably the best-known band to come out of Birmingham. Formed in the post-punk haze called New Romanticism, they broke quickly and in a big way. Helped by the advent of MTV, the band spent the first half of the eighties traveling the world and shooting videos with supermodels. Their first album, **Duran Duran**, released on Capitol in 1981, is the one that I owned, with singles like **Girls on Film** and **Planet Earth**. With this album New Wave arrived in the United States.

The **AU PAIRS**' light shone brightly but briefly as they confronted the political climate of Margaret Thatcher's Britain in the early eighties. The band was led by feminist activist Lesley Woods and guitarist Paul Foad. Their 1981 debut album, **Playing with a Different Sex**, reissued on CD with bonus tracks by RPM, is a significant classic of the post-punk era.

OCEAN COLOUR SCENE are fronted by Steve Craddock, an avid fan of the Small Faces and the Jam (he's also done double duty in Paul Weller's band since 1993). Carrying the mod flag with a heavy dose of R&B and a Beatlesque pop sensibility, the group went through some tough times before achieving success. Their big break in the UK came in 1996 with their second album **Moseley Shoals** on MCA, named after the studio it was recorded at in Birmingham's bohemian suburb of Moseley.

BROADCAST formed in 1995, and with their keyboard- and synthesiser-based recordings and sporadic releases have gained a reputation as perfectionists. They've released several singles and EPs but only two full-length albums, both highly regarded for their take on avant-pop. The 2003 release **Haha Sound** on Warp has a little more depth and weight than their earlier work and shows the group pushing to find the edges of their music.

BOYS & GIRLS AND COMMON PEOPLE: BRITPOP

S ince rock and roll first became a cultural phenomenon in the mid-1950s and made its way from the United States over to England, there has been a constant shifting back and forth, with musicians being influenced by what was happening on either side of the Atlantic Ocean. The Beatles and the Rolling Stones could never have existed without their American influences, such as Elvis Presley, Little Richard, Buddy Holly, and Muddy Waters. In much the same way, the British Invasion of the States in the 1960s influenced a whole generation of American bands.

In the mid 1990s the UK saw the phenomenon known as Britpop, which in some ways was a response to the American grunge bands that were surfacing, as well as a reaction to much of the indie and electronic music of the previous ten years. It was a movement that had been brewing since the Stone Roses had released their eponymous debut in 1989; Britpop was in effect a return to the sound and style of the guitar-based bands of the 1960s and 1970s. For a period of about five years it ruled the charts in England with the help of the press, who set up a clash between Oasis and Blur in an effort to recreate the rivalry of the Beatles and the Stones in the early sixties. Oasis crossed the Atlantic, achieving platinum success before imploding, though Blur were never quite able to duplicate their huge UK following in the States. Nonetheless, the movement spawned several really good groups and turned a whole new generation of kids onto guitar-based pop music. Here's a list of ten bands and albums that defined Britpop:

[LONDON] SUEDE: *Suede* (Columbia, 1993)

BLUR: *Parklife* (Capitol, 1994)

OASIS: *Definitely Maybe* (Epic, 1994)

PULP: *Different Class* (Island, 1995)

ELASTICA: *Elastica* (DGC, 1995)

SLEEPER: *Smart* (Arista, 1995)

GENE: *Olympian* (Polydor, 1995)

KULA SHAKER: *K* (Columbia, 1996)

THE BLUETONES: *Expecting to Fly* (A&M, 1996)

SUPERGRASS: *In It for the Money* (Capitol, 1997)

THE BRITISH INVASION, PART 1

In the sixties, the Beatles opened the door for a whole slew of British bands and artists. In what became known as the British Invasion, groups like the Dave Clark 5, the Who, and others dominated the U.S. charts from 1963 to 1966. Here are some of the classic albums that got American teenagers screaming and their parents worried.

THE BEATLES led the invasion, and although I explore their work in a little more detail in another section (see "Beatles Top 10"), it's important to recognize that there would never have been a British Invasion without the loveable mop tops from Liverpool. In 1964 when the Beatles appeared on *The Ed Sullivan Show* (in the theater that *The Late Show with David Letterman* now calls home), popular culture was changed forever. **Please Please Me**, released on Capitol in 1964, was apparently recorded in just one day and consequently has an edge that can only be created by urgency. It features a couple of hit singles, including the title cut, as well as a number of covers (as did most of the early albums by their contemporaries). This became the prototype for the sound of the British Invasion.

It's hard to believe now, but when **THE ROLLING STONES** first came to the United States, they were considered a danger to American youth. The band just oozed bad boy sexuality, and they played up their role as the anti-Beatles (who in their early days were considered goody two-shoes by those looking for a little adventure). Many of the early British invasion U.S. releases were cobbled together from already-available singles and cuts from different UK releases. **The Rolling Stones, Now!**, released in 1965 on ABKCO, was just such an album. It catches the band's original lineup swaggering through covers such as Bo Diddley's **Mona** and Chuck Berry's **You Can't Catch Me**, as well as a couple of early Mick Jagger/Keith Richards originals and the out-and-out blues rocker **Little Red Rooster**.

THE WHO were also bad boys, although they didn't have the same sex appeal as the Stones—they were just downright scary. With Pete Townsend's permanent scowl and guitar-breaking antics on stage and Keith Moon's hotel-wrecking escapades, they helped create rock-and-roll myths that are still retold today. Their 1965 debut album **The Who Sings My Generation** on MCA records included a couple of James Brown covers and ten original songs, including the classics **The Kids Are Alright** and **My Generation**.

Like the Who and the Stones, **THE KINKS** came out of London. Based around two brothers, Ray and Dave Davies, their sibling rivalry became legendary (see "Bands of Brothers" for more details). Although they never achieved the level of fame that their contemporaries did, they are considered to be just as influential with bands like the Jam and the Pretenders name-checking them in the eighties. Like most of the British Invasion groups, the Kinks' music was rooted in R&B; although their later work became more intrinsically English and then more pop rock–based, the early albums have the classic British Invasion sound. **Kinda Kinks** from 1965, reissued on Rhino, features a couple of hit singles—**All Day and All of the Night** and **Tired of Waiting for You**—and is a good place to begin.

Between 1964 and 1967, **THE DAVE CLARK 5** had a string of hits on both sides of the Atlantic and for a while were considered the Beatles' most serious rivals. As with the Beatles, the sound centered around vocal harmonies and nifty melodies, although unlike the Fab Four, they were self-produced (by Dave Clark). **Coast to Coast** was released in 1965 and is probably the definitive Dave Clark 5 album. It includes one of their best singles, **Anyway You Want It**, and is available as an import on German reissue label Rock-in-beat Records.

At one time or another **THE YARDBIRDS** featured three of the most important guitar players in contemporary music: Eric Clapton, Jeff Beck, and Jimmy Page. In fact, the band eventually morphed into Led Zeppelin. Back in 1965, with Clapton in residence, the band was still exploring the blues, and at the end of that year **Having a Rave Up**, a collection of singles, B-sides, and live tracks, was released on Charly Records. The album was remastered and reissued recently as an import, on the Repertoire label.

Graham Nash and Allan Clarke were friends as kids growing up in Manchester and by 1962 had formed **THE HOLLIES**. They rapidly moved through the standard R&B covers to start writing and recording their own pop material that revolved around their vocal harmonies (a skill that Nash would perfect later in the decade as a member of Crosby, Stills & Nash). Although successful and popular in England from the start, they didn't crack America until 1966 with a single and album of the same name, **Bus Stop**, that appears to be unavailable at this time. There's a very good compilation, **The Hollies Greatest Hits**, that was released on Epic in 1972.

THE ANIMALS hailed from the northern town of Newcastle, about as working-class a city you could find in England back in the sixties. (Check out the original *Get Carter* movie with Michael Caine, filmed in Newcastle around the same time, to get a sense of how bleak it was.) Fronted by singer Eric Burdon, the band's membership shifted constantly throughout the decade, but the original lineup featured Alan Price on keyboards, as well as Chas Chandler (who went on to produce and manage the Jimi Hendrix Experience) on bass. The band's second album, recorded in 1965 just prior to Price leaving the group, was **Animal Tracks** on Columbia (reissued on CD by EMI) and is pretty much R&B-based rock, mainly covers. It's interesting to note that back in those days, singles were usually left off of albums, so if you want to hear Animals hits like **We've Gotta Get Out of This Place** and **House of the Rising Sun**, pick up a best-of compilation.

THE BRITISH INVASION, PART 2

In 1981, MTV unwittingly launched the second British Invasion. The new round-the-clock music channel desperately needed videos to fill its schedule, and the idea of making promotional videos to promote songs was relatively new and unsophisticated. The Brits had been working on it for a while, though, making videos to give to the weekly UK chart shows such as "Top of the Pops," and so MTV's lineup was soon dominated by artists coming out of London's New Wave/New Romantic scene. For a while the Brits were back.

The video for **A FLOCK OF SEAGULLS** single **I Ran (So Far Away)** was all over MTV in 1982 and showed Americans just how weird the New Romantics' haircuts could get. The band didn't make it too far past the one-hit-wonder category and never broke at all in their homeland. In fact, the band's hairdos got almost as much attention as their songs—fitting given that lead singer Mike Score had been a hairdresser! Their self-titled album **A Flock of Seagulls** was released on Jive Records in 1982.

DURAN DURAN probably benefited from MTV more than any other band. Combining their synth pop with a series of stylish, model-draped videos helped turn Duran Duran into global pop superstars. Although their fame faded later in the decade, and the band fragmented with various members leaving and returning through the years, the group is still making records and touring. Back in 1982 their second album, **Rio**, on Capitol Records was the one that broke them not only in the States but worldwide, and includes the hits **Hungry Like the Wolf** and the title cut.

Led by the Kemp brothers (Martin and Gary) and vocalist Tony Hadley, **SPANDAU BALLET** were, along with Duran Duran, the leading lights in the UK New Romantic movement. Their early singles did well in the UK and achieved moderate success in the

United States. In 1983 their third album, **True**, on EMI saw the band shedding the New Romantic style for a more sophisticated sound and look, and was their breakthrough U.S. release. The band continued until the end of the decade and racked up additional hits before calling it quits, with the Kemp brothers moving on to acting careers.

Annie Lennox and Dave Stewart had been a couple and played together in a band called the Tourists before setting off as a duo, calling themselves **THE EURYTHMICS**. Their synth pop followed from where the New Romantic fad had fizzled out, and they had a string of hits throughout the eighties. In 1983 the video for **Sweet Dreams (Are Made of This)** was in heavy rotation on MTV and helped propel the album of the same name into the upper reaches of the Billboard charts. Their next album, **Touch**, was released later that same year on RCA and was the one that made Dave and Annie eighties superstars.

While Annie Lennox was bringing a subtle androgyny to the Eurythmics, Boy George, with his flamboyant dress(es) and make-up, was causing a huge stir on both sides of the Atlantic and scoring a string of hit singles and videos with his band **CULTURE CLUB**. Their second album, **Colour By Numbers**, released on Virgin in 1983, made them the hottest pop group in the world. The album had four hit singles, including **Karma Chameleon**. A musical time capsule for sure.

BROTHERS AND SISTERS

If you begin making music at an early stage, chances are that you have a sibling on hand to fight over that first toy drum, piano, or guitar. Though there are a number of examples of brothers who formed groups together and several groups formed around sisters (see the "Bands of Brothers" and "Sister, Sister" essays in this book), this list covers several brother and sister teams, which are more rare.

THE CARPENTERS were Richard Carpenter, who played piano, and his sister Karen on drums (they both sang). The duo had been in a couple of short-lived trios in the latter part of the 1960s before setting out on their own in the early 1970s. They had a string of soft pop hits, including a cover of the Bacharach/David song **(They Long to Be) Close to You** and others such as **Rainy Days and Mondays** and **Top of the World**. Their sound was simple, good arrangements and easy-to-hum melodies. Unfortunately, they were both victims of compulsive/addictive behaviors. In the late seventies Richard had to enter a facility to deal with an addiction to painkillers, and Karen succumbed to the eating disorder anorexia nervosa, dying from the illness in 1983. **A Song for You**, released in 1972 (A&M), is probably their most cohesive album release: It's full of well-crafted pop songs as well as a couple of Top-10 hits.

The Mormon family five-piece band of brothers, **THE OSMONDS**, achieved huge chart success in the first few years of the seventies as leading proponents of the bubblegum pop movement. Their rise was in no small part due to the youngest brother Donny, whose adoring fanbase of young girls bought the group's records in droves. This was pretty much a carbon-copy repeat of the formula that had proved so successful for the Jackson 5, so it was an obvious next step when Donny Osmond followed Michael Jackson down the path toward a solo career. Around the same time, younger sister Marie established herself as a successful singer as well. After **DONNY AND MARIE OSMOND** had achieved considerable chart success as solo artists, they teamed up for a weekly television variety show and a couple of albums of duets. (They returned to TV at the end of the nineties for a short-lived talk show.) Most of their recordings are a little too wholesome, but there's no denying the quality of their voices; the 20th Century Masters series release **The Millenium Collection: The Best of Donny and Marie Osmond** (Universal, 2002) collects their highlights.

Bruce and Erica Driscoll grew up in Grand Rapids, Michigan. With their Brazilian mother and a childhood that included many trips to Brazil, it's not surprising that when they decided to make music together as **ASTAIRE**, their influences would include artists such as Caetano Veloso and Astrud Gilberto, as well as European bands like New Order and Saint Etienne. In late 2004, they released their debut EP, **Don't Whisper Lies**, on their own label, Wax Divine.

Hailing from Chicago, Matt and Eleanor Friedberger grew up with a grandmother who was a choir director and a mother who was a fan of the comic operas of Gilbert and Sullivan. When the siblings began making music together as **THE FIERY FURNACES**, they combined the lyrically fun approach of Gilbert and Sullivan with a potpourri of sixties psychedelia, blues, folk, and indie rock. Moving to the musically happening New York borough of Brooklyn in 2000, they began playing live and recording demos, which led to a record deal with the then-recently resurrected Rough Trade label. Their second album, **Blueberry Boat**, released in 2004, showcases their unique approach and adds beats and samples to an already intriguing mix.

THE CALL OF WALES

If you look at a map of Great Britain, Wales is the chunk about halfway up on the left-hand side jutting out into the Irish Sea. Like the Irish and the Scots, the Welsh are descended from the Celts, a proud, ancient warrior people who gave the

Romans a run for their money back in the day. Most of Wales is spectacularly beautiful, particularly the north, with mountains, lakes, and valleys that draw tourists year-round. It's also famous for sheep-farming, coal-mining, and singers. There's a long tradition of male choirs that sprung up from the coal industry in the south of the country. And there have been a couple of Welsh singers who've become world-famous stars, and many others who've had successful singing careers. Here are a few of my favorites.

TOM JONES is often referred to back in Wales as "The Voice" because his voice is so strong and recognizable. He'd been singing with a couple of bands in the early sixties before doing solo gigs, when he was discovered by manager Gordon Mills (who also went on to manage Tom's great rival Engelbert Humperdinck). Mills got Tom a record deal with Decca, and in 1965 he had a huge international hit with the orchestrated pop song **It's Not Unusual**. Tom was an instant pop star and sex symbol, with a sexy hip-swiveling technique borrowed from Elvis. In the same year he also recorded the theme songs for the James Bond movie *Thunderball* and the Peter Sellers comedy *What's New, Pussycat?*—classic sixties pop.

By the early seventies he had moved to the States and become one of the biggest draws in Las Vegas, where normally mild-mannered, middle-aged women threw their underwear at him on stage every night for the best part of a decade. Although he has continued to record and has worked on projects with a number of contemporary artists, his recent career has been largely defined as a club act, and he still regularly tours the world. The album **Live in Las Vegas**, recorded in 1969, captures him at his peak vocally and as a performer, covering a couple of Beatles tunes as well as his own hits. The album is available on CD as an import from London records.

SHIRLEY BASSEY was born in Tiger Bay, Cardiff, to a white mother and a Nigerian sailor father. She started singing as a little girl and began her career at age sixteen in a touring show called "Memories of Al Jolson." Apparently, it was her desire to get out of Cardiff that took her on the road rather than her need to sing, although she's said that when she first heard applause from an audience, that's when she knew she was a singer.

Bassey's early recordings were in the mold of Judy Garland, whom she very much admired, and they scored her a couple of No. 1 hits in the UK as the calendar turned from the fifties to the swinging sixties. Her international breakthrough came when she was asked to record the title song for the James Bond movie *Goldfinger*, and it made her a star. The hits continued for her in the UK throughout the seventies. She had her own TV show during this time as well and scored another hit with another James Bond theme song, **Diamonds Are Forever**. She also recorded the theme for *Moonraker*, which gives her the distinction of being the only artist to record songs for three Bond movies.

In 1962 Bassey teamed up with conducter/arranger Nelson Riddle for an album called **Let's Face the Music and Dance** on EMI. It's fascinating to hear her run through songs by the likes of Irving Berlin, Cole Porter, and Rogers and Hart, and to hear the subtlety in her voice, when she later became known as a belter. Also worth checking out is a remix album of her various hits called **The Remix Album: Diamonds Are Forever** from Nettwerk Records, released in 2000. Although she officially retired in the early eighties, she still pops up every couple of years or so to do live dates and make the occasional recording.

JEM is the nom de plume for Gemma Griffiths, a relatively new artist whose voice is wonderfully seductive and haunting at the same time, but whose real talent is as a songwriter and producer. Jem left Wales to go to university in Brighton, where she became friends with Norman Cook (aka Fatboy Slim), one of dance music's biggest stars. She began to DJ, promoting shows herself and learning the ropes of the music business before heading back to Wales to make her own music. I first heard Jem's music a few years ago when she dropped off a demo of a song called **Finally Woken** at my office. As soon as I heard it I wanted to hear more. I was fortunate enough to hear a number of other songs over the next year or so as she was in the process of recording them. She mixes electronic beats with hip-hop, samples, and good pop hooks, creating something that has a truly unique feel. All of those songs and more ended up on her debut release from 2004 called **Finally Woken**, on ATO Records.

Also from Wales, **CHARLOTTE CHURCH** has sold several million records of mainstream classical music beginning at just twelve years of age with the album **Voice of an Angel** on Sony Classical. Blessed with a magnificent soprano voice, she is a major star in the UK and has had a reasonable amount of success in the States. As she's grown older she has expanded her repertoire to include show tunes and operatic pieces. She's currently undergoing the difficult transition from rebellious teenager to young woman.

CHOCOLATE POPSICLES

Chocolate has been around for centuries, hailed by many as an aphrodisiac, feared by others whose cruel metabolism makes it an unwanted desire. Plus, it's a great word to include in a band name. The following is a list of artists who have done just that, and some recommended listening for when you get that cocoa craving.

HOT CHOCOLATE were a multi-racial pop/funk band out of Britain who favored an intimate approach to music with songs that in the mid-seventies would've been on many a bachelor's playlist. Shaven-headed singer Errol Brown exuded an earthy sexuality, and the band had a couple of big R&B hits in the seventies, including **You Sexy Thing**, which shows up on the 1997 compilation **14 Greatest Hits** on EMI.

CHOCOLATE GENIUS is the alter ego of Marc Anthony Thompson, a New York City–based songwriter. Having released a couple of albums under his own name in the mid-eighties (for Warner Brothers), he adopted his new moniker after playing with folks like guitarist Marc Ribot, and John Medeski and Chris Wood (of avant-jazz outfit Medeski, Martin & Wood). His first album released under the name Chocolate Genius—**Black Music** in 1998 on V2 records—is a wide-ranging brew of styles and songs that moves from jazzy R&B grooves through alternative rock to acoustic and folk-tinged tunes that together seem to poke fun at and question the label "black music."

DEATH BY CHOCOLATE is a four-piece British band who released a self-titled album in 2001 on Jetset records that featured a potpourri of sixties-style, surreal space-age pop. Vocalist Angie Tillett basically speaks in a playful kiddie-style voice over almost all of the tracks, creating an eccentric collection that would fit in nicely with a bizarre cartoon series that is still to be created.

MILES DAVIS: ICON

Miles Davis is without a doubt the most important jazz musician ever. He was born in Alton, Illinois, in 1926 but grew up in St. Louis. It seems like he got the music bug early, as he picked up his first trumpet at twelve years of age. By the time he was a teenager, he was playing out in bars and clubs and getting paid for it. When he was eighteen he went to see a performance by Billy Eckstein's big band, which at that time included Charlie Parker and Dizzy Gillespie among its lineup, and Miles made up his mind right there to move to New York and become a full-time jazz musician. It was shortly after the end of World War II, and Manhattan was as exciting as it had ever been when Miles jumped into the city, spending his first few years there playing with Charlie Parker's band and sitting in with a number of other bands. He eventually began putting together his own band, and his first record deal (with Capitol) followed in 1949.

Miles was to spend the next forty years at the forefront of jazz constantly pushing at the boundaries of the music, and reinventing himself and jazz along the way. At one time or another he worked with many of history's most important jazz musicians, including John Coltrane, Gil Evans, Sonny Rollins, Art Blakey, Cannonball Adderley, and Herbie Hancock. Not only was Miles an accomplished soloist, but he was also a bandleader, composer, and musical innovator, as well as a man who nurtured the talent of others. His creative approach to everything he did pushed jazz into new realms right from his first album, **Birth of the Cool**, and continuing throughout his career right up to his last release before his death in 1991, **Doo Bop**, a collaboration with rapper Easy Mo Bee. What follows is a list of ten essential Miles Davis recordings:

Birth of the Cool (Blue Note, 1949)
Miles Davis Quartet (Prestige, 1953)
'Round About Midnight (Columbia, 1955)
Miles Ahead (Columbia, 1957)
Kind of Blue (Columbia, 1959)
Sketches of Spain (Columbia, 1959)
Seven Steps to Heaven (Columbia, 1963)

Miles Smiles (Columbia, 1966)
Bitches Brew (Columbia, 1969)
On the Corner (Columbia, 1972)

DEADHEADS AND JAM BANDS

In 1965 San Francisco was the place to be. The counterculture was rising out of the ashes of the beat movement, and artists and musicians were flocking to the Haight Ashbury district, attracted by its cheap rents and bohemian lifestyle. Jerry Garcia, an accomplished bluegrass musician, teamed up with guitarist Bob Weir, keyboardist Ron "Pigpen" McKernan, drummer Bill Kreutzmann, and bass player Phil Lesh to form a group called the Warlocks. They soon changed their name to the Grateful Dead, and not only were they about to begin a long, strange journey of their own, but they also started a movement that gave birth to the jam band phenomenon.

THE GRATEFUL DEAD quickly became synonymous with drug use, which was hardly surprising considering that Ken Kesey, the writer of *One Flew Over the Cuckoo's Nest* and the host of renowned "Acid Test" parties, invited them to perform at his LSD soirees. A large part of the hippie aesthetic of outrageous clothes and confronting conformity that came out of San Francisco began with Kesey's movement, and the Grateful Dead were right there at the beginning.

The Dead became local stars with their eclectic mix of folk, bluegrass, and psychedelic rock. They also started making recordings, although without much success initially. In 1967 they began recording sessions that embraced the extended and improvised versions of songs, the way they performed them in concert. As a result the band had a number of successful albums in the seventies, including one of their best, **American Beauty**, released by Warner Brothers in 1970. The eighties, however, was difficult for the group, with several band members dying as a result of drug abuse and tragic accidents. But the band continued on as if it had a life of its own—which it did for the "real" fans, the community of Deadheads, as they became known, who followed them around the country from show to show. The group experienced a second wave of commercial success at the end of the eighties in large part due to a hit single **Touch of Grey**, which surprisingly brought them to a new, younger audience.

But it was all about the live shows. The band had always improvised their set at each concert, with no two shows ever being the same, and as a result, fans started bootlegging tapes of the shows. A whole subculture of tape trading and sales soon sprang up and continues to this day. With Jerry Garcia's death in 1995, the band effectively ended, but the surviving members have continued to perform under various other names.

PHISH would not exist if it hadn't been for the Grateful Dead. The band, led by guitarist Trey Anastasio, formed in 1983 in Vermont and began their career playing college campuses in the Northeast. Their reputation as heirs to the Dead has come about not just because they share musical styles, but because they also have focused on live performance as a major part of their music. Phish concerts are "events," and like the Dead, the band allows fans to record and trade tapes of their concerts. The band took what many thought would become a permanent break in 2000 but came together once more in 2002 and hit the road for an extended tour. At the end of 2004 they apparently quit for good, but their legions of fans live in hope that the road will beckon Phish again sometime in the future. The group recorded several successful studio albums, including the 1996 Elektra release **Billy Breathes**, which found U2 and Dave Matthews Band producer Steve Lillywhite reining in the band's rambling jazz-rock tendencies (most of the tracks are under four minutes) and helping fashion a solid, cohesive set of songs.

THE DAVE MATTHEWS BAND, led by transplanted South African singer/songwriter Dave Matthews, has managed to do amazing business on the concert circuit and also sold a lot of records, with every studio album achieving platinum status. The band's mix of neo-hippie rock and world-influenced pop music struck a chord with music fans almost immediately. Their first studio album, **Under the Table and Dreaming**, released in 1994 on RCA, set the ball rolling for one of the most consistently successful U.S. acts of the last decade.

BLUES TRAVELER were one of the most successful roots rock groups of the mid-nineties, and like the Dave Matthews Band were able to sell a lot of records as well as concert tickets. Led by the (then) oversized singer and harmonica player John Popper, they had a unique sound and were a mainstay on modern rock radio. The 1994 album **four** on A&M catches them at their commercial peak.

Formed in Athens, Georgia, **WIDESPREAD PANIC**, as befits a band from the South, incorporates a little southern rock into the jazzy psychedelic blues mix that is the hallmark of a good jam band. Their 1991 self-titled release on Capricorn records is the highlight of their studio releases.

MOE began life as "Five Guys Named Moe" in and around Buffalo, New York, before realizing that they should at least simplify the band's name. Their hard work on the northeast live circuit through the mid-1990s earned them a short-lived record deal with Sony, but as with many bands who create marvelous improvisational moments on stage, they found it hard to simplify things in the studio. The group released their next few albums on their own Fatboy label. They get major props for the innovative album **Wormwood**, released on Artist Direct in 2003, on which they used live recordings of the basic rhythm tracks and added all the other instrumentation and vocals in the studio.

STRING CHEESE INCIDENT formed in Boulder, Colorado, in 1993 and apparently began their career performing around various ski resorts and getting paid with lift tickets before getting serious about their job as musicians. The band have a Grateful Dead–like mix of bluegrass and jazzy, psychedelic rock, but also throw in elements of world music. They release their albums on their own label, Sci Fidelity, and their 2001 album **Outside Inside** comes closest to grabbing the energy of their live shows, many, many of which have been recorded and are available from the band's own label.

THE SAMPLES also hail from Colorado (what is it about that thin air?) and are a little more jazz influenced than most of the bands in this category. They have put out most of their albums on independent labels. Try **Underwater People** from 1992 on the What Are Records? label.

DESERT ISLAND DISCS

There's a BBC radio program called *Desert Island Discs* that has been running in the UK since 1942. The premise is quite simple: Famous guests are invited to select eight records they would want to have with them if they were stranded on a desert island, and the show's host then interviews them in between the tracks as they're played. Through the years I myself have been asked many times which songs I would like to have with me if I found myself in such a position. I've rounded my list up to ten songs and listed them in the format that they were originally released. As we now live in the age of portable digital-music players, these are the songs I would hope to have on my iPod should I find myself a castaway like Tom Hanks or Robinson Crusoe, awaiting the arrival of either a passing ship or Ursula Andress.

FRANK SINATRA
I've Got You Under My Skin
Songs for Swingin' Lovers! (Capitol, 1956)

PETULA CLARK
Don't Sleep in the Subway
Single (Warner Brothers, 1967)

THE BAND
The Weight
Music from Big Pink (Capitol, 1968)

MARVIN GAYE
I Heard It Through the Grapevine
I Heard It Through the Grapevine (Motown, 1968)

THE BEATLES
Here Comes the Sun
Abbey Road (Capitol, 1969)

LED ZEPPELIN
Whole Lotta Love
Led Zeppelin II (Atlantic, 1969)

T. REX
Ride a White Swan
Single (Fly, 1970)

NEIL YOUNG
Old Man
Harvest (Reprise, 1972)

GANG OF FOUR
To Hell With Poverty!
Another Day/Another Dollar (EP) (Warner Brothers, 1982)

RADIOHEAD
The National Anthem
Kid A (Capitol, 2000)

DON'T QUIT YOUR DAY JOB: TV ACTORS WHO'VE TAKEN THE PLUNGE

There are many actors who sing. After all, if you're stage-trained, there are two things that you might just need in your future career: the ability to swordfight and a singing voice for those Broadway auditions. What is it, though, that possesses TV actors in particular to release albums of love songs or covers of their favorite tunes? While you ponder that question, here are some actors who felt they had what it takes to crack the charts.

Although the "Star Trek" character of Captain Kirk only lasted three television seasons back in the sixties, his fame was such that **WILLIAM SHATNER** was able to record **The Transformed Man** (1968, reissued by Varese Sarabande in 1994), a collection of poetry and spoken word performances of songs like Bob Dylan's **Mr. Tambourine Man** and The Beatles' **Lucy in the Sky With Diamonds**. Only Shatner knows for sure if it was deliberately camp or if he was serious, but either way it's a classic. In 2004 Shatner returned with a new release, **Has Been**, on Shout! Factory records. Aided and abetted by Ben Folds and Joe Jackson, it featured a terrific cover of **Common People**, a song originally written and recorded by the British group Pulp. Before we come back to earth, we must also recognize Captain Kirk's former shipmate Mr. Spock. Actor **LEONARD NIMOY** also made a number of records, the best of which is **Mr. Spock's Music from Outer Space** (1967, also reissued by Varese Sarabande), which includes some spoken word pieces, as well as songs that were written specifically for the album (with titles such as **Highly Illogical**) and a number of instrumentals, including the "Star Trek" theme song.

TELLY SAVALAS appeared in many movies but is perhaps best known as the TV cop "Kojak" one of the most popular TV series of the 1970s. He recorded a couple of albums at the height of the show's popularity, and **Telly** (MCA, 1974) featured a cover of the David Gates song **If**, originally recorded by Bread in 1971. Telly's version hit the top of the UK singles charts for six weeks!

DAVID SOUL's career-defining role was as Hutch, one half of the hip seventies TV team "Starsky & Hutch." He had, however, a previous stint as a singer, calling himself variously "The Covered Man" or "The Mystery Singer" and appearing on talk shows singing and playing guitar while wearing a mask or hood! After the show's success, Soul was able to show his face and released a string of albums in the latter half of the seventies, including **David Soul** (Private Stock, 1976), which featured the No. 1 single **Don't Give Up On Us Baby**. The album appears to be out of print at this time, although there is an import **The Best of David Soul** collection available on Music Club Records.

CHERYL LADD leapt to fame when she replaced Farrah Fawcett Majors in the original "Charlie's Angels" TV series in 1977. Several years earlier she had been featured as one of the singing voices (Melody Valentine) in the animated TV series "Josie & the Pussycats," and she went on to release two albums at the height of her "Angels" fame. The first of which, **Cheryl Ladd** (Capitol, 1978), included a minor pop hit **Think It Over**.

While most of the above-mentioned actors can safely be said to have released records that fit into the novelty category, **DAVID HASSELHOFF** has been a multiplatinum recording artist and has performed in front of concert crowds in the thousands . . . in Germany. In much the same way that the French are fascinated with and have deified Jerry Lewis, the Germans took to David Hasselhoff as if he were one of their own. The star of "Knight Rider" (where he shared the screen with the talking car KITT) and later on "Baywatch" (where he shared the screen with Pamela Anderson and other scantily clad women), he found his music audience in Europe. The album **Is Everybody Happy** (BMG,1995) catches him at his rock and pop Eurotrash best.

DOUBLE YOUR PLEASURE

When my twins, son Sam and daughter Luna, were born, so began my education into and observation of the unique relationship that twins share with one another. I recently had a band on my radio program called Blonde Redhead that featured twin brothers Simone and Amadeo Pace. Watching their interaction got me to thinking about sets of twins who've made music together through the years. I found that there actually aren't that many, but there were also a handful of artists who, while not biological twins, came up with group names that included "twins." Here's a list of the two kinds of musical twins.

THE ARMSTRONG TWINS, Lloyd and Floyd (really), were country and bluegrass musicians out of Little Rock, Arkansas, who performed on guitar and mandolin in and around their home state in the 1940s, before relocating to Los Angeles where they performed during the 1950s. They were frequent radio guests and were well known for their trademark harmonies and matching stage outfits. They made a number of recordings in the early part of their career as well as a reunion album in 1979. That later release, along with some of the early recordings, is available on CD as **Mandolin Boogie** from Arhoolie Records.

Identical twins Kim and Kelley Deal grew up in Dayton, Ohio, and although they played music together as teenagers, Kelley was not as interested in pursuing it as a career. On the other hand, Kim was determined to be a musician by trade and became the bass player in the legendary alternative rock band the Pixies. She also formed her own band **THE BREEDERS** with Tanya Donnelly, but when Tanya left after their first album, Kim drafted her sister into the band; their next album, **Splash**, was released in 1993 on 4AD. It ended up going platinum and establishing the band as bona fide alternative stars. Kim later started a side project called the Amps while the Breeders continued on and off until Kim joined up in 2004 with the reformed Pixies.

COCTEAU TWINS were a Scottish group formed by guitarist Robin Guthrie, bass player Will Heggie (who was replaced fairly early on in their career by Simon Raymonde), and vocalist Elizabeth Frasier. Okay, no real twins were in this group, but they did have a cool name and a truly distinct sound created by layers of Guthrie's shimmering guitars and Frasier's otherworldly vocals, carefully created from vocal sounds rather than lyrics. Their 1990 release **Heaven or Las Vegas**, on the UK label 4AD, is my favorite.

Also from Scotland, **THE PROCLAIMERS** featured twin brothers Craig and Charlie Reid. In the mid-1980s they released a couple of albums of mainly acoustic, melodic songs that, although well reviewed, didn't sell well commercially. That was until their song **I'm Gonna Be (500 miles)** from the 1988 Chrysalis release **Sunshine on Leith** was included as a featured track five years later in the movie *Benny and Joon*. It catapulted them briefly to success and made the album a surprise hit.

Simone and Amadeo Pace are Italian twin brothers who along with Japanese art students Kazu Makino and Maki Takahashi formed the group **BLONDE REDHEAD** in New York in 1993. Their guitar-driven downtown art rock attracted the attention of Sonic Youth drummer Steve Shelley, who recorded and released their first couple of records on his own label. (Takahashi left after the first.) The brothers and Makino evolved their songwriting skills over the next few albums and added strings and keyboards to their guitar-based sound. In 2004 they released their sixth album **Misery is a Butterfly** on 4AD.

Sisters **TEGAN AND SARA QUIN** created an early stir in their hometown of Calgary, Alberta, then signed in 2000 to fellow Canadian Neil Young's label Vapor Records. Their first few releases were rooted in acoustic punk and drew comparisons to Ani DiFranco. Their 2004 CD **So Jealous** finds them hitting their stride with a collection of hooky power-pop songs that make good use of their vocal harmonies and show them maturing as songwriters and performers.

Led by Alannah Currie and Tom Bailey, **THE THOMPSON TWINS** were a hugely successful eighties pop band with big hair and many, many big synth-pop hits. Their 1983 Arista release **Quick Step & Slide** was probably their most complete album and kicks off with the hits **Love on Your Side** and **Lies**.

THE GLIMMER TWINS is actually the alias that Keith Richards and Mick Jagger of the Rolling Stones use as producers of the Stones' records. One of these is the generally underappreciated and overlooked 1976 release **Black and Blue** on Virgin. It was the first album to feature Ron Wood as a member. Please note: There is an artist out there also called The Glimmer Twins, an electronic act from Belgium.

BOB DYLAN: ICON

Bob Dylan (original last name Zimmerman) was just 19 years old when he left his hometown of Hibbing, Minnesota, and arrived in New York City in 1961. He was, however, already an accomplished guitar and harmonica player who had modeled himself on Woody Guthrie. Plugging into the burgeoning Greenwich Village folk scene, he quickly began to make a name for himself playing the coffeehouse circuit. He was signed to Columbia Records in 1962 and after releasing his self-titled debut (consisting mainly of covers) he followed it the next year with **The Freewheelin' Bob Dylan**, an album that established him as a songwriter whose observations resonated with his contemporaries.

His subsequent albums began to incorporate his love of poetry and blues music, and it was only a matter of time until he plugged in his guitar and crossed over to a pop audience. While the folk community felt betrayed by this switch to an electric sound, the rock audience embraced him, and by 1966 he was consistently topping the charts, as were his songs, covered by numerous artists, including Joan Baez and the Byrds. When he toured the UK that year he took a new backing group with him, the Hawks (later to become the Band). Later that summer Dylan was involved in a motorcycle accident outside his home in Woodstock in upstate New York, and when he recovered, he bought recording equipment, set up a studio in a rented house, and called the Band to begin recording new material. A sea change was inevitable.

Dylan's new work incorporated more country influences and heralded his willingness to take risks musically and to tour extensively, something he still does to this day. Throughout the seventies his work became more political, and the decade ended with his announcing that he was a born-again Christian; his early eighties releases reflected this new faith but were commercially and critically disappointing. As Dylan's career continued into the nineties, his releases received mixed reviews, although there was renewed interest in his work at the turn of the millennium. Bob Dylan remains probably the most influential and important songwriter of his generation. Here are ten of his best albums, spanning his 40-plus-year recording career:

> **The Freewheelin' Bob Dylan** (Columbia, 1963): Dylan's second release, it heralded the arrival of an important new talent.
>
> **The Times They Are A-Changin'** (Columbia, 1964): This was the first Dylan album comprised solely of self-penned songs, with protest songs perfectly in tune with those uncertain times.
>
> **Highway 61 Revisited** (Columbia, 1965): Though Dylan had already "gone electric," this was his first down and dirty rock album.
>
> **Blonde on Blonde** (Columbia, 1966): Using his touring group, the Hawks (later to become the Band), this album incorporates his many influences into a sprawling double album.

John Wesley Harding (Columbia, 1967): This was Dylan's first album after his Woodstock motorcycle accident, and it's one of his most carefree. At times, the album sounds almost like a country record.

Blood on the Tracks (Columbia, 1975): Dylan's marriage to Sara Lowndes was on the rocks, and this served as his break-up record. With the idyllic Woodstock lifestyle giving way to a mansion in Malibu, the Dylans lost something in the transition, and we find a bitter man, spitting out his disdain toward himself and his soon to be ex-wife. Artistically, it's probably his best album.

The Basement Tapes (Columbia, 1975): Recorded in 1967 (with the Band) just before *John Wesley Harding* and not intended for release, this is a loose, fun collection capturing both Dylan and the Band at their creative best.

Empire Burlesque (Columbia, 1985): After a few albums that focused on his born-again Christian beliefs, Dylan released this collection of fine songs. It's somewhat over-produced, but nonetheless a return to form.

Oh Mercy (Columbia, 1989): With Daniel Lanois in the producer's seat, Dylan wrapped up the eighties with an understated, atmospheric collection of songs.

Love and Theft (Columbia, 2001): Another comeback, his best album since the seventies finds Dylan jumping back and forth between rock, folk, and country, and doing what made him famous, telling stories.

ELECTRONIC PIONEERS

Long before DJ culture and electronica launched a thousand clubs in major cities across the globe, the pioneers of electronic music were hard at work experimenting with primitive computers and music created without traditional musical instruments. In 1918 Russian scientist **LEON THEREMIN** took his interest in music (he played cello and piano) and physics and created the world's first electronic instrument, appropriately called the theremin. The instrument is surrounded by a magnetic field and equipped with two antennas, and a sound pitch is created by the movement of one's hands within the magnetic field. The theremin's sound is most recognizable from sci-fi movies of the fifties (quite notably it was used in the theme song to the original "Star Trek" TV series), although there have been a number of rock bands who've used it in recent years as well.

Probably the most important invention in electronic music was the Moog synthesizer, invented by **DR. ROBERT MOOG** in 1964. It became the first widely used electronic musical instrument. One of the first artists to use the instrument for serious composition was **WALTER CARLOS** (later to become **WENDY CARLOS**). Carlos's 1968 adaptations of various Bach compositions, **Switched-On Bach**, was the first full-length album to explore the Moog, and her 1972 soundtrack for Stanley Kubrick's *A Clockwork Orange* was a pioneering score performed on the Moog. A side note: The album also introduced the vocoder to recorded music. These albums were reissued in 1998 on East Side Digital recordings.

KRAFTWERK rose out of the late-sixties music scene in Germany. The scene at that time was experimenting with electronic sounds and instruments. Florian Schneider and Ralf Hütter created a unique sound that focused on the use of Moog synthesizers and their own homebuilt drum machines. While their early work and releases were minimalist, by 1974 they began to incorporate arrangements and melodies into their compositions. The album **Autobahn** (reissued in 1998 on Astralwerks) and the single of the same name were hugely successful and put the band on the musical map. Throughout the seventies they continued recording and putting out songs like **Trans-Europe Express** that have since been recognized as genre-defining recordings. In the eighties, the charts were dominated by drum machines and manufactured pop music and Kraftwerk faded away. However, by the end of the nineties, with the rise of electronica and DJ culture, Kraftwerk found themselves revered as innovators, and as the new millenium dawned they reconvened to tour and record again.

Michael Rother and Klaus Dinger were early members of Kraftwerk but left in 1971 to form **NEU!**. Their first album, also called **Neu!**, was released the next year (and was reissued in 2001 on Astralwerks). Unlike the robotic sounds of their former group, Neu! featured much more groove-based electronic sounds, coupled with nominal melodies. They recorded two more albums in the seventies, **Neu! 2** and **Neu! 75** (both on Astralwerks), followed by **Neu! 4** in 1996 on the Captain Trip label.

TANGERINE DREAM have had one constant member throughout their history: founder Edgar Froese. In fact, at the time of this writing, Tangerine Dream is just Edgar and his son Jerome. From the group's beginnings in Berlin at the end of the sixties this was a band that created experimental music using a variety of both regular instruments and objects found around the house (such as vacuum cleaners), using reverb and delay processors to change the sound. After a couple of early German releases, in 1974 the group became a three-piece ensemble with Froese joined by Christopher Franke and Peter Baumann. In that year they became one of Richard Branson's early signings to his then-fledgling Virgin Records label and recorded the album **Phaedra** at his Manor Studios, where Mike Oldfield recorded **Tubular Bells**. The title track is almost eighteen minutes long and is considered a landmark recording of electronic music. Championed by legendary British DJ John Peel, the album established the band as an important new arrival. Tangerine Dream went on to become something of a revolving door as musicians came and went. They were also early innovators of electronic keyboard-based movie scores in the eighties, probably the best known being **Risky Business**.

Completing the "Krautrock" domination of this category are **CAN**, whose core members were Holger Czukay, Irmin Schmidt, Jaki Leibezeit, and Michael Karoli. (The group's first vocalist was American Malcom Mooney, followed by Japanese singer Damo Suzuki.) They were more of an experimental rock band than an electronic group but nonetheless were early innovators in the use of electronic instruments in their music. They were only a group for ten years (primarily in the seventies), but they recorded a body of work that was wildly experimental; they managed to combine ambient soundscapes with sprawling jazzlike improvisations and constantly evolving rhythms. The 1971 double album **Tago Mago** and 1972's **Ege Bamyasi** with Suzuki (both reissued on Mute Records) laid a musical foundation for a number of artists who've followed, including **GARY NUMAN**, **SONIC YOUTH**, and **STEREOLAB**.

ERIN GO BRAGH: IRISH MUSIC

As a result of its troubled political and religious past, Ireland's history is full of tragedy. It seems that much of the art that has come out of the country has been touched in some way by this, and its music is no different. The country is naturally the home of many traditional Celtic musicians, as well as a number of successful rock and pop artists who have enriched the world's music stages with their unique talents over the years. It seemed until quite recently that there was a cultural cringe in Ireland, due in large part to its past and a feeling that London was the place to be if you wanted to break through as an artist. But no longer—the vibrancy of Ireland's artistic community is there for all to see, as the country has embraced its role as part of the European community.

VAN MORRISON was the first true Irish rock superstar, breaking out of Belfast in the north in the mid-1960s with his band Them and the now-classic song **Gloria**. With a mix of influences ranging from blues to jazz and R&B, Van Morrison was clearly going somewhere, and in 1967 the now-solo Van moved to the States. His second album, **Astral Weeks**, released by Warner Brothers in 1968, is considered a classic, a subtle mix of folk and jazz. His subsequent work has veered from equally brilliant to quite ordinary, and his live shows are known to be either remarkable or just not good. But when you catch Van Morrison at his best, he can be transcendental, with a voice that is a mystic combination of blues heroes like Ray Charles and an ethereal otherworldliness. His work through the years has reflected his deepening sense of spirituality, and although he still spends a lot of time in the United States, he now lives back in Belfast.

CHRISTY MOORE's early musical heroes were rockers like Little Richard and Elvis Presley; his understanding and embracing of traditional Irish music didn't come until later, when he lived in London in the late sixties. Back in Ireland he began recording as a solo artist and eventually formed the band Planxty. Their combination of rock and traditional Celtic music proved very successful. With Christy playing acoustic and rhythm guitar and the traditional Irish drum known as bodhran, as well as singing, he was in the group on and off for over a decade. His first stint as a solo artist was in the mid-seventies and was documented by a couple of live recordings; he resumed his career in earnest in the mid-1980s with a number of well-produced albums, but his live work has been sporadic at best due to health problems. The 1994 concert album **Live at the Point** on Grapevine Records features some of his finest ballads, political comments, and tales of giving up the drink. Christy Moore is one of those performers whose essence is released when he's on stage.

RORY GALLAGHER was a blues guitarist, one of the best. He grew up in Cork and as a child began listening to blues records by the likes of Muddy Waters, Albert King, and John Lee Hooker. His first recording was with the band Taste, which he formed while living in London at the end of the sixties. He went solo in 1971 and put out eight albums in that decade, as well as releasing a couple of live recordings. He also did a lot of session work and got to record with some of his music idols, including Muddy Waters, on **The London Sessions**, a 1972 album that was recently reissued by MCA. He continued recording and performing throughout the eighties and into the nineties, but Rory suffered from the disease of alcoholism and eventually his liver gave out. He passed away far too young at just 46 years of age in 1995. Check out his 1974 live album **Irish Tour**, reissued in 1999 on Buddha Records. It was recorded in Dublin, Cork, and Belfast. This is a document of one Ireland's great live performers.

Dublin's **THIN LIZZY** were one of those rock aberrations that come along once in a while and shine brightly for a brief moment before passing on. The band were led by vocalist and bass player Phil Lynott, a black man playing music that was deemed white, writing lyrics that wove stories together with hard-driving rock and smart melodies. Forming in 1970, the band, after a couple of earlier releases, hit their stride and found their moment in 1976 with the album **Jailbreak** on Mercury, which included the huge radio hit **The Boys Are Back in Town**. The irony of timing was that just as Thin Lizzy were breaking through at the end of the seventies, punk rock was on the ascent and rapidly changing the musical landscape. Within a few years hard rock was out of favor. By 1983 Thin Lizzy decided it wasn't worth carrying on; tragically, Phil Lynott wasn't far behind, succumbing to drug abuse in 1986 at the age of 35.

With one or two exceptions, most notably the Ramones, punk rock is by definition unlikely to lead to lengthy careers. In Ireland The Undertones from Derry in the north and the Boomtown Rats from Dublin in the south blazed short but important trails for young Irish musicians. **THE UNDERTONES** never really broke any further than the UK, but they had a number of hits including **Jimmy Jimmy** and **Teenage Kicks**, which featured their trademark frenetic garage guitar pop and singer Feargal Sharkey's distinct vocals. Their 1979 debut (reissued on Rykodisc), **The Undertones**, sums up just how powerful punk pop can be. The band broke up in the early eighties, with Sharkey having a brief solo stint followed by a successful career as an A&R executive in the record business. Other band members went on to form the highly regarded group **THAT PETROL EMOTION**. They reunited (surprisingly to good reviews) without Sharkey in 2003.

THE BOOMTOWN RATS' career lasted a little longer as their music evolved past punk and into New Wave. In the UK they had nine Top-40 singles. Their American success came in 1979, when they recorded a song called **I Don't Like Mondays**. The lyrics referred to a San Diego teenager, Brenda Ann Spencer, who went to school one day in January of that year and opened fire on teachers and students, killing the school's principal and custodian. When asked why she did it, her answer was, "I don't like Mondays, this livens up the day." The band's chilling song became their biggest hit, and the album it was from, **The Fine Art of Surfacing**, on Columbia, is a collection of New Wave pop that outclasses most of its peers. After the band's singer Bob Geldof put together the Ethiopian famine relief concerts Band Aid and Live Aid in 1985, the band broke up and Geldof went solo.

Ireland's rock coming-out party is in large part due to the success of **U2**, who formed in Dublin at the tail end of the seventies. Bono, the Edge, Adam Clayton, and Larry Mullen, Jr., came out of Dublin's post-punk scene and signed with Island Records, who released their first album, **Boy**, in 1980. With their third album, **War**, released in 1983, the band became an MTV staple and broke through in a major way in the United States—quite surprising for an album that was so clearly political, with songs like **Sunday Bloody Sunday**. Their views on world politics have continued to inform their work through the years, and they are one of just a handful of successful artists not afraid to use their fame to draw attention to various human rights and political issues they feel are important. Their 1987 album **The Joshua Tree** was the album on which the band incorporated the influences they had picked up on their countless treks across America, and it turned the band into global superstars.

SINÉAD O'CONNOR seemingly came out of nowhere in 1987 with her debut album, **The Lion and the Cobra**, on Ensign Records. It was a passionately intense, confrontational collection of songs that pushed an unprepared 21-year-old woman out into the frenzied world of rock music. In 1990 her cover of Prince's **Nothing Compares 2 U** from her equally stellar album **I Do Not Want What I Haven't Got** (also on Ensign) took her to the giddy heights of stardom, and she never really recovered either personally or artistically. She was extremely outspoken on subjects as diverse as the IRA and marriage. In 1991 she refused to play a show in New Jersey if the "Star-Spangled Banner" was to be played before she went on, and then followed that up the next year by tearing up a picture of Pope John Paul II on live TV during "Saturday Night Live." Her career, at least in America, effectively ended as a result of those actions. Her subsequent work has been eclectic and diverse but largely ignored, and at this point she says she has retired from music.

A pop band from Limerick with a cute name, **THE CRANBERRIES** conquered American pop radio in the early nineties with a string of hits and a couple of multiplatinum albums. Brothers Noel and Mike Hogan formed the band with Fergal Lawler, and after the original male singer left, Dolores O'Riordan joined after bringing them a demo of the song **Linger**, which would later become a huge hit. The boys were big Smiths fans, and the acoustic sensibility Dolores brought with her, as well as her unique voice, led to their debut album (released in 1993 on Island Records), **Everybody Else Is Doing It, So Why Can't We?** It was an instant hit both in Europe and the States, and why not? It's an album of finely crafted pop that offered an alternative to the grunge/punk movement that was just beginning to break. The band's 1994 follow-up,

No Need to Argue (Island), was just as effective and similarly well received. Their releases since then have not been as commercially successful, but nonetheless the group are still performing and recording albums.

Singer/songwriter/painter **DAMIEN RICE** is a young artist who is continuing the Irish tradition of fine storytelling in his music. His first band, Juniper, was signed to a major label in 1997. After battling with the label over creative control, he decided he'd rather not make music for a while and promptly took himself to Italy where he busked for a living. He returned to Ireland, and after setting up a home studio recorded and self-produced his debut solo album, **O**, in 2002. It was initially also self-released, in Ireland only. The album is a collection of simple acoustic songs that build layer upon layer into sometimes fully orchestrated anthems before quickly subsiding into simpler or more dissonant arrangements. The passion with which he imbues these songs is constant in both the playing and the forceful yet sometimes subtle vocal delivery. The addition of vocalist Lisa Hannigan adds an ethereal element to an already delicate recording. The album was released in the United States on Vector Recordings in 2003. For what it's worth, this is my pick for best album of this decade (so far).

THE FIFTH BEATLE AND OTHER COLLABORATIVE PRODUCERS

There were two guys who played with the Beatles before they hit it big. One was Stu Sutcliffe, the band's original bass player. He went with them to Hamburg in 1960 and 1961, where they played a string of club residencies and honed their live show. Stu was really only in the band because of his friendship with John and ended up staying on in Germany to be with his girlfriend, Astrid Kirchherr, when the band headed back to Liverpool. Tragically he died the next year from a brain hemorrhage.

The other former Beatle was Pete Best, the band's original drummer, who was unceremoniously dumped in favor of Ringo Starr just prior to the band recording their first studio single, **Love Me Do**. For my money though, the true Fifth Beatle was George Martin, the band's producer, who worked with them throughout their career and whose creative contributions helped shape their musical direction. This essay takes a look at George and explores the work of a number of other producers whose collaborations with certain artists have been integral to the artists' body of work.

After a short-lived job with the BBC, **GEORGE MARTIN** became an in-house producer for the EMI label Parlophone Records. At that time the label was best known for classical and spoken word recordings, and for records by comedians like Peter Sellers. Martin is credited for realizing early on the songwriting potential of John Lennon, Paul McCartney, and George Harrison; when he signed the Beatles in 1962, nobody could have envisioned the success they would have together.

Throughout their career, Martin brought suggestions to the recording process, such as the use of orchestral strings and horns, as well as tape segments running backwards on their more psyche-delic albums. His most important contribution, however, was to encourage them to experiment with instruments such as French horn, sitar, and harpsichord and to develop their songwriting techniques. There's little doubt that George Martin helped the Beatles redefine popular music in the sixties and beyond, as their influence led other bands and musicians to rethink the way they made and recorded music.

In 2001 EMI released a box set called **Produced by George Martin**, which features 151 songs spanning a career of fifty years and ranging from big band and skiffle (a late-fifties form of British folk music), through some of the comedy work he did with Peter Sellers and Spike Milligan, to music by the Beatles, Gerry & The Pacemakers, Cilla Black, Ella Fitzgerald, Jeff Beck, America, and Celine Dion. It also includes tracks performed by his own band, the George Martin Orchestra.

The first time I remember seeing **BRIAN ENO** was on the British TV show "Top of the Pops" when he was a member of Roxy Music. He was playing a synthesizer that looked like an old tele-phone operator's exchange, the type you'd see in old hotel lobbies in 1930s movies, with cables patched in and out of various jack sockets and operators listening in on calls that were supposed to be private. (Hey, maybe it *was* an old telephone operator's exchange.) Brian Eno went on from that early career in glam rock to become a hugely influential ambient musician and innovative producer, putting his mark on records by artists such as David Bowie, Talking Heads, and U2.

His work with Bowie originally encompassed the trilogy **Low**, **Heroes**, and **Lodger**. Recorded between 1977 and 1980, they find Bowie experimenting with electronics, minimalism, and avant-garde pop. Around the same time that Eno was working with Bowie, he also struck up a friendship and working relationship with Talking Heads front man David Byrne, and as the producer of the band's second (**More Songs About Buildings and Food**), third (**Fear of Music**), and fourth (**Remain in Light**) records, he helped define their songwriting structure and sound. In fact, by 1980's *Remain in Light* (which was in many ways the group's break-through record), Eno played on and cowrote all of the tracks.

Eno's next challenge as a producer was to work with U2. Along with Daniel Lanois, he produced the band's 1987 milestone release **The Joshua Tree** and their next studio album, the career-rede-fining (and Bowie-influenced) **Achtung Baby** from 1991, as well as its follow-up, 1993's **Zooropa**. And he returned as one of the producers on the 2000 release **All That You Can't Leave Behind**. He's also worked as a collaborator with experimental musicians such as John Cale, Harold Budd, and Jah Wobble. His own album **Ambient 1: Music for Airports**, released in 1978 on EG Records, features just four pieces of ambient music that drift in and out of the listener's consciousness.

DAVID BRIGGS worked as an engineer and producer with Neil Young from his self-titled debut album in 1968 until the 1994 release with Crazy Horse, **Sleeps with Angels**. Briggs wasn't hung up on studio gadgets or technical wizardry, and through the course of their work together he became known as a producer who could capture the sound of a rock band's performance and transfer it to record—not an easy feat. Although his career was defined by his work with Neil Young, he also made records with other artists, including Nils Lofgren, Alice Cooper, Spirit, and Nick Cave and the Bad Seeds.

Young's **Tonight's the Night** is a very emotional collection of songs written just after the deaths of Crazy Horse guitarist Danny Whitten and Neil's friend and roadie Bruce Berry, both deaths due to drug overdoses. Young's grief and mourning, together with the questioning of his celebrity, are inherent to the songs. Capturing those real emotions in the performance is what made Briggs such a unique producer. Their collaboration ended when Briggs died of lung cancer in 1995.

NIGEL GODRICH began his career as a teaboy in a London studio called Audio One. His next job was at the famous RAK Studios, where he progressed to being an assistant engineer, finally getting his break when the producer John Leckie, who liked bringing projects into RAK, gave him the opportunity to engineer Radiohead's second album, **The Bends**. It was a meeting of the minds that would impact both his and the band's future. He left RAK to go freelance, and with friends and former RAK alumni Sam Hardaker and Henry Binns (later to form the group Zero 7) set up a small studio and started producing records himself.

Over the years Nigel has produced artists such as Pavement and Air, as well as two albums by both Beck and Travis. But it is as Radiohead's producer that he's made his reputation as a studio wizard who brings another dimension to a project. Beginning with **OK Computer**, the band's 1997 follow-up to *The Bends*, Nigel has produced each successive album, including **Kid A** in 2000, **Amnesiac** in 2001, and **Hail to the Thief** in 2003. This covers a period of time in which Radiohead assumed the mantle of most revered band in the world, with each new album pushing the envelope a little further than the last. With Nigel at the helm, the band, who are at best leery of outsiders, have a friend whose judgment they trust.

FRENCH KISSES

The French have long prided themselves on resisting the onslaught of American pop culture. They feel (and who's to argue?) that after centuries of their own artistic, political, and culinary offerings to the world, it's important to maintain their own identity. They even have a government department that invents new French words for English slang and modernisms. They have, however, always been big fans of American movies and music while at the same time supporting their own artists, few of whom have succeeded outside of France, most likely due to the language barrier. Here's a list of albums by French artists of various genres that are worthy of your inquisitive nature.

JOHNNY HALLYDAY was brought up in post-WWII France mainly by his cousins Desta and Menen, who were touring dancers. He lived on the road with them and began singing and playing guitar at an early age. By the time he discovered Elvis Presley in the late 1950s he knew he wanted to be a rock-and-roll singer. Through a series of French-language covers of American rock-and-roll hits, he soon became the French Elvis. In the early 1960s he also became a teen idol and, somewhat like the "British Elvis" Cliff Richard, through the years Johnny was able to reinvent himself, adapting to the musical styles of each decade, including psychedelia and R&B. He has also been featured in dozens of movies through the years and is one of France's best-known cultural icons.

In 1996 Johnny celebrated his fiftieth birthday by performing in Las Vegas and flying in plane loads of fans from France to be in the audience. The 1997 live album **Destination Vegas**, on Philips (a French import), features tracks from throughout his career, including a couple from his rock-and-roll beginnings.

I could spend pages on **SERGE GAINSBOURG** and not even scratch the surface of how important he was to French popular culture. In America he also attained cult status despite only having one song hit the charts, **Je T'Aime . . . Moi Non Plus** (**I Love You . . . Me Neither**). In his homeland he was regarded as a mischief-maker and playboy. After his early musical explorations of cabaret and jazz, Gainsbourg found his place in French musical history with a series of sensual songs often performed with women he was involved with, such as Brigitte Bardot and Jane Birkin. Much of his subject matter directly challenged what was considered acceptable, with explicit lyrics about sex and drug use. His duet **Lemon Incest**, with daughter Charlotte, certainly raised eyebrows, and there's no doubt that after his commercial peak in the early seventies his art became more confrontational and questionable. Nonetheless, his influence on musicians—not just in France—is immeasurable. There are a number of compilations of his work worth checking out. I suggest trying **Initials B.B.** (Polygram) from 1968.

A classic French chanson, **EDITH PIAF**, also known as the "Little Sparrow," is widely regarded as France's most important singer. Many of the songs she sang throughout her career captured the dark times in her own life. And the difficulties began young, when as a small child she was sent to live with her grandmother, who ran a brothel. Later on Edith became a street performer, and the hard lessons she learned during those times infiltrated her performances and singing style. Her friends and acquaintances were criminals and pimps, and she lived dangerously for a number of years, until she was discovered singing on a street corner by a cabaret club owner just a few years before World War II. Throughout the war her career continued to blossom, and her personal life entertained audiences as well; she moved through a string of lovers who were usually songwriters or singers, many of whom became protégés. The self-written **La Vie en Rose**, released just after the war, was a huge international hit and is probably her best-known song. Toward the end of her life alcohol and substance abuse became an issue, and her ill health ended in cancer and an early death at age 47 in 1963. **Live at Carnegie Hall** (Capitol) from 1957 is one of just a few well-recorded live documents of her performances.

Okay, so Roger Jouret (the man behind **PLASTIC BERTRAND**) was actually Belgian, but at the risk of being guillotined I'm including him in this section because everyone outside of France thought he was French, and he did at least sing in French! His claim to fame is really just one song, but it's a New Wave masterpiece, **Ca Plane Pour Moi (This Life's for Me)**. The song was a huge hit in the summer of 1978 across most of Europe and found its way across the Atlantic as well. It was a silly song, really, with lyrics that didn't say anything, but it was fun to listen to. It was on the album of the same name but is probably easier to find on **King of the Divan: Best of Plastic Bertrand** (EMI), released in 2003.

AIR, aka Nicolas Godin and Jean-Benoît Dunckel, began playing music together in the mid 1990s after meeting at a university in Paris. They shared a love of old synthesizers and Serge Gainsbourg, and the early music that they made had the feeling of a sixties Italian movie soundtrack with light atmospheric and Brian Wilson–like pop melodies. They've made three albums and also scored Sofia Coppola's first movie, *The Virgin Suicides*. Their first full-length album, **Moon Safari** (Astralwerks), was released in 1998 and is considered a chill-out classic today.

DJs Guy-Manuel de Homem-Christo and Thomas Bangalter created **DAFT PUNK** out of the ashes of their indie rock band Darling. In Daft Punk they shot to the forefront of house music, which in mid-1990s France was taking over the dance floors and throwing up homegrown re-mixers and producers. Their first full album, **Homework** (Virgin), released in 1997, was groundbreaking in its fusion of disco, funk, and beats.

GENIUS LOVES COMPANY

The human voice is a remarkable instrument. It can reveal intimate secrets or shout loud proclamations, and throughout this book many singers are listed who've explored the gift that is their voice to create work that resonates with audiences. When two voices come together to sing a duet, though, something truly unique can happen. Of course, most duets are love songs of one type or another, so be prepared for all the sappiness that can come along. Nonetheless, here's a list of duet albums worth a spin in your CD player.

One of the most highly regarded pairs to ever record together, **MARVIN GAYE AND TAMMI TERRELL** made three albums, the first of which was **United**, released in 1967 on Motown.

Recorded for Columbia Records in 1967, the year before they married, **Carryin' On** was **JOHNNY CASH AND JUNE CARTER**'s first collaboration and features an eclectic collection of material, including the classic single **Jackson**.

The quintessential duet couple of country music, **GEORGE JONES AND TAMMY WYNETTE** recorded **Golden Ring** in 1976 as their marriage was crumbling, and you can hear the impending divorce in their performances. It has since been reissued on Razor & Tie.

Two of the founders of "Outlaw" country music, **WAYLON JENNINGS AND WILLIE NELSON** got together in 1978 to record **Waylon & Willie**, a collection of five duets and three solo songs from each of them, and a celebration of what they had achieved in breaking free of the Nashville system. It has since been reissued on BMG.

Early on in her career, Motown's biggest female star, **DIANA ROSS**, recorded with a whole host of her label mates including Smokey Robinson, Stevie Wonder, and the Temptations. In 1982 the label released a compilation consisting of ten of those songs, called **Diana's Duets**. Diana also recorded an album of duets in 1973 with Marvin Gaye called **Diana & Marvin**.

At the time of **RAY CHARLES**'s death in 2004, the finishing touches were being put on **Genius Loves Company** (Concord Records), an album of duets with artists including Elton John, Norah Jones, and Van Morrison. In 1998 Rhino Records also released a compilation album called **Duets** that Charles recorded throughout his career with artists such as Johnny Cash, Betty Carter, and Aretha Franklin.

GOOD ENOUGH TO EAT

It's not that easy to come up with band names relating to food without appearing goofy. For example, Toast would be just too weird, or the Pickles. Who knows? Perhaps somewhere there may be bands with those names, but they're not exactly well known if they are out there; hence my point. But then who's to say naming yourself after a foodstuff can't work? There have, in fact, been a number of groups who've come up with names from the menu; listed below are a few of the best.

VANILLA FUDGE were assumed by many to be an English band because of their mix of psychedelic rock and blues, but they were actually from Long Island, New York. If you think Vanilla Fudge is a strange name, they were originally called the Electric Pigeons! Their debut album, **Vanilla Fudge**, released on Atco in 1967, featured a collection of covers, including songs by the Beatles (**Eleanor Rigby**), the Zombies (**She's Not There**), and Curtis Mayfield (**People Get Ready**), performed as blissed-out psychedelic jams.

Originally formed by former Small Faces singer/guitarist Steve Marriott and soon-to-be-famous-in-his-own-right guitarist Peter Frampton, **HUMBLE PIE** went on to become a hugely successful rock band known for their heavy blues sound. However, the group's early recordings were largely acoustic based. The band's second of three albums with Frampton, 1969's **Town & Country** (A&M), catches them at perhaps their most idyllic, conjuring up images of the genteel English countryside.

BREAD are probably the biggest-selling band named after a food staple! Formed by songwriters David Gates and James Griffin in Los Angeles in 1968, and with a string of early-seventies hit singles like **Make It With You** and **Everything I Own**, they came to define 1970s middle-of-the-road soft rock. Take a bite out of **Baby I'm-a Want You**, released on Elektra in 1972.

THE JAM are also featured in the UK punk section of this book. They get a double entry for naming themselves after the best way to preserve fruit. Try to find a copy of the 1992 Polygram compilation album **Extras**, a collection of B-sides, rarities, and covers that helps spread the word about just how great this band was.

BLANCMANGE named themselves after the quintessential English pudding of the same name (it's a cross between custard and Jello). The group was comprised of Stephen Luscombe on keyboards, Neil Arthur on guitar and vocals, and a couple of drum machines. They recorded three extremely well-crafted New Wave synth-pop records in the first half of the 1980s, the final one being **Believe You Me** on Sire in 1985.

THE SOUP DRAGONS named themselves after a character in a delightful 1970's kid's stop-animation English TV show called "The Clangers." In the show, the Soup Dragon was the gatekeeper of the subterranean soup wells, which were the Clangers' main source of food. The band stirred up a musical pot that included punk, funk, rock, and dub reggae. They had a big modern-rock hit with a cover of the Rolling Stones **I'm Free**. Their 1992 album **Hotwired** on Big Life Records catches the band at its peak.

CAKE, led by John McCrea, were formed in Sacramento, California, in the early 1990s. Often compared with New York band Soul Coughing because of the similarity in vocal styles between McCrea and Soul Coughing's frontman Mike Doughty, Cake are really more of a blue-collar alternative rock band with smart-arse lyrics that have enabled them to consistently get singles such as **The Distance** and **Never There** played on alternative radio. Grab a slice with 1996's **Fashion Nugget** from Capricorn.

SQUIRREL NUT ZIPPERS formed in Chapel Hill, North Carolina, in 1993 and named themselves after a type of candy. They played a style of music that was a mix of retro swing and alternative pop, and carved out a surprisingly successful couple of years at the top of the alternative charts in the second half of the 1990s, in large part due to the single **Hell**. Their 1998 album **Perennial Favorites**, from Chapel Hill label Mammoth Records, will give you a good taste of the neo-swing movement of which they were at the forefront.

GREAT FIRST ALBUMS

They say you have your whole life to write the songs on your first album. And up to the point the work is written and recorded, that's true. The second album is often the tough one, and some artists only ever get one album released. Here are some debut albums that heralded the arrival of important new artists or groups:

LITTLE RICHARD: *Here's Little Richard* (Specialty, 1957)

CHUCK BERRY: *After School Session* (Chess, 1958)

THE WHO: *My Generation* (MCA, 1965)

THE JIMI HENDRIX EXPERIENCE: *Are You Experienced?* (MCA, 1967)

THE VELVET UNDERGROUND: *The Velvet Underground & Nico* (Polygram, 1967)

THE BAND: *Music from Big Pink* (Capitol, 1968)

LED ZEPPELIN: *Led Zeppelin* (Atlantic, 1969)

FUNKADELIC: *Funkadelic* (Westbound, 1970)

STEELY DAN: *Can't Buy a Thrill* (MCA, 1972)

BOB MARLEY & THE WAILERS: *Catch a Fire* (Tuff Gong, 1973)

PATTI SMITH: *Horses* (Arista, 1975)

THE CLASH: *The Clash* (Epic, 1977)

TALKING HEADS: *Talking Heads 77* (Sire, 1977)

TELEVISION: *Marquee Moon* (Elektra, 1977)

KATE BUSH: *The Kick Inside* (EMI, 1978)

JOY DIVISION: *Unknown Pleasures* (Qwest, 1979)

R.E.M.: *Murmur* (IRS, 1983)

RUN-D.M.C.: *Run-D.M.C.* (Profile, 1984)

THE SMITHS: *The Smiths* (Sire, 1984)

SINÉAD O'CONNOR: *The Lion and the Cobra* (Chrysalis, 1987)

THE STONE ROSES: *The Stone Roses* (Silvertone, 1989)

MASSIVE ATTACK: *Blue Lines* (Virgin, 1991)

BECK: *Mellow Gold* (DGC, 1994)

JEFF BUCKLEY: *Grace* (Columbia, 1994)

AIR: *Moon Safari* (Astralwerks, 1998)

COLDPLAY: *Parachutes* (Capitol, 2001)

HAPPY TRAILS: COWBOY CROONERS

Nowadays, portable digital recorders can record just about any sound anywhere in the world. Unfortunately, they weren't around when cowboys were singing around campfires out in the high plains in the nineteenth century. But luckily for us, there were a number of movie cowboys in the middle of the twentieth century who did record those old songs and more. Three of them were larger-than-life characters who, as we barrel ahead into the new millennium, deserve their own category in this book.

GENE AUTRY was the original singing cowboy and probably the biggest American music star of the first half of the twentieth century. His career spanned records, movies, television, and radio, and he helped define country and western music for more than three decades. He was originally from Tioga, Texas, and received his first guitar at the age of twelve. He began singing and playing around local cafes while holding down a "real job" working as a telegraph operator for the railroad. One night he was spotted by the actor Will Rogers, who suggested that he try his luck in New York, and in 1929 Autry headed off to the big city and began his recording career. With a mix of yodeling, folk, and cowboy songs his career took off, and it wasn't long before Hollywood called and Gene Autry headed to his next career as a singing cowboy in B-movie westerns.

He became one of the top movie stars of his day, and his career continued to rise until he joined the military for the last two years of World War II. When he came home, he just picked up where he left off. However, by the early 1950s the B-movie genre was in decline, and Autry switched to television and produced his own show for a number of years. Through some smart early investments, he also owned a number of radio and television stations. As the music business changed, he gradually pulled back from performing to focus on his businesses, which he did until his death in 1998. There aren't too many Gene Autry recordings in print at this time, but **Back in the Saddle Again**, originally released in 1968, was reissued on CD a few years ago on Sony and is a good representation of the cowboy songs for which he became famous.

ROY ROGERS was not just a cowboy—he also had one of the most famous horses in entertainment history. When I was a kid growing up in Birmingham, England, my mum told me how she remembered when she was a little girl in the 1940s, and Roy Rogers came to town and stayed at the poshest place in town, the Queens Hotel. On his arrival he marched right into the lobby with his horse Trigger, who apparently had his own room. Such was the celebrity of Roy Rogers, who began life in Cincinnati as Leonard Slye.

Like a lot of young men in the 1930s, Roy (then known by his given name) headed off to California to seek his fortune. After playing guitar and singing in a number of combos, including

Sons of the Pioneers, he eventually broke into the movies. This happened after he snuck into a casting call for Republic Pictures (Gene Autry's employer), which was impressed enough to offer him a contract and his new, catchier name. Gene Autry was the main man at the time, but there was room for another singing cowboy, and after Autry signed up for the military during World War II, Roy found his place. He also found a screen partner in singing actress Dale Evans. After his first wife passed away, the two were married and spent the next several decades in movies, radio, and on television as the king and queen of western music. His best-known song is one that was used as the theme for "The Roy Rogers Show" on television, **Happy Trails**. For a good all-around collection that includes some of Roy's work with the Sons of the Pioneers, check out **King of the Cowboys**, a compilation released by ASV/Living Era in 1999. Roy Rogers passed away at age 86, just a few months before Gene Autry, in 1998. (A bit of Roy Rogers trivia: Yes, he was the man who started the fast food chain that still bears his name!)

TEX RITTER was another Texan who headed to New York looking for fame and fortune, but unlike Autry, Tex began his showbiz career as an actor on and off Broadway. After he began playing guitar on stage he graduated to radio with his own cowboy show and eventually went to Hollywood, where every studio and producer were looking for their own Gene Autry. By the mid 1930s he was making seven or eight westerns a year and wound up doing some eighty-plus movies over a ten-year period.

He was pretty much out of the film business by the end of World War II and began to focus on his music career, moving away from exclusively recording country music to more pop-oriented material. He had several Top-10 singles and a couple of No. 1 tunes as well, with songs like **I'm Wastin' My Tears on You** and **You Two-Timed Me One Time Too Often**. (Now if that's not the name of a country song, I don't know what is!) He too moved into television as host of the show "Town Hall Party," and his son was the popular TV sitcom actor John Ritter. Tex also recorded the hit theme song to the classic 1953 western *High Noon*, and continued recording on and off until his death in 1974. There's a 28-song collection of his recordings called **High Noon** released on CD in 1992 by Bear Family records.

HEADBANGERS BALL

Long before MTV devoted a whole show to it, headbanging had become a legendary pastime for (usually) long-haired teenage boys. While there is some debate (which I don't wish to join in on) about who actually coined the phrase "heavy metal," the music is generally agreed to have originated, or at least begun to flourish, in the British Midlands in the late 1960s, around the time that Led Zeppelin formed. The genre is now approaching its late thirties and has gone through a number of mutations over the years while crisscrossing the continents, but it has always represented rebellion in some form or another. The following are considered to be some of the most important heavy metal bands and albums that rocked through the years, all of which have given both kids and their parents headaches. If you want to let your hair down and risk an aneurysm, any one of these should do the trick.

After the demise of his previous band the Yardbirds in 1968, guitarist Jimmy Page formed **LED ZEPPELIN** with bassist John Paul Jones, singer Robert Plant, and drummer John Bonham. The new group turned the blues into what became known as heavy metal beginning with their first release, **Led Zeppelin** (Atlantic 1969). But it was their next album, **Led Zeppelin II** (also released in 1969 on Atlantic), that completed the transformation and laid down the blueprint for the genre, as well as turning the band into the biggest touring act of the seventies. Led Zeppelin's influence on rock music is hard to quantify but in their eleven-year career (which ended in 1980 with the alcohol-related death of Bonham) they made a series of albums that fused rock and folk music together with Middle Eastern influences, creating a unique body of work that stands alone in the history of rock, and has inspired countless bands in the years since.

Before Ozzy Osbourne became head of TV's most dysfunctional family, he was the singer in probably the most prototypical heavy metal band ever, **BLACK SABBATH**. Formed in Aston, Birmingham, they took their name from a book title by occult novelist Dennis Wheatley. The band's second and third albums, **Paranoid** and **Master of Reality** (both on Warner Brothers and released in 1971), catch the band at their best, with the simplicity of Ozzy's lyrics, taking on the subjects of death and destruction, combining with Tony Iommi's crashing guitar riffs in a way that influenced every heavy metal band to follow.

Like Black Sabbath, **JUDAS PRIEST** formed in Birmingham in 1970 and after a couple of early membership changes (one of the band's trademarks), the two musicians who were to turn the band into a major act joined the group, Glenn Tipton on guitar and Rob Halford on vocals. The band borrowed the guitar thrash of Zeppelin and the dense, dark blues of Sabbath to create their own brand of metal, but it was Halford's semi-classical voice that elevated their sound beyond anything that had come before. By 1980 the band were wearing a lot of studded leather and looking to America for their future, and that year's **British Steel** (Columbia) is the album that broke them into the international mainstream. Rob Halford left the band in 1993 and was replaced by American "Ripper" Owens, who had been the singer in a Judas Priest tribute band. Halford rejoined the group in 2004.

In 1973, while the Brits were setting the stage both at home and in the United States for hard rock to become heavy metal, down under in Sydney, Australia, guitarists Malcolm and Angus Young were forming a new group. A year later the band moved to Melbourne (at that time the center of the Australian music industry) where they recruited singer Bon Scott and **AC/DC** were born. By 1979 they had established themselves as one of the most important up-and-coming heavy metal acts in the world. The album **Highway to Hell** (Epic, 1979) broke them in the United States. But just as AC/DC were poised for major stardom tragedy struck, as Bon Scott joined the long list of senseless rock-and-roll early demises when he choked to death on his own vomit after a night of binge drinking. But success was not to elude AC/DC, who immediately recruited Brian Johnson from the British band Geordie to replace Scott, then promptly recorded their best and biggest-selling album, **Back in Black** (Epic, 1980). With its simple, hefty power chords and the classic song **You Shook Me All Night Long**, this is up there with the best hard rock and heavy metal albums ever recorded.

Another Brit band, **IRON MAIDEN**, can lay claim to being one of the most important groups to ever suit up in leathers and lay down heavy guitar riffs. They originally formed in the mid seventies and, like Judas Priest, underwent many personnel changes through the years. However, it was the arrival of singer Bruce Dickinson in 1982, adding his trademark piercing vocals to the band's sound, that led them to become a major band. Their album from that year, **The Number of the Beast** (Sony), set the stage for a decade of rock star success throughout the world. The band today continues to record and tour.

As the 1980s became the era of MTV and videos became de rigueur for any band that wanted to sell records, a lot of metal bands morphed into mannequins, and it all became about image. Los Angeles group **METALLICA** would have no part of that. Not only did they doggedly stay true to the grit of the music, they also ratcheted things up a notch with the speed of their playing. Metallica pretty much reinvented heavy metal in the 1980s, and their 1986 release **Master of Puppets** (Elektra) catches the band recording an album of epic anarchy. It was the biggest-selling release they'd had up until that point—all with no radio airplay or MTV support, just word of mouth. Of such things are rock legends created.

JIMI HENDRIX: ICON

In just a few short years at the end of the 1960s, Seattle-born Jimi Hendrix staked his claim as probably the most important electric guitarist ever. He also gained considerable attention for his onstage antics, which included playing the guitar with his teeth, smashing the instrument, and even pouring lighter fluid over it and setting it on fire. Hendrix certainly got everybody's attention.

His rise to stardom seemed surprisingly sudden, when in fact he had been working away at his craft touring on the R&B and soul circuit for a number of years as a sideman and session player with people like Little Richard, and Ike and Tina Turner. When Hendrix decided to go solo, he moved to New York and began playing under the name Jimmy James and the Blue Flames around the city's clubs. In one of those clubs, Café Wha? in Greenwich Village, he met Chas Chandler, the bass player for the Animals, who became his manager and persuaded Jimi to move to London. It didn't take long for things to happen as the band that was to become the Jimi Hendrix Experience was put together, with Noel Redding on bass and Mitch Mitchell on drums.

A string of singles in the summer of 1967, including **Hey Joe** and **Purple Haze**, hit the UK Top 10, followed by the debut album **Are You Experienced?**, which launched psychedelic rock onto an unsuspecting British public. America was next, and over the next three years Jimi Hendrix recorded some of the most important and influential rock music ever made, as well as giving legendary performances at the Monterey, Woodstock, and Isle of Wight music festivals. Like several of his contemporaries, Hendrix lived stardom full tilt, overindulging in alcohol and drugs and dying at the tragically young age of 27 in September 1970. At the time of his death, he had recorded much unreleased material that has found its way onto numerous posthumous releases, some good, some poor. Listed below are the studio albums that were recorded and released during his lifetime, all of which are essential listens:

> **Are You Experienced?** (MCA, 1967)
> **Axis: Bold as Love** (MCA, 1967)
> **Electric Ladyland** (MCA, 1968)

Also worth seeking out is the **Band of Gypsys** live album from 1970, released on Capitol. The Experience had broken up the previous summer, and this band was assembled in New York with Buddy Miles on drums and Billy Cox on bass. The album was put together from a 1970 New Year's Eve performance at the Fillmore East and shows Hendrix exploring the boundaries of his guitar-playing even further. The album includes a number of previously unreleased demos and is considered a truly great live album. It is also the only album of his live material that was released while he was still alive and with his approval.

HEY HO, LET'S GO: PUNK IN THE U.S.A.

The Brits would have you believe that they came up with punk rock circa 1976 with the Sex Pistols. Not so fast. The Pistols and their contemporaries did indeed kick it into gear, but punk rock started in New York City a year or two prior. Here are the essential American punk bands and their classic albums.

Though not part of the punk movement proper, **THE VELVET UNDERGROUND** need to be mentioned, as their importance and influence on the early New York punk rock scene cannot be overstated. From their formation in the mid-sixties, they defied convention and set about their music as one giant experiment, bringing together disparate musical styles and the intellectual avant-garde to create a body of work that most certainly sat on the left-hand side of the mainstream, thus setting the stage for an explosion of new bands willing to push the envelope even further. Their second album, **White Light/White Heat**, released in 1967 on Verve Records, catches them exploring and probing the edges of rock music. With lyrics covering sex, drugs, and violence, it was almost a blueprint for what was to come eight years later.

THE STOOGES weren't really a punk rock band; they actually formed almost a decade before the punk revolution in 1967. But front man Iggy Pop's attitude was certainly punk way before anybody came up with the genre-defining term. He would perform with self-inflicted cuts on his chest and throw himself around the stage in wild abandon while the band played its hard-edged brand of blues and garage rock. Their 1973 release **Raw Power**, reissued recently on Columbia's Legacy label, catches them at their most engaged and inventive.

THE NEW YORK DOLLS were part punk, part glam, part like nothing on earth! But there's no doubt about their importance to the story of punk rock. Malcolm McLaren, who went on to put together the Sex Pistols in 1976, managed the Dolls for a while in 1975 and learned a lot of lessons about how to shock, which he later put to good use with the Pistols. The Dolls' 1974 release **Too Much Too Soon**, on Mercury, was their second and final album.

THE RAMONES came together in Queens, New York, in 1974 and are acknowledged as the first punk rock band. All the band members took Ramone as their last name, and the image was simple: leather jackets and blue jeans. They quickly made a name for themselves with a string of two-minute, fast-paced rock songs, and there's no doubt that with their residency at the club CBGB's on New York City's Bowery they helped create and influence a scene that changed the face of music. Their third album, **Rocket to Russia**, released on Sire in 1977, features classic songs like **Rockaway Beach, Teenage Lobotomy**, and **Sheena Is a Punk Rocker**. With fourteen songs, the album clocks in at just a little over thirty-two minutes.

TELEVISION were also around before the punk rock explosion that hit New York in the mid-seventies. After playing around town since forming in 1973 and recording some demos for Island that were never released, they eventually scored a record deal with Elektra in 1977, but only released two albums before calling it a day. (They did reunite for another album in 1991.) The first album, **Marquee Moon**, with its ten-minute title track, showcases the unique talents of guitarists Tom Verlaine and Richard Lloyd.

JOHNNY THUNDERS & THE HEARTBREAKERS originally formed as a trio in 1975, with Richard Hell from Television and Johnny Thunders and Jerry Nolan from the New York Dolls, expanding later to a four-piece with Walter Lure. Hell left within a year to form his own band. The rest of the band actually moved to London for a year as the British punk scene ramped up, but they returned to the States by 1977 and broke up. They reunited on and off until Thunders's drug-overdose death in 1991. Their debut release **L.A.M.F.** on Track Records (1977) is hard to find these days but shows up as a Japanese import from time to time.

Richard Hell was an original member (playing bass) of Television, although he'd left the band by the time they released **Marquee Moon**. He went on to form the Heartbreakers with ex–New York Dolls Johnny Thunders and Jerry Nolan, but his time with that band was also short-lived, as he knew he needed to be a bandleader. With the formation of **RICHARD HELL & THE VOIDOIDS** that's exactly what happened. The band's first album, **Blank Generation**, released on Sire in 1977, is considered a punk rock classic.

THE DEAD BOYS formed out of a defunct Cleveland band called Rocket from the Tombs. When various members of that band moved to New York City and started their new group, they plugged right into the burgeoning scene at Hilly Kristal's CBGB's. With their basic three-chord attack and singer Stiv Bators's onstage mayhem, it was only a matter of time before they landed a record deal. This was another short-lived band that only made two records. The first one, **Young Loud & Snotty**, released in 1977 on Sire, says it all, really.

THE GERMS were an LA punk band led by eccentric singer Darby Crash. Crash's stage persona was somewhere between Sid Vicious and Iggy Pop. He was never going to last long. They only recorded one album, **(GI)**, in 1979 for Slash Records, which was produced by Joan Jett. It features Crash's full-throttle theatrics and guitarist Pat Smear ripping his way through the songs. Crash (real name Jan Paul Beahm) lived up to his name, flaming out at age 21 as a result of a heroin overdose.

THE DEAD KENNEDYS formed in San Francisco in 1978 and almost immediately ruffled the establishment with their mix of hardcore punk rock music and politics, not to mention their name. Led by Jello Biafra, they were at the forefront of a new movement of West Coast punk bands that took American punk into the eighties. Their music and onstage performance were incendiary, and they captured this on record with the 1980 album **Fresh Fruit for Rotting Vegetables**, released on IRS. The album was re-mastered and reissued on Cleopatra records in 2002. It's a slice of full throttle, left-wing, in-your-face punk that challenges the American status quo head on, kicking the door open for the West Coast hardcore punk scene.

FLIPPER were another band that came out of the San Francisco Bay Area hardcore punk scene of the early eighties. Unlike the Dead Kennedys, though, they allowed space within the music and, in fact, at times slowed the music down so much that they were considered "post hardcore." Their 1982 release **Generic Flipper** on Def American established them as one of the most important underground rock acts of their time. It closes with the classic seven-and-a-half-minute song **Sex Bomb**.

BLACK FLAG are probably the best known of all the LA punk bands. After forming in 1977 and going through several lineup changes, everything clicked when Henry Rollins, a fan of the band from Washington, D.C., joined as their singer. They blasted out of California in the early eighties, touring relentlessly across the United States, no doubt planting punk rock seeds along the way for hundreds of young musicians who followed. Their first album, 1981's **Damaged** on their own SST label, was savage in its musical and political onslaught and kick-started some serious rethinking in the California hardcore scene as to just what the music could achieve.

THE MINUTEMEN were formed by school friends D. Boon and Mike Watt, who later enlisted George Hurley to form a tight three-piece band that went on to record some of the most eclectic short punk rock tracks ever committed to vinyl. They weren't afraid to take on covers of unlikely songs either, and their fourth album, 1984's **Double Nickels on the Dime** (originally a double album) on SST, includes stripped-down versions of Creedence Clearwater Revival and Steely Dan songs. With forty-three tracks, the album clocks in at seventy-three minutes.

Hardcore punk never really went away; it mutated and survived underground in pockets around the country waiting for another opportunity to arise. When Nirvana exploded onto the alternative music scene in the nineties, punk did indeed return—see the "Smells Like Teen Spirit: The Sound of Seattle" essay in this book for details.

HIGHWAYMEN

In the summer of 1992, I had the good fortune to spend a week working on a crew that was putting up a stage for a benefit concert in Montauk, at the tip of New York's Long Island. The event was an annual fundraiser for the Montauk Lighthouse and had been hosted in alternate years by Long Island rock star residents Paul Simon and Billy Joel. The year I was working the event, Paul Simon topped the bill, but the other headliner was a band called **THE HIGHWAYMEN**, a supergroup of sorts comprised of some of country music's biggest legends: Willie Nelson, Waylon Jennings, Kris Kristofferson, and Johnny Cash. I'd never been a country music fan until the day I stood on the side of the stage I'd helped erect and saw these guys perform—right then and there my whole musical outlook was turned on its ear. These were real men, singing about real things: no pretense, no wannabe-rock-star attitude. Any attitude they had, had been earned from living through the stories they were telling in the music.

In 1985 these four giants of country music, all music outlaws in their own way, got together to record the album **Highwayman** on Columbia Records. It went straight to the top of the country music charts and spawned a couple of hit singles: the title cut, a cover of a Jimmy Webb song, and another cover, **Desperados Waiting for a Train**, written by Guy Clark. The album also included a couple of Johnny Cash originals. Over the next decade they got together to record two other collections, **Highwayman 2** (Columbia, 1990) and **Road Goes on Forever** (Capitol, 1995). The following gives some background on each artist and recommended listening from their individual careers.

Raised in Abbott, Texas, by his grandparents, **WILLIE NELSON** received his first guitar at just five years of age and began writing his first songs just a few years later. As a young man he played in various bands with his sister, Bobbie, before trying his hand as a DJ and then a singer. He eventually moved to Nashville in 1961 and worked as a songwriter for other country singers. After a few minor successes, Patsy Cline recorded his song **Crazy**, turning it into a huge pop hit, and his songwriting career began to flourish.

By the early 1970s Willie was out front singing and recording his own songs; with his friend Waylon Jennings he pioneered the "outlaw" sound of mixing rock with country music. **Shotgun Willie**, recorded for Atlantic Records in 1973, is regarded by many as one of his finest collections. While it fuses a number of musical styles, the essence of the record is Willie's ability to tell a tale. Through the years Willie has recorded an album almost every year, sometimes two or three, and has been both a prolific writer and performer. When the IRS came after him in 1990 Willie had to work even harder to pay off a big tax bill, but he weathered the storm and became a bigger cult hero than before.

One of the highlights of my radio career was sitting in a studio with Willie Nelson in October 2000 and having him play solo acoustic guitar accompanied only by a harmonica player. In between songs like **Crazy** and **Milk Cow Blues**, we chatted up a storm about his career and just had a grand ole time. A cut from that session, **Healing Hands of Time**, appears on the KCRW compilation **Sounds Eclectic**, released in 2001 on Palm Records.

Another Texan who began playing guitar as a young boy, **WAYLON JENNINGS** also became a radio DJ as a young man before his music career took off. His first break came when he filled in on bass for Buddy Holly's band the Crickets. (He was actually supposed to fly on the plane that crashed and killed Holly in 1959, giving up his seat to the Big Bopper, who was feeling unwell.)

After Holly's death, it took Waylon a few years to get back on his feet emotionally. After a stint in Los Angeles he moved to Nashville, where he became great friends with Johnny Cash. Waylon began recording his own style of honky-tonk and country but began to feel restricted by the country music machine that was Nashville. He also became friends with songwriters Kris Kristofferson and Willie Nelson, and separately and together they began to write and record country music outside of the constraints of the Nashville system. His 1972 album **Lonesome, On'ry and Mean**, recorded for RCA, catches him in full throttle, producing and recording songs by a number of songwriters, including his future Highwaymen bandmates. Throughout the seventies and into the early eighties, Waylon was a genuine country superstar and continued recording and releasing records up to his death in 2002.

Growing up in England with no concept of what country music was or who its stars were, my only exposure to **KRIS KRISTOFFERSON** was seeing him as an actor in movies like *A Star Is Born* and *Convoy*. Little did I know that he had written some of the most popular songs ever recorded, such as **Me and Bobby McGee, Help Me Make It Through the Night**, and **One Day at a Time**. His personal history includes studying creative writing at college in Claremont, California, receiving a Rhodes scholarship to Oxford University in England, and serving a stint in the Army as a helicopter pilot.

While many of his songs have been recorded by artists as diverse as Gladys Knight, Willie Nelson, and Marianne Faithfull, Kris's own recordings have met with mixed reviews. However, his second album for Monument Records, **The Silver Tongued Devil and I**, released in 1971 and featuring a mix of affectionate love songs and observations on life, was the album that saw him establish himself as a successful recording artist and heralded a diverse career as a performer of music and a film actor.

JOHNNY CASH was one person I wanted to get on my radio program and never did. I did get to meet him on that stage in Montauk in 1992, and he was indeed that big man in black. But he was also a giant in the sense that he was one of a kind, an original in so many ways. Johnny was born and raised in Arkansas, and just like Willie and Waylon learned to play music and write songs as a young boy. He did a stint in the Air Force in the 1950s, during which he became serious about writing songs. He moved to Memphis with his first wife, performing with a country music trio; he also worked as a radio announcer, again like Willie and Waylon.

After auditioning for Sun Records owner Sam Phillips in 1955, it wasn't long before Johnny's songs began making waves. By the end of the decade he had topped the charts with a couple of hits, including **I Walk the Line** and **Folsom Prison Blues**, and moved on to Columbia Records. In the early sixties he began his struggle with amphetamine addiction but still managed to record and release music. When he cleaned up and married his second wife, June Carter, in 1968 and embraced Christianity, his music returned to some of his gospel roots. His two legendary live albums from this time were **Folsom Prison** (1968) and **At San Quentin** (1969), both for Columbia Records and both recorded in front of prison audiences as he sang songs about murder, loss, remorse, and prison. Both albums were reissued on CD a few years ago with bonus material that didn't make it onto the original vinyl releases.

Throughout the seventies Johnny's success continued as he hosted his own network TV show for two seasons and acted in a number of movies, but as the eighties arrived and country music began to turn to more manufactured contemporary artists, his record sales dropped. Apart from the Highwaymen records his career was, by his own standards, in decline. It wasn't until 1993 when he signed with Rick Rubin's American Recordings that Johnny's career was revitalized. He recorded a collection of acoustic songs over the course of four albums produced by Rubin that brought him to a younger audience. Ironically, this new audience was not a country audience but more geared toward rock. The albums' material was for the most part his own, but he also covered the work of such artists as Tom Waits, Nick Cave, Soundgarden, and U2. In fact, his last hit from his final studio album, **American IV: The Man Comes Around** (Universal, 2002), was a sparse but powerful recording of the Nine Inch Nails song **Hurt**. It found him getting significant airplay on alternative rock radio. Johnny had been in and out of the hospital a number of times during the nineties and been close to death; however, it was a surprise to everyone when his wife June suddenly died in May 2003. Without his "rock," Johnny himself passed away that September at the age of 71.

HIP-HOP, DON'T STOP

From the moment the first slaves arrived in America, African-American artists have used their voices to keep their spirits alive and sung lyrics that have camouflaged and hidden their true meanings from those not in the know. Many trends in American popular music have begun in the black music community. Take the beginning of rock and roll: There could never have been an Elvis Presley without black artists like Roy Brown, Clyde McPhatter, and Big Joe Turner. Likewise, the Beatles and the Rolling Stones owe a huge debt to artists such as Chuck Berry, Little Richard, and Howlin' Wolf. It seems that every generation or so, a new musical style bubbles up from the underground and scares the hell out of the keepers of the nation's morals, as well as a whole host of teenagers' parents, before being co-opted by corporate America and finding itself the next big marketing tool. Such is the case with hip-hop.

The history of hip-hop goes back to the mid-1970s when rap first appeared, so called because that's what the vocalists did, with no singing as such, but rather a rapid-fire delivery of words (not unlike Jamaican reggae toasters) over drum machine beats and records scratched by DJs. It started on the streets of the Bronx and Brooklyn and soon spread across all five boroughs of New York City, and eventually jumped across the country to California before working its way inland from both coasts. As the artists developed their craft, sampling became a more and more important part of creating new sounds. This caused problems, as the owners of the work being sampled quite rightly wanted payment; in many cases they were black artists from another generation such as James Brown and George Clinton. By the early 1990s an unspoken agreement was made within the record and music publishing industries whereby a percentage of ownership for the owner of the sample would be negotiated by their lawyers for any new song featuring a sample. The rate varies depending on the usage. It's usually somewhere between 10 and 50 percent, although in extreme cases the owner of the sample may demand complete control of the new composition.

The music found mainstream success in the mid-1980s as white kids in middle America began to discover that the alienation so many of the rappers spoke about wasn't exclusive to the projects of New York or the rundown blocks of East Los Angeles. It was also significant that the Beastie Boys, a group of white rappers from New York City, arrived on the scene in 1986 and made rap more attractive to white kids. As the eighties ended, rap featured social commentary in a way not seen since the folk movement of the early sixties. It was also around this time that hip-hop took two distinctly different paths. On the commercial side of things, rappers such as MC Hammer and Vanilla Ice (the first white rapper to attract a significant audience) took their brand of smooth-edged hip-hop to the masses and cleaned up on the pop charts. At the other end of the spectrum came gangsta rap, with lyrics that were often misogynist, homophobic, and threatening. In fact, in the early nineties a war erupted between rival factions from the East and West Coasts that led to the (still unsolved) murders of a number of rap artists including Biggie Smalls (aka The Notorious B.I.G.) and Tupac Shakur.

As the decade and century closed, hip-hop continued to mutate and gave us Eminem, a white rapper from Detroit who pretty much everyone in the community agreed was one of the best to ever pick up a microphone. His lyrics were controversial, causing outrage among society's "moral guardians" and a resulting media frenzy—which predictably ensured that almost every disaffected teenager bought his records. As the new millennium began, hip-hop also saw a big crossover into the pop world, but this time with groups who were well respected, such as OutKast and Black Eyed Peas, selling millions of records worldwide. Listed below are twenty albums that cover the history of hip-hop in all its various incarnations:

THE SUGARHILL GANG: *The Sugarhill Gang* (Sugar Hill, 1980)

GRANDMASTER FLASH: *The Message* (Castle Music, 1982)

RUN-D.M.C.: *King of Rock* (Arista, 1985)

AFRIKA BAMBAATAA: *Planet Rock—The Album* (Tommy Boy, 1986)

BEASTIE BOYS: *Licensed To Ill* (Def Jam, 1986)

PUBLIC ENEMY: *It Takes a Nation of Millions to Hold Us Back* (Def Jam, 1988)

N.W.A: *Straight Outta Compton* (Priority, 1989)

DE LA SOUL: *3 Feet High and Rising* (Tommy Boy, 1989)

QUEEN LATIFAH: *All Hail the Queen* (Tommy Boy, 1989)

GANG STARR: *Daily Operation* (Capitol, 1992)

GURU: *Jazzmatazz, Vol.1* (Capitol, 1993)

A TRIBE CALLED QUEST: *Midnight Marauders* (Jive, 1993)

US3: *Hand on the Torch* (Blue Note, 1993)

SNOOP DOGG: *Doggystyle* (Death Row, 1993)

2PAC: *Me Against the World* (Interscope, 1995)

THE FUGEES: *The Score* (Columbia, 1996)

PUFF DADDY: *No Way Out* (Bad Boy, 1997)

BLACK EYED PEAS: *Behind the Front* (Interscope, 1998)

EMINEM: *The Marshall Mathers LP* (Interscope, 2000)

OUTKAST: *Stankonia* (La Face, 2000)

HIT THE ROAD, JACK

Taking a road trip is a great opportunity to assemble a whole bunch of music for the drive. Sometimes you might want to pick music that reflects or matches the mood you're in, and other times you might want to select your music to get you in the mood for a long day or night ahead. Growing up in England, my early road trips weren't that long—it's hard to drive much more than two or three hours on any given trip in a country that's about the same size as Delaware. In fact, for most trips, one or two cassettes would do the job. It wasn't until I lived in Australia for a while in the eighties and then later when I moved to the United States that I really got to understand the value of a well-chosen half dozen or so CDs. It really can make the difference between an enjoyable twelve-hour drive or an unbearable half day in a tin can on wheels. Here's a list of albums I think will make it a little easier next time you head out on the interstate:

> **VAN MORRISON**: *Astral Weeks* (Warner Brothers, 1968): This album is folk blues at its best with Van playing acoustic guitar and a string section accompanying him. Top it off with his evocative lyrics of growing up, and it's the perfect album for a drive under the stars.
>
> **THE ROLLING STONES**: *Sticky Fingers* (Virgin, 1971): You cannot drive across America without a Rolling Stones album, and this one's bluesy and dark. It's perfect as you're driving through those twilight zone towns in the middle of nowhere.

NICK DRAKE: *Pink Moon* (Island, 1971): If your nighttime drive takes you into the early predawn hours, then pop this in for the final stretch. Nick Drake had a sublime voice, and this is a beautiful collection of unadorned, acoustic, melancholic songs.

AC/DC: *Highway to Hell* (Epic, 1979): The quintessential road trip record: No one has ever fallen asleep at the wheel with this on the sound system. Pop this in for any highway that goes around or through a major metropolis.

FRANKIE GOES TO HOLLYWOOD: *Welcome to the Pleasuredome* (Island, 1984): Frankie appeared from nowhere in the summer of 1984 and disappeared shortly thereafter, but they left this great album of powerful dance pop music, which is especially good for coastal road driving.

N.W.A: *Straight Outta Compton* (Priority, 1989): This is intense rap music right out of the ghetto, lyrically questionable at times, but there's no doubt about its authenticity. If you're feeling pissed off about the state of the world, hit the road and crank this one up.

THE DANDY WARHOLS: *Thirteen Tales from Urban Bohemia* (Capitol, 2000): It's a baker's dozen of solid head-bopping power pop, perfect for that drive through the Corn Belt.

THE FLAMING LIPS: *Yoshimi Battles the Pink Robots* (Warner Brothers, 2002): My friend Gary Jules likes this record because it's positive, and let's face it, you need some positive vibes out there on the roads. It's also rich with lyrical fantasy, an essential for UFO-spotting during long drives at dusk.

HONKY-TONK ANGELS AND A COAL MINER'S DAUGHTER

Before country music became just another demographically guided marketing tool, there were country singers who had lived the hard lives they sang about in their music. Female artists like Dolly Parton, who grew up with eleven siblings and parents who could barely afford to feed them, let alone buy them clothes, and Loretta Lynn, who was married at thirteen, led the way in the sixties and seventies for strong, independent women in country music.

KITTY WELLS was probably country music's first true female star and one of the few actually born in Nashville. After singing in various duos and groups, including with her sisters and her husband, Johnnie Wright, her solo career took off in 1952 with a hit single recording of **It Wasn't God Who Made Honky Tonk Angels**. For most of the fifties and the first half of the sixties she racked up a string of hits on the country charts, many of them with feminist lyrics that responded to the misogynistic male country music of the day. She paved the way for a lot of the women below. **Country Music Hall of Fame Series** (MCA, 1991) is a collection of sixteen of her singles recorded for Decca between 1952 and 1965.

Dying in a plane crash in 1963 at the age of just thirty all but assured **PATSY CLINE**'s legendary status. However, the recordings she left behind back it up. Her early 1950s records are in more of a rockabilly style, but her breakthrough came with lush production by Owen Bradley and more romantic songs like Willie Nelson's **Crazy** and Hank Williams's **Your Cheatin' Heart**. Check out 1962's **Sentimentally Yours** on MCA for some of her best work.

When you have a movie made about your life (*Coal Miner's Daughter*), chances are you've already made a few people sit up and take notice. **LORETTA LYNN** was one of the biggest stars in country music through the late sixties and seventies, with a string of hits. What was unusual, though, was that she was a pioneer in writing about women's issues. Songs such as **Don't Come Home a Drinkin' (With Lovin' on Your Mind)** and **The Pill** were not only overtly feminist but also written from experience. Her 1971 album **Coal Miner's Daughter** on MCA is a solid collection of songs featuring Loretta at her best and isn't connected with her autobiography or movie of the same name (which was released in theaters nearly a decade later). In 2004 Loretta Lynn also released a comeback album of sorts on Interscope, produced by Jack White of the White Stripes, called **Van Lear Rose**.

Originally from Oklahoma, **JEAN SHEPARD** was raised in Bakersfield, California, and began her career as a honky-tonk singer with early success singing duets with Ferlin Husky. She recorded consistently for Capitol Records and United Artists throughout the fifties, sixties, and seventies, her breakthrough coming in the mid-sixties after her husband, Hawkshaw Hawkins, was killed in the plane crash that also took the life of her friend Patsy Cline. Few of her original albums have been released on CD; however, **This Is Jean Shepard** (1959) was recently reissued on First Generation Records.

At age thirteen **WANDA JACKSON** had her own radio show in Oklahoma and by age sixteen she was on tour with Elvis Presley. Her career encompassed both country and rockabilly styles, and she also recorded several gospel albums in the seventies after becoming a born-again Christian. Her 1960 release on Capitol, **Rockin' with Wanda**, is a terrific collection that showcases her rockabilly singles.

Born in McMinnville, Tennessee, and raised with her nine siblings by a single mother, **DOTTIE WEST**'s background paved the way for a career as a country singer. After starting out as a traditional interpreter of country music, she surprisingly became known as one of Nashville's first pop crossover successes in the early seventies, with several singles in the Top 40 as well as a string of duets with Kenny Rogers that included a couple of chart-toppers. Not many of Dottie's albums have been reissued on CD; try **The Essential Dottie West** compilation from RCA (1996).

DOLLY PARTON's song **Coat of Many Colors** pretty much sums up where Dolly came from. Its lyrics tell the tale of how her folks were so poor, her mom made her a coat out of cast-off material scraps. She went on to become the most successful country singer ever, on an international scale. She's also well known for her acting skills in television and movies and has written many of the songs she's recorded. Stylistically she's gone from country to pop, with a few stops in between. My favorite album is a recent release from 1999 on Sugar Hill Records called **The Grass Is Blue**, where she revisits her bluegrass roots.

After her father died when she was a baby and her mother moved away, **TAMMY WYNETTE** was raised by her grandparents in Mississippi. By the time she was in her mid-twenties she was divorced with three children and began singing to pay the bills. She went on to become the most successful country singer of her generation with a string of hits in the seventies. I recommend her third album, 1967's **D-I-V-O-R-C-E**, reissued on CD by Koch.

Born into the famous musical Carter family, it was inevitable that **JUNE CARTER CASH** would write and perform country music. She did so originally with her sisters Anita and Helen as the

Carter Sisters, as well as with the whole family. When the Carter Family went on tour opening for Johnny Cash (June cowrote his hit **Ring of Fire**) in the early sixties, the seeds were planted for a romance that led to June and Johnny marrying in 1968 and to June largely retreating from performing. Toward the end of her life she recorded several albums, and 2003's **Wildwood Flower** on Dualtone Records features contributions from Johnny as well as various children and grandchildren. Both June and Johnny passed away within months of its release.

HUSBANDS AND WIVES

B eing in a relationship can be complicated enough at the best of times. The pressures of everyday life, financial decisions and careers, and raising children can all take their toll on even the most secure marriages. It takes a brave (or naïve) couple then to decide that they want to work together as well. So, okay, maybe opening a flower shop together might work, but just how crazy are you to be a married couple in a rock-and-roll band?

When songwriter Salvatore Bono met Cherilyn Lapierre in 1964, a rock-and-roll legend was in the making. They began making music together as **SONNY AND CHER**, fell in love, and then married. Success came quickly with a string of hit singles between 1964 and 1967, including **I Got You Babe** and **The Beat Goes On**. But their biggest success was to come in the early seventies, after the initial burst of stardom. When the hits dried up, Sonny and Cher took their act on the road, and in between the songs they developed a sitcom-like routine with Sonny as the straight man and Cher as the joker. They were spotted in Las Vegas and offered a show on television.

In 1971 "The Sonny & Cher Show" debuted on CBS and became an instant hit. During the next three years, their career as a duo hit new heights, as did Cher's solo career. Their personal relationship soured as the TV show's numbers were dropping, and they separated around the same time that the show ended in 1974. Cher went on to an acting career with lead roles in movies like *Silkwood* and Sonny became a restaurateur and later on a politician, first as mayor of Palm Springs and later as a Republican congressman. He died tragically in a skiing accident in 1998. Cher went on to become a huge international solo artist and gay icon, who continues, it seems, to hit the road every couple of years for a farewell tour! As with most singles acts, the albums they made during their career were a little inconsistent. Pick up **The Beat Goes On: The Best of Sonny & Cher**, released on Rhino in 1993. It has all of the early hits.

Ike Turner had been playing piano and guitar in an R&B ensemble called the Kings of Rhythm in Memphis and later St. Louis in the first half of the 1950s. The band had been extremely successful in both cities but was lacking that one special ingredient, a charismatic singer. When Ike met Annie Mae Bullock, things were about to change. Ike added her to his band's revue, Annie Mae changed her name to Tina, and before long she was the star of the show. **IKE & TINA TURNER** were married soon afterwards, and renamed the band the Ike & Tina Turner Revue, taking the band on the road to stardom.

While Ike was happy about the success, he had a tough time with Tina getting all the attention. He had long been a control freak and an active alcohol and drug abuser. It was unknown to all but a few on the inside, but as the group topped the charts with a series of clever covers and songs of their own, there was another type of hit happening, spousal abuse. Throughout their relationship Ike violently beat and terrorized Tina. As is the story with many battered wives, Tina took a long time to leave, but eventually she made the break and left him. As she walked out, she gave up control of any of the music they had made together, and it took a while for her to establish herself as a solo artist. When she did, though, she became the biggest rock and soul diva of the 1980s while Ike's career largely went up in smoke. Because Ike & Tina never stuck with one record label for more than a couple of singles their album output is decidedly spotty; however, the album **River Deep, Mountain High** recorded in 1966 on A&M with Phil Spector producing five of the album's twelve songs, including the glorious title track, showcases Tina's hugely powerful voice against Spector's classic "wall of sound." Be aware, though, it's pretty tough to find this on CD.

Nickolas Ashford and Valerie Simpson, who performed as **ASHFORD & SIMPSON**, began their careers as songwriters in the mid sixties, penning such hits as **Let's Go Get Stoned** for Ray Charles and **Ain't Nothing Like the Real Thing** for Marvin Gaye and Tammi Terrell. They also wrote songs for several other Motown artists before getting married and embarking on their own recording career in the early seventies. They recorded several gold albums in that decade and into the eighties, consistently placing singles on the R&B and pop charts. Though largely retired from performing, they continue to write for other artists and occasionally release records. **Is It Still Good to Ya**, released on Warner Brothers in 1978, is a short album, clocking in at just over 34 minutes and with only eight songs, but it catches them at their peak as recording artists.

PAUL AND LINDA MCCARTNEY became a couple as the Beatles were disintegrating. When the group called it quits in 1970 and Paul decided to form a new band, **WINGS**, he wanted his wife—who had proved such an inspiration to his songwriting on his solo album **Ram**—with him, so she joined the band as a keyboard player. She had only studied piano for a couple of years, and her skills were rudimentary at best, but despite some nasty criticism she stuck with it and toured and recorded with the group throughout its career (1971–78). **Band on the Run**, released on Capitol in 1973, is the highlight from their group.

TINA WEYMOUTH AND CHRIS FRANTZ were the rhythm section that laid down the groove for the band **TALKING HEADS**. They first met in college at Rhode Island School of Design. Chris was then playing in a band with David Byrne called the Artistics. Eventually, Weymouth, Frantz, and Byrne all found themselves back in New York, where Chris and David decided to team up again to play music. Tina picked up a bass guitar, and with Chris on drums and David as frontman, they formed Talking Heads in 1974, initially as a three-piece band. The group went on to success, first as a cult band breaking out of the CBGB's scene in New York's Lower East Side, and then after adding keyboardist Jerry Harrison with their debut release **Talking Heads: 77** on Sire records. That same year Tina and Chris married.

After Talking Heads hit it big worldwide, Tina and Chris, needing to let off steam, formed a side project called the **TOM TOM CLUB**, which has been a sporadic recording and touring project over the years. Their first album, **Tom Tom Club**, featuring the much-sampled single **Genius of Love**, was released on Sire in 1981. It was a surprise hit and still stands up well. Although Talking Heads called it quits on 1991, Chris and Tina have continued to write and record with various projects and also work as producers for other artists, including the Happy Mondays and Ziggy Marley.

THURSTON MOORE AND KIM GORDON were dating when they formed **SONIC YOUTH** along with Lee Ranaldo in New York in 1981. With Thurston and Lee both playing guitar and Kim on bass, they added drummer Richard Edson (who went on to become a highly regarded indie film actor in such films as *Do the Right Thing*) and keyboard player Anne DeMarinis. The band made their first live performance at the "Noise Festival," which was a celebration of the "no wave" movement that had immediately followed the punk scene. They soon became known for their trademark washes of guitar feedback, and throughout the eighties built a solid underground reputation, releasing a series of independent EPs and albums. Thurston and Kim married in 1984. In 1990 the group signed to DGC records, who promised them the freedom to record the music that they wanted to make and give them the marketing and promotional support that they had always lacked. As a result, the group's profile was raised significantly and they were hailed as the "godfathers" of alternative rock. When alternative radio exploded across the country in the early nineties with bands like Nirvana and Pearl Jam, Sonic Youth achieved significant commercial success. Their 2002 album **Murray Street**, on Interscope, pays its respects to their guitar-drenched past, but also has a melancholic feel that shows the band has grown and matured over their twenty-plus years.

WIN BUTLER AND RÉGINE CHASSAGNE are a married couple at the heart of the Montreal-based indie rock band **THE ARCADE FIRE**. Along with Win's brother William, Tim Kingsbury, and Richard Parry, the band formed in 2003 and released their highly acclaimed debut **Funeral** on Merge records in 2004. The album covers a lot of musical (think Belle & Sebastian meets the Polyphonic Spree) and emotional (several members of the group lost family members during the album's making) ground with powerful songs of despair, loss, and ultimately, love.

ICELAND ROCKS

The windswept, almost arctic island of Iceland was until recently best known for its natural hot springs and cod-fishing fleet. In the last fifteen years it's given birth to more bands per habitable square mile than just about anywhere on Earth. As one of the members of Gus Gus told me a few years ago, "There's really nothing to do except make love and play music." Here's a list of some Icelandic artists and their albums.

BJÖRK is Iceland's best-known musical export to date. Before embarking on a solo career, she was a member of **THE SUGARCUBES**, a group that evolved out of Iceland's early eighties punk scene into a band with a unique brand of melodic pop. The Sugarcubes' 1988 debut **Life's Too Good** (Elektra) was well received and broke out of Iceland and onto U.S. college radio charts. The band made two more albums that were also well reviewed but, due to internal tensions (members getting divorced and so forth), they broke up in 1992. The following year Björk released her debut solo album, **Debut** (Elektra), and shifted her music in a more dance and electronic direction. Her 2001 release **Vespertine** (Elektra) is also worth picking up.

Also hailing from Iceland are **GUS GUS**, a collective of filmmakers, musicians, and DJs, who in the late nineties managed to endear themselves to both the indie rock and dance communities. Their debut release **Polydistortion** (4AD, 1997) showcases the band at its eclectic best.

SIGUR RÓS are named after Victory Rose, the younger sister of one of the band members. In 1999 they recorded their second album, **Ágaetis Byrjun** (PIAS America). Frontman Jon Thor Birgisson sings falsetto in a made-up language he calls Hopelandic. He also plays his guitar with a violin bow. The group's music fuses wild, windswept, and otherworldly elements that crystallize into one of the most unique records I've ever heard.

IT'S RAINING CATS AND DOGS

When I was about seven years old, my mum persuaded me to convince my dad that I wanted a cat. Of course it was my mum who wanted the pet, but nonetheless we ended up with a beautiful blue point Siamese cat we called Dolly, after the song and movie *Hello Dolly*, which had been a big hit that summer. I remember how Dolly got on top of the kitchen cupboards and the mice I brought home from school to feed during the holidays died of fright! I've always had pets ever since. Gosh, I don't know . . . through the various relationships I've been in I must have fed and changed litter trays for almost fifteen kitties. At the time of this writing, my family has four cats and a dog living with us in our small house.

What is it about humans that compels us to have these little creatures in our lives? I guess it depends on the individual, but I think that one way or another it probably all comes down to the need for company. It's also intriguing to me that some people will only have cats, while others would never have a cat and insist that they are "dog people." Interesting, as well, that so many artists and groups would include some type of cat or dog in their name. Here's a few such artists, with recommended listening for each.

CAT STEVENS was one of the most prolific singer/songwriters of the late sixties and early seventies, recording a string of hit singles (such as **Matthew & Son, Morning Has Broken**, and **Peace Train**) and albums that sold well on both sides of the Atlantic. Toward the end of the seventies, he became a Muslim, changing his name to Yusuf Islam and retiring from the music business to focus on his religious studies and charity work. He provoked huge outrage in 1988 when he surfaced to voice what was interpreted as support of Iranian leader Ayatollah Khomeini and his fatwa (death sentence) ordered against author Salman Rushdie in response to the book *The Satanic Verses*. Islam/Stevens has consistently denied ever supporting the fatwa, insisting that he only tried to explain the Islamic religious texts that supported Khomeini's edict. (Visit catstevens.com to read his statements on this matter.) The Cat Stevens back catalog was remastered and reissued by A&M in 2000, including a compilation **The Very Best of Cat Stevens**. Listening to it recently for the first time, I was amazed at just how many recognizable hits the twenty-song compilation contains; I thoroughly recommend it as a starting point for anyone who wants to explore Cat Stevens's body of work.

JOSIE AND THE PUSSYCATS had their own weekly TV series in the seventies and were one of the most successful all-girl trios of the decade. Of course, they also had tails and ears, which made them different, but then again, they were animated characters. The cartoon series inspired one self-titled album of bubblegum pop, released on Capitol in 1970.

THE STRAY CATS were an early-1980s Long Island rockabilly band that achieved a short-lived but huge popularity in both the UK and the United States. Their 1982 release **Built for Speed**, reissued on DCC, catches them at their best. Singer Brian Setzer went on to later successes with his own swing orchestra.

CAT POWER is the alter ego of Chan Marshall, a compelling songwriter who has released several albums since 1995. My favorite is **You Are Free**, released in 2003 on Matador.

ATOMIC KITTEN are quite simply three very attractive, sexy girls who followed in the footsteps of the Spice Girls with a series of dance-pop singles on the UK charts. Their debut album from 2001 on EMI was called **Right Now**.

ACTUAL TIGERS were an alternative band that released a good collection of pop songs called **Gravelled and Green** in 2001 on Nettwerk records. The album's sound is reminiscent of Paul Simon and Elliott Smith.

PEDRO THE LION is essentially the solo project of Seattle musician David Bazan, who apparently made up the name for a children's book character before using it for his musical nom de plume. His 2004 album **Achilles Heel**, on Jade Tree records, is a collection of indie folk-rock songs.

THREE DOG NIGHT were a hugely successful rock/pop band in the first half of the 1970s that featured three vocalists. They recorded a string of hit singles, the best known being Mama Told Me (Not to Come). I suggest listening to **The Complete Hit Singles**, a compilation released by Universal in 2004.

THE DINGOES named themselves after the wild dogs that roam the Australian outback. The group was formed by guitarist Kerryn Tolhurst and singer/harmonica player Broderick Smith in 1971, after they both returned from a stint in Vietnam with the Australian army. After playing in a couple of blues bands together, they formed the Dingoes. The band was uniquely Australian in its reference points, but they were also influenced by the California sound of bands like the Eagles and the Byrds. Their 1977 release **Five Times the Sun** is available as an import on Universal.

SKINNY PUPPY formed in Vancouver, British Columbia, in 1982 and throughout the next decade took their dark electronic goth sound and recorded a series of multilayered dissonant albums that were at the forefront of what became industrial music. **VIVIsectVI**, released in 1988 on Nettwerk, pretty much laid out the blueprint for the industrial artists who followed, such as Nine Inch Nails.

Los Angeles–based punk pop band **THAT DOG** included Anna Waronker and sisters Petra and Rachel Haden (daughters of jazz great Charlie). The group released three well-received alternative rock albums in the mid-1990s before calling it quits. **Totally Crushed Out!** is a collection of songs about first loves that was released in 1995 on Geffen.

Though **DOGS DIE IN HOT CARS** may sound like a public service announcement, it is actually the name of a young Scottish group whose sound is reminiscent of New Wave bands like XTC and Talking Heads. Their debut album **Please Describe Yourself** was released on V2 in 2004.

JAZZ VOCALISTS: THE LADIES

Though by and large the world of jazz has been very much a man's world, many of the best-known jazz artists are women. Through the years it's been the female vocalists, many of whom started out as gospel or blues singers, who've helped put the music on the map and taken it to a wider audience. Here is a list of some of those pioneering women and their essential albums.

Certainly, the most recognizable female jazz vocalist is **BILLIE HOLIDAY**. Check out my essay "Naughty Girls" for more details on her and her best albums.

ELLA FITZGERALD was a major star of the Swing Era and a bandleader early in her career, when she took over the reins of the orchestra led by Chick Webb, whom she had been working for when he passed away. Over the years she sang with all the great bands, including those led by Dizzy Gillespie (she learned to scat while working with his band), Count Basie, and Duke Ellington. She also recorded a huge amount of material—the American Songbook series for Verve, featuring the work of artists such as Cole Porter, the Gershwins, Duke Ellington, Johnny Mercer, and others, took her most of the second half of the fifties. She had a very wide vocal range and was considered one of the finest popular song interpreters, and pretty much the quintessential jazz singer. Her 1945 release for Decca, **Lullabies of Birdland** (available on CD as an import from Universal), is a great place to start.

BESSIE SMITH was first and foremost a blues singer. She recorded and performed regularly throughout the 1920s and achieved a stardom that others could only hope for. As the Roaring Twenties gave way to the Great Depression, though, blues unsurprisingly fell out of favor, as did artists like Bessie. She did, however, continue making music and began working with jazz musicians and songs. She was on the verge of a comeback when she was killed in a car accident in 1937 at age forty-three. Most of her recordings have been reissued by Columbia in some form or another, though rarely as the original albums; **The Collection** (1989) is a sixteen-track introduction to her work and includes some truly wonderful collaborations with Louis Armstrong.

As a child, **SARAH VAUGHAN** became her local church's organist in her hometown of Newark, New Jersey, where she had sung in the choir. When she won a talent contest in 1942 at the famed Apollo Theater in Harlem, she was offered a gig as pianist and singer in Earl Hines's big band. There was no looking back from that moment on for Sarah, who possessed a remarkably expressive voice and could scat with the best. After a short stint in another big band led by Billy Eckstine, she spent most of the rest of her career as a solo artist, performing mainly with a trio of piano, double bass, and drums. At various times her trio consisted of the best players available; all the guys wanted to play with her. One of her best releases with a trio is **Swingin' Easy** from 1954, available on CD from Polygram.

One of the most abstract and innovative jazz singers, **BETTY CARTER** was equally comfortable singing standards and ballads. She grew up in Detroit and began her career sitting in with whomever was in town; artists like Charlie Parker and Duke Ellington would always call her, and consequently she developed a wideranging style before she was hired by Lionel Hampton. After she left Hampton's band she toured with Miles Davis for the last few years of the fifties, and when Davis suggested her to Ray Charles in 1961, she and Charles cut a now classic album together, **Ray Charles and Betty Carter**. The album was combined with another Charles album, **Dedicated To You**, for a 1998 CD reissue on Rhino.

Carter spent most of the sixties being a mom to her two sons. When she returned to the music world in the seventies and couldn't get a record deal, she showed an amazing amount of confidence in herself by starting her own label, Bet-Car, to release her recordings. In 1988 she signed a new record deal with Verve and enjoyed a renewed interest in her work up until her death in 1998. **The Audience With Betty Carter**, originally released as a double album on her own label in 1979, is now available from Verve and shows off her incredible diversity.

Probably the most respected jazz singer of the nineties, **CASSANDRA WILSON** has a beautifully husky voice and has gained a reputation as someone who constantly challenges herself and her audience. Her choice of material has veered from standards to blues and, most recently, folk and country music. Her 1993 Blue Note release **Blue Light 'Til Dawn** shows off her versatility as she sings several of her own compositions alongside covers of material by Robert Johnson, Van Morrison, and Joni Mitchell.

It might seem a bit premature to include **NORAH JONES** on a list like this, but any artist who can seemingly arrive from nowhere, sell more than 14 million copies of her debut record, and single-handedly reinvigorate what was a decidedly stagnant jazz music industry deserves to be here. I first met Norah in 2001 when she performed a song on my radio program with the Charlie Hunter Quintet. I was struck immediately by her smoky voice and warm personality, and invited her to come back with her own band a few months later, on the day her first album, **Come Away with Me**, was released on Blue Note. Everyone in the studio that day knew we were witnessing a special artist, but none of us could have predicted her huge success.

JAZZ VOCALISTS: THE MEN

Now let's look at some of the men who put jazz singing on the map. Some of them went on to have careers that eclipsed their humble beginnings; others stayed true to their roots. Either way, all of them created memorable music and legacies that can be heard on CD. (A brief note: One vocalist not listed here is Frank Sinatra; you can read more about him in the essay "The Rat Pack.")

Although he's remembered as one of the biggest pop singers of the forties and fifties, **NAT KING COLE** began his career as a jazz pianist, influencing a generation of other players, such as Oscar Peterson and Bill Evans. As a successful African-American entertainer amidst a time of bubbling social upheaval, he was often in a no-win position: On the one hand, his career was impacted profoundly by racism; on the other, he was branded a sellout. When he found fame as a singer he was shunned by jazz fans in much the same way Bob Dylan was treated by folk purists when he first plugged in his guitar. Before Nat primarily became a more mainstream singer he recorded with his band the Nat King Cole Trio; the 1956 Capitol release **After Midnight** showcases his piano playing as well as his voice, and proves beyond any doubt that he was first and foremost a jazz musician.

Beginning with Earl Hines's orchestra and later fronting his own big band (which included the likes of Charlie Parker, Dizzy Gillespie, and Miles Davis, as well as just about every other cool cat of the time), **BILLY ECKSTINE** began his early career as a singer of novelty songs until he realized that his deep baritone voice was best suited to singing ballads. He was also an accomplished trumpet player and guitarist and would often play those instruments with his band when they toured. He disbanded the orchestra at the end of the forties and shifted toward more pop-oriented material, scoring a number of chart hits on both sides of the Atlantic and, in the process, becoming the first African-American romantic idol. Several fine collaborations with artists such as Count Basie and Sarah Vaughan found him exploring his roots in the sixties. He also recorded a handful of albums for Motown, before pretty much retiring from recording in the seventies, save for a couple of later albums before he passed away in 1993. His 1958 album **Billy's Best!** (for Mercury, now on Polygram) is a terrific collection of jazz-pop, which is ultimately where he excelled.

For a period of time from the 1930s through the 1950s (before rock and roll changed everything), there was no more omnipresent entertainer than **BING CROSBY**. Records, radio, movies, and television—he conquered them all. Embraced by America as a warm, everyday kind of guy, he was a multifaceted performer whose success stemmed from his singing voice, a deep, unique baritone that branded whatever type of material he recorded—and he recorded pretty much every musical style at one time or another—as "Bing Crosby songs."

Growing up in Tacoma, Washington, he began singing in his high school jazz band before joining a local outfit, led by Al Rinker, as drummer and singer. At the end of the 1920s both Crosby and Rinker headed to California and joined a band led by Paul Whiteman, as well as performing as the Rhythm Boys with pianist Harry Barris, after which Crosby became a solo artist and began his movie career. The 1991 compilation **1926–1932** on Timeless Records collects a number of his early recordings with the Rhythm Boys and Whitehead as well as cuts with orchestras led by Duke Ellington and the Dorsey Brothers; it is a good overview of Crosby the jazz singer.

Born in Chicago in 1925, **MEL TORMÉ** grew up listening to big bands on the radio. He was something of a child prodigy, singing in vaudeville at a very young age and auditioning a song he had written for bandleader Harry James when he was just fifteen years old. He began his career as a drummer before becoming a singer and moving to Los Angeles, where he also began working in movies and continued writing his own songs. His best-known song is **The Christmas Song (Merry Christmas to You)**, made famous by Nat King Cole.

During World War II Tormé achieved success with his vocal group the Mel-Tones, who performed with Artie Shaw. The 1950s was a busy decade for him as a solo artist; he recorded and performed relentlessly and found himself in demand for movie roles, either as himself or as an actor in low-budget films. Somewhere along the way he acquired the nickname "The Velvet Fog" for his silky-smooth voice. It probably explains why he had such a tough time being taken seriously as a jazz vocalist, as successive record labels saw him more as a commercial singer. However, as the West Coast jazz scene heated up, he found himself at the forefront and picked up a scatting reputation second only to that of Ella Fitzgerald.

In 1955 Bethlehem Records released **It's a Blue World**, the first of several collaborations with arranger Marty Paich, and the album captures Tormé as a vital thirty-year-old singer. The sixties were a lean time for many jazz musicians, and Mel took other jobs, including a stint as the musical director on TV's "The Judy Garland Show," as well as recording several albums of commercial pop material that he later distanced himself from. By the mid-seventies, however, jazz began a comeback, and Tormé found record labels who allowed him to be himself. He recorded regularly up until his death in 1999.

Born in Cleveland, Ohio, **JIMMY SCOTT** acquired the nickname "Little Jimmy Scott," reflecting his physical stature. As a result of Kallman's syndrome, a rare hereditary condition, Jimmy stopped growing and never went through puberty. It left him at just five feet tall and with the soprano voice of a young boy. Jimmy Scott's life and career were to be profoundly impacted by his childhood misfortune. In the 1940s he began traveling through the south singing in tent shows and received his first break when he was asked to sing in Lionel Hampton's band. After going solo in the fifties and recording a couple of albums, Scott got caught up in a contractual dispute at the beginning of the sixties that effectively stopped him from recording for almost ten years. In fact, his output was sporadic from that time on until he was "rediscovered" in 1991 by Seymour Stein, then head of Sire Records. Since then he has enjoyed something of a renaissance, both in his career and as an artist with full control, something he never had as a younger man. He made several well-received albums in the early part of his career; his 1955 album for Savoy, **If You Only Knew**, is one of the best.

Chicago-born **JOHNNY HARTMAN** cut his teeth in the same Earl Hines–led band that gave Billy Eckstine his start, and also in Dizzy Gillespie's big band. Hartman went on to become one of the finest ballad singers of the 1950s, recording his best work in 1963 with **John Coltrane and Johnny Hartman**, a collection of wonderfully performed standards for Impulse Records. His output was intermittent during the rest of the sixties and most of the seventies, although he did return in 1980 with a couple of acclaimed albums prior to his passing away in 1983.

KINDERGARTEN POP

There are so many albums of children's music out there and so many artists making music for children that I thought more than a couple of times about whether or not to even include this category. You can choose from myriad Barney, Sesame Street, and other television characters' CDs, or soundtracks to well-loved movies like *Mary Poppins*, *The Little Mermaid*, or *Finding Nemo*. Artists like Dan Zanes and Raffi have made careers out of recording albums for children. Any of these albums will most likely please your little ones. However, as a recent parent myself of Sam and Luna (who are twins—I know I'll sleep again one day, right?), I've selected four albums that were given to us and seemed just a little more individual than the obvious choices.

THE LIMELITERS were one of the best selling and most highly regarded folk groups ever. In the early 1960s, the original lineup of Glenn Yarbrough, Alex Hassilev, and Lou Gottlieb were everywhere—live performances, radio, television, and even commercials. They also found time in 1962 to record **Through Children's Eyes: Little Folk Songs for Adults** (Folk Era), a live recording with a chorus and an audience of kids. My girlfriend's parents played this album for her and her siblings back in the sixties and seventies. While it does sound a little dated to older ears, there are fun tracks like **Run, Little Donkey, Lollipop Tree**, and **Marty**, as well as covers of the Carter family's **Stay on the Sunny Side** and Woody Guthrie's **This Land Is Your Land**. Though it was recorded more than 40 years ago, and it's funny to think that the kids who originally listened to it are now middle-aged, our little guys love it.

I was given **Punk Rock Baby: Lullaby Versions of Punk Classics** by a couple of friends in the music business when our twins were born, and we parents have actually had more fun with it than the kids. But it's not just a novelty record—it actually works! The songs are reworked as soothing lullabies, and tracks like the Clash's **London Calling**, the Buzzcocks' **Ever Fallen in Love**, the Sex Pistols' **Pretty Vacant**, and Ian Dury's **Sex and Drugs and Rock 'N' Roll** are just a few of the songs getting the sleepytime treatment. The CD, released in 2002, is an import from Fulfill Records.

Here Come the ABCs finds John Flansburgh and John Linnell, aka **THEY MIGHT BE GIANTS**, swapping their eccentric post-punk pop for an album that takes kids on a unique tour through the letters of the alphabet. Some of the tracks are simple little ditties, while others are full-blown songs and not that dissimilar in style to some of the songs on their rock albums. In fact, this doesn't seem like that much of a stretch at all for these two pranksters! Highlights include **Alphabet of Nations, Pictures of Panda's Painting, The Alphabet Lost and Found**, and **Who Put the Alphabet (in Alphabetical Order?)**. The CD was released by Disney in 2005 and there's also a DVD version with puppets and animation to help tell the stories within the songs.

THE WIGGLES star in an Australian kids TV show that's been running down under since 1992; it's one of the most popular shows for youngsters under the age of four both there and in the U.S. The program was conceived and fronted by four teachers-turned-musicians from the Melbourne music scene: Anthony Field, Jeff Fatt, Murray Cook, and Greg Page. Together with their friends Captain Feathersword, Henry the Octopus, Dorothy the Dinosaur, and Wags the Dog, the guys created a program that features a mix of skits, stories, and songs that are educational and fun. Their album and DVD releases have been hugely successful and any one of them will probably be a hit with your little guys. My twins' favorite is **Yummy Yummy** from 2000. It includes songs like **Fruit Salad, Hot Potato**, and **Shake Your Sillies Out**. The CD is available in the U.S. on KOCH records.

LIVIN' LARGE: THE BIG BAND BOOM!

Big band's popularity began in the 1930s in dance halls and ballrooms across America, with bandleaders like Duke Ellington and Count Basie leading the charge. The

"Swing" movement, as it became known, had a huge impact on popular culture during the late thirties and World War II, and also launched several singers to international stardom, including Frank Sinatra. This was the music of my dad, who, as a young boy in London during the war, was evacuated along with thousands of other children to the countryside south of the English capital so as to be away from Hitler's bombs. As those kids watched the Royal Air Force and Luftwaffe do battle in the sky, their radios were tuned to the latest craze from America. Today's teenagers might find it difficult to believe, but this was the music that scared the pants off many a 1930s parent! My thanks to my dad for his help with this list of ten essential big band artists and recordings.

COUNT BASIE started in the 1930s, and although many jazz aficionados will tell you that the group of musicians he worked with from that time was the better band, he is best remembered for his 1950s ensemble and recordings of tunes written by Neal Hefti. The thirties recordings don't stand up too well by modern technological standards, so when looking for an entrée into his music, check out his highly regarded **Atomic Mr. Basie** from 1958 on Blue Note.

LES BROWN worked as an arranger before starting his own band. Doris Day began singing with him in the 1940s, and he later worked extensively with Bob Hope, which enabled Brown to keep the orchestra together. Many of his early albums are unavailable on CD, but try **Best of the Big Bands: Les Brown**, a 1989 compilation of his forties recordings, from Columbia.

TOMMY DORSEY was a trombone player and worked for many years in a variety of bands alongside his older brother Jimmy. He is also remembered for launching the careers of several jazz instrumentalists such as Buddy Rich (drums) and Ziggy Elman (trumpet)—and a young singer called Frank Sinatra. **This Is Tommy Dorsey and His Orchestra, Vol. 1** is a good all-around collection of his work compiled in the early seventies and reissued on the Collectables label.

The biggest name in the 1930s and 1940s was **DUKE ELLINGTON**. But he wasn't just a bandleader—he was a composer of extraordinary depth and probably the most outstanding jazz composer ever. A true giant of American music, not only did he write for his band, he also worked on show tunes for Broadway and movie scores for Hollywood. His concerts were always different, as the bands he worked with constantly found new ways to interpret the music. **En Concert Avec Europe 1: Theatre des Champs Élysées, Paris France** is a magical recording from two nights of concerts in 1965, available on the French label RTE.

The "King of Swing," **BENNY GOODMAN** was a clarinetist who led several combos as well as his orchestra and was one of the earliest stars of the Swing movement. His mid-1930s band at one time included future bandleaders such as trumpeter Harry James and drummer Gene Krupa. In 1938 his band was the first to play a jazz concert at Carnegie Hall. That night's music is available from Columbia as a double-CD set called **Carnegie Hall Jazz Concert**.

Of all the big band leaders, **WOODY HERMAN** lasted the longest. He started in the late 1930s and was still fronting a big band in the 1980s. One of the reasons for Woody's longevity was that over the years his playing evolved and adapted to the music of the day. Later in his career he even included current pop and rock pieces in his repertoire. There is a two-disc Columbia CD of Woody's glory days in the mid-1940s, entitled **Blowing Up a Storm**.

STAN KENTON made his name in the 1940s with his "Progressive Jazz" sound. Kenton experimented over the years and at one time had a brass section with several people playing mellophonium, a cross between a bass trombone and a French horn that is actually a mellophone with its tubing straightened so that the bell points straight ahead, like a trumpet, instead of backward. In 2001 Capitol issued a four-disc master-tape collection called **The Complete Capitol Years: 1943–47**.

GLENN MILLER had only four years in the big time before joining the war effort in 1943, never to return when his light aircraft went missing somewhere in the sea between England and France. Of such mysteries legends are created, and the Glenn Miller sound lives on, with more bands playing his music today than any other big-band composer. **The Essential Glenn Miller** (RCA, 1995) is a two-CD set.

BUDDY RICH was the drummer at Benny Goodman's Carnegie Hall concert in 1938 and was also in Tommy Dorsey's band with Frank Sinatra. Buddy, a great showman, later formed his own band with Sinatra's help and survived the rock-and-roll years with his driving modern jazz sound, fully earning his title as the world's greatest big-band drummer. **Mercy, Mercy** is a live album from 1968 on Blue Note, on which he pushes both himself and his band to the limit.

ARTIE SHAW was the first bandleader to hit the big time in Hollywood in the late 1930s and early 1940s. He was married six times to women who included actresses Ava Gardner and Lana Turner. Musically, his rival was Benny Goodman: The experts said Goodman had the better technique, but Artie had the warmer sound. A good place to start would be **The Very Best of Artie Shaw**, a 2001 compilation from RCA.

LIVING IN PERFECT HARMONY

No, I'm not talking about the schlocky duet **Ebony and Ivory** that Paul McCartney and Stevie Wonder did back in the eighties. I'm talking about great records that feature sweet vocal harmonies.

The best place to begin this category is with **THE BEACH BOYS**, which included the three Wilson brothers—Brian, Dennis, and Carl—together with their cousin Mike Love and friend Al Jardine. The group's trademark surf rock sound was enhanced by their complex harmonies. Although the group's creative engine, Brian, withdrew from the band in the latter part of the sixties as a result of severe drug addiction, the Beach Boys carried on with a variety of lineups into the nineties. Examples of what they did best and recorded before their innocence was lost are **Surfin' U.S.A**. (1963), **Today!** (1965), and **Pet Sounds** (1966), all on Capitol Records.

You can't talk about the Beach Boys without mentioning **JAN & DEAN**. Jan Berry and Dean Torrence were high school friends in Los Angeles who started off singing doo-wop and went on to form one of the most influential partnerships in the California surf music scene. They are best known for a string of singles, including a song called **Surf City**, co-written by Berry and Brian Wilson, with Wilson contributing additional vocals. They were never taken as seriously as the Beach Boys, probably in part because their songs were so much fun and their output wasn't as prodigious. **The Little Old Lady from Pasadena** (Liberty, 1964) shows off those glorious harmonies, as well as their Dick Dale–influenced guitar sounds and some nice studio production touches.

Coming from the folk world, the **KINGSTON TRIO** (hilariously spoofed in the 2003 movie *A Mighty Wind*) were comprised originally of Dave Guard, Nick Reynolds, and Bob Shane and are arguably the most popular folk act ever. Their first album **The Kingston Trio** (Capitol, 1958) is a good introduction.

THE MAMAS AND THE PAPAS (Denny Doherty, John Phillips, Michelle Phillips, and Cass Elliot) were probably the biggest vocal group of the second half of the sixties. They also ended up becoming the prototypical incestuous band as a result of the carefree lifestyle of the time and its free-love ethos. Their debut album **If You Can Believe Your Eyes and Ears** (MCA, 1966) is a classic slice of sunshine pop and also contains the hits California Dreamin' and Monday, Monday. For a brief moment they held the world in their hands, but ultimately a little too much bed-hopping and the tensions it raised tore them apart.

THE BYRDS were one of the first bands to fuse folk and rock, and their early work was recognized as groundbreaking in its use of chiming guitars and Beatlesque interweaving harmonies. Their debut release, **Mr. Tambourine Man** (Columbia, 1965), named after their cover of the Bob Dylan song, is the first in a series of albums that helped shape the music of the second half of the sixties. David Crosby was a founding member of the Byrds and went on to found another group that achieved even bigger success, **CROSBY, STILLS, AND NASH**, together with Stephen Stills and Graham Nash. The band released their first album, **Crosby, Stills, and Nash**, on Atlantic in 1969; while the songs for the most part reflect the times in which they were written, the three-part harmonies on this album are boundless. Also worth checking out is the band's 1970 follow-up, **Déjà Vu**, also on Atlantic. **NEIL YOUNG** joined the band for this album, and as well as adding his songwriting talents to the mix, he contributed his unique falsetto voice that made the group's vocal options even more intricate than before.

LOVE IS A MANY-SPLENDORED THING

Throughout the ages, love has been the inspiration for just about anything you care to name. Art, literature, food, wine, even war—and of course, songs. It's impossible to know how many millions of songs have been written, but it's a safe guess that love was involved in the vast majority. Needless to say, writing about love songs could take up the entirety of this book and several others. But instead, this list is of the many great groups and artists who either have *love* as a part of their given name or who have used the word as part of their band name.

Led by Arthur Lee and formed in Los Angeles in the mid-sixties, **LOVE** were the West Coast's best-known psychedelic rock band at the time, and in their first incarnation recorded three albums that are considered among the best examples of the genre. Their 1967 album on Elektra Records, **Forever Changes**, consistently shows up on all-time best-album lists.

When early goth pioneers Bauhaus called it a day, three of the four members—David J, Daniel Ash, and Kevin Haskins—

formed **LOVE AND ROCKETS** and, interestingly enough, went in a completely different musical direction. Bauhaus had been known for their gloomy demeanor, but Love and Rockets were much brighter and enjoyed moderate chart success on both sides of the Atlantic. The 1987 album **Earth, Sun, Moon** (Beggars Banquet) is probably their most consistent release.

The group **LOVE SPIT LOVE** were led by Richard Butler, former vocalist of the successful British band the Psychedelic Furs. He formed his new band in New York in 1992 with his brother Tim, who'd also been in the Furs, drummer Frank Ferrer, and guitarist Richard Fortus. The first of their two albums was 1994's **Love Spit Love**, released on the short-lived Imago record label. On that album, Butler brought his eighties sound up to date and into the early alternative rock world.

THE HOUSE OF LOVE were a British band who at the end of the 1980s briefly looked like they could become seriously big. Their mix of post–punk pop and shimmering guitars led their debut album, **The House of Love**, released on Creation Records in 1988, and considered to be one of the best albums of that year. The album is available on Relativity records and should not be confused with their second album, also self-titled, released in 1990 on Fontana.

Coming out of Philadelphia, **G. LOVE & SPECIAL SAUCE** are a three-piece band led by Garrett Dutton (aka G. Love). The band's trademark and somewhat idiosyncratic sound mixes soul, blues, and R&B with a vocal delivery that's both laconic and hip-hop–flavored at the same time. The group's second album, **Coast to Coast Motel**, from Epic (1995) finds the band at their best.

LOVE INC. is just one of several names used by the German house and electronic musician/producer Mike Ink. (He also uses the names M:I:5 and Gas.) Love Inc. is usually reserved for his house music releases, most of which have been on EPs and singles.

There is a full-length collection called **Life's a Gas** from 1996 on his own Force Inc. label.

DARLENE LOVE was in the Phil Spector stable of great female vocalists, singing on such hits as **He's a Rebel** and **Da Doo Ron Ron** for the Crystals, as well as with other groups like the Blossoms and Bob B. Soxx and the Bluejeans. She sang backup for Dionne Warwick and Aretha Franklin but never really got the recognition she deserved. In 1998 she released a solo album on Harmony Records called **Unconditional Love**, which collects some of her favorite gospel classics. On a side note, she later turned to acting, playing Danny Glover's long-suffering wife in the *Lethal Weapon* series of movies.

COURTNEY LOVE's name is sure to bring up lively debate among a generation of music fans who were around when alternative rock hit the mainstream in the early nineties. She was married to Nirvana frontman Kurt Cobain; as a couple, they were constant subjects of scrutiny, with the media and public speculating about their alleged heroin use. Courtney had never been the cheerleader/prom queen type and had spent a good deal of time bouncing around Europe and the States before she met Kurt. When he killed himself in 1994, Courtney found herself a single mom and widow at the age of 29. She has seemingly been on an emotional rollercoaster ride ever since. Courtney has veered from the heights of rock success with her band **HOLE** and as a critically acclaimed actress with her role in the 1996 movie *The People vs. Larry Flynt*, to the depths of drug addiction and the unpredicatble behavior that goes with it. Although recorded prior to Cobain's death, Hole's second album **Live Through This** (DGC, 1994) was released just afterwards. It was a big commercial and critical success and is among the best alternative albums of the period.

MADCHESTER

Head north out of London on the M6 motorway, and about three hours and 160 miles later you'll arrive in Manchester, a city founded as a Roman camp in AD 70; it later became famous in the nineteenth century as a center of the cotton and textile industries. It is also home to arguably the best-known soccer club in the world, Manchester United.

The city has consistently produced some of the biggest names in the British music scene. One of the earliest stars was George Formby, a household name in the 1930s and 1940s, who played ukulele and sang saucy songs in an era when war-weary Brits needed a laugh. In the sixties bands like the Hollies, Herman's Hermits, Freddie & the Dreamers, and the Bee Gees topped the charts. The seventies began with progressive rock artists such as Barclay James Harvest and Roy Harper and also saw one of the best pop groups ever to come out of Britain, 10cc; it ended with the punk explosion of the Buzzcocks and Magazine, followed by the post-punk outfit Joy Division.

Into the eighties things really got cooking with the Smiths, who made a huge mark on the Manchester and British music scenes, giving hope and inspiration to the many bands who have followed in their footsteps. At the end of the eighties and continuing into the nineties came the rise of a new dance club–influenced scene that was dubbed Madchester, so named because of the sheer number of new bands that surfaced around the Hacienda nightclub and the alcohol- and ecstasy-fueled rave culture that went along with it (documented with all its warts intact in the 2002 movie *24 Hour Party People.*) During this time bands like Happy Mondays and the Charlatans (who had to tag their name with "UK" in the states) ruled the British charts. As that scene faded and Britpop surfaced, Oasis arrived to take the music to the world. The city's music scene has continued to thrive. The following is a breakdown by decade of some of the artists and representative works from the Manchester scene:

The Sixties

FREDDIE & THE DREAMERS: *You Were Made for Me* (EMI, 1964)

WAYNE FONTANA & THE MINDBENDERS: *Wayne Fontana & The Mindbenders* (Badfro, 1965)

THE HOLLIES: *For Certain Because* (Phantom, 1966)

JOHN MAYALL & THE BLUESBREAKERS: *Bluesbreakers with Eric Clapton* (Deram, 1966)

GEORGIE FAME: *Two Faces of Fame* (Sony, 1967)

HERMAN'S HERMITS: *Blaze* (Repertoire, 1967)

THE BEE GEES: *Odessa* (Polydor, 1969)

The Seventies

ROY HARPER: *Stormcock* (Griffin, 1971)

BARCLAY JAMES HARVEST: *Barclay James Harvest* (EMI, 1972)

ELKIE BROOKS: *Rich Man's Woman* (A&M, 1975)

10CC: *The Original Soundtrack* (Polygram, 1975)

MAGAZINE: *Real Life* (Caroline, 1978)

SAD CAFÉ: *Misplaced Ideals* (Renaissance, 1978)

THE BUZZCOCKS: *A Different Kind of Tension* (Nettwerk, 1979)

THE DURUTTI COLUMN: *The Return of the Durutti Column* (Polygram, 1979)

THE FALL: *Dragnet* (Resurgence, 1979)

JOY DIVISION: *Unknown Pleasures* (Qwest, 1979)

The Eighties

NEW ORDER: *Power, Corruption, & Lies* (Qwest, 1983)

LEVEL 42: *World Machine* (Polygram, 1985)

THE CHAMELEONS: *Strange Times* (Geffen, 1986)

THE SMITHS: *The Queen Is Dead* (Sire, 1986)

HAPPY MONDAYS: *Bummed* (Elektra, 1988)

MORRISSEY: *Viva Hate* (Sire, 1988)

RAILWAY CHILDREN: *Recurrence* (Atlantic, 1988)

808 STATE: *90* (Universal, 1989)

A GUY CALLED GERALD: *Automanikk* (Sony, 1989)

THE STONE ROSES: *The Stone Roses* (Silvertone, 1989)

LISA STANSFIELD: *Affection* (Arista, 1989)

The Nineties

INSPIRAL CARPETS: *Life* (Elektra, 1990)

ELECTRONIC: *Electronic* (Warner Brothers, 1991)

SIMPLY RED: *Stars* (Atlantic, 1991)

THE CHARLATANS: *Between 10th and 11th* (Beggars Banquet, 1992)

JAMES: *Seven* (Polygram, 1992)

OASIS: *Definitely Maybe* (Epic, 1994)

BLACK GRAPE: *It's Great When You're Straight . . . Yeah* (MCA, 1995)

THE CHEMICAL BROTHERS: *Dig Your Own Hole* (Astralwerks, 1997)

THE VERVE: *Urban Hymns* (Virgin, 1997)

MINT ROYALE: *On the Ropes* (MCA, 1999)

The Twenty-first Century (So Far)

BADLY DRAWN BOY: *The Hour of Bewilderbeast* (XL, 2000)

DOVES: *Lost Souls* (Astralwerks, 2000)

WITNESS (UK): *Under a Sun* (MCA, 2001)

ALPINESTARS: *White Noise* (Astralwerks, 2002)

STARSAILOR: *Love Is Here* (Capitol, 2002)

LAMB: *What Sound (Deluxe)* (Koch, 2003)

ELBOW: *Cast of Thousands* (V2, 2004)

JONI MITCHELL: ICON

The legendary Joni Mitchell was born in Fort McLeod, Alberta, Canada, as Roberta Joan Anderson. Her first musical loves were classical composers like Mozart and Schubert, which led to piano lessons at the tender age of seven. At age nine, she contracted polio and while recovering in the hospital discovered her love of drawing and painting. Her first string instrument was actually a ukulele, but a guitar soon followed, and by age 19 she was playing the Canadian folk circuit and living in Toronto. An early unsuccessful marriage to folksinger Chuck Mitchell (they also performed together for a while) gave her the name that would become famous around the world.

When Joni moved to New York City in 1967, as a result of constant gigging up and down the East Coast, other artists began recording her songs, leading her to a record deal with Reprise and her first album (produced by David Crosby), a self-titled acoustic release in 1968. It was, however, her third and fourth albums— **Ladies of the Canyon** in 1970, which included the songs **Big**

Yellow Taxi and Woodstock, and Blue the following year—that cemented her status as a songwriter and performer who would help define a musical generation. In the following years Joni refused to follow convention and consistently tried on new musical clothing with jazz, pop, and avant-garde recordings. While never achieving ongoing commercial success, Joni Mitchell is without a doubt one of the most outstanding and influential female performers of the twentieth century.

Other releases by Joni that are too good to miss:

Clouds (Reprise, 1969): Her second album, and more assured than her first.

For the Roses (Asylum, 1972): Joni takes a more commercial turn and scores a hit single with **You Turn Me On (I'm a Radio)**.

Court and Spark (Asylum, 1974): Joni's first real foray into jazz and one of her best.

Hejira (Asylum, 1976): This album finds Joni pushing her jazz influences even further.

Mingus (Asylum, 1979): An album that began as a collaboration with jazz great Charles Mingus, Joni had to finish the record alone after he passed away.

Night Ride Home (Geffen, 1991): This album featured some of her strongest material in years.

Travelogue (Reprise, 2002): Joni revisits twenty-two tunes drawn from her songbook and reworks them with various jazz greats and a seventy-piece orchestra.

MORE THAN JUST BACKGROUND MUSIC: MOVIE SOUNDTRACKS

M usic in movies should help tell the story, whether it be an original score or an existing song. Far too often music is used in films in a way that distracts from the story (sometimes with good reason), but there are exceptions. Here are two lists of those exceptions that can be listened to and enjoyed as CDs.

Rock Movie Soundtracks

A Hard Day's Night (Capitol, 1964): The Beatles' first movie yielded an album that contained fourteen new songs, eight of which were included in the movie itself. The film is a wacky caper, in which the boys spend most of the movie running around on a train and in the city of London avoiding their hordes of screaming fans. The album was also a turning point for the Beatles, with the songs manifesting a depth that hadn't been seen in their earlier work.

Woodstock (reissue, Atlantic, 1995): Originally released in 1970 and remastered and reissued as a four-CD box in 1995 (with additional songs not in the movie), *Woodstock* is considered the ultimate "rockumentary." It was shot at the original Woodstock Festival on Yasgur's Farm in upstate New York in August 1969. Live performances include Crosby, Stills, Nash & Young; Joan Baez; Janis Joplin; the Who; Richie Havens; Jefferson Airplane; Joe Cocker; and Jimi Hendrix, among others. Not all of the performances or recordings are great, but it's a record of one of rock's defining moments. I suggest picking up the DVD as well.

Quadrophenia (MCA, 1973): The Who's second rock opera is much more accessible than **Tommy** and tells a story that connected with the band's own history as London mods. The soundtrack features seventeen Pete Townshend originals, including songs like **The Real Me, Bell Boy,** and **5:15**.

Purple Rain (Warner Brothers, 1984): This film and soundtrack heralded the arrival of Prince as a major star. The story of boy meets girl, boy loses girl is a backdrop for Prince's talents as he gathers all of his influences—guitars, funk, and R&B—and delivers a collection of music widely regarded as his best album.

Singles (Sony, 1992): Just as alternative rock was breaking out of Seattle and putting the Northwest city on the musical map for the first time since Jimi Hendrix, director Cameron Crowe used the city's music scene as the setting for his movie about a group of single people in their twenties. The soundtrack includes many songs written for the movie by the likes of Pearl Jam, Soundgarden, Alice in Chains, and Mudhoney.

Velvet Goldmine (Polygram, 1998): Director Todd Haynes's movie vividly recalls glam rock's glory days with a story about an arty, snot-nosed kid's rise to debauched stardom, based loosely on David Bowie's early days. No surprise then that Bowie wouldn't allow the filmmaker to use any of his music, but the soundtrack is packed with songs by artists who were around in the early seventies, such as Roxy Music, Steve Harley & Cockney Rebel, T. Rex, and Lou Reed. Haynes also hired Shudder to Think and Grant Lee Buffalo and put together two other groups of musicians to record new material that captured the sound of the time.

Almost Famous (DreamWorks, 2000): This film is Cameron Crowe's homage to the innocence of his adolescence and the music that accompanied it. With songs by Led Zeppelin, Simon & Garfunkel, Elton John, and Thunderclap Newman, the soundtrack puts us at a moment in time that promised so much but ultimately failed to live up to a generation's expectations.

High Fidelity (Hollywood, 2000): The movie, based on the book of the same name by Nick Hornby, follows a record store owner and DJ, Rob Gordon (played by John Cusack), who lives his life around his record collection. The soundtrack is a truly eclectic bag, including songs by the Kinks, Velvet Underground, Bob Dylan, the Beta Band, Stereolab, and Stevie Wonder.

24 Hour Party People (FFRR, 2002): The movie tells the story of the music scene that exploded out of Manchester, England, in the late 1970s and throughout the 1980s. Its main protagonist was former journalist Tony Wilson, the man who founded Factory Records and the infamous club the Hacienda, both of which have become synonymous with the "Madchester" scene. The movie and its soundtrack feature music from some of the best bands to ever come out of England, such as Joy Division, New Order, the Buzzcocks, Happy Mondays, and the Clash.

School of Rock (Atlantic, 2003): The film follows the adventures of Dewey Finn (played by Jack Black), who has just been kicked out of his own band, as he attempts to teach a class of school kids the history of rock music by forming them into a band with himself as the singer. It's a loose comedy that should get you laughing, especially if you're a music fan. Its great soundtrack is "Rock and Roll 101," with classic tracks by the Doors, the Ramones, the Who, Led Zeppelin, and Cream.

Original Scores

Citizen Kane (Varese Sarabande, 1941): Orson Welles was just twenty-five when he shot his masterpiece, a movie considered by many to be the best film ever made. The story is a barely disguised attack on one of the most powerful media giants of his day, William Randolph Hearst. Bernard Herrmann was thirty when he provided the memorable score to this, his first movie as a composer.

Laura (1944): Directed by Otto Preminger and starring Gene Tierney, Dana Andrews, and Clifton Webb, the film is a story full of twists and turns about a girl's murder and the policeman investigating it, who falls in love with the dead girl's portrait. But who was really murdered? David Raksin provided a memorable score which is, alas, not available at this time on CD.

The Magnificent Seven (Koch, 1960): Directed by John Sturges, this film, starring Yul Brynner, Steve McQueen, Charles Bronson, and James Coburn, was based on the Japanese movie *The Seven Samurai*. The energetic score, with its Mexican musical flourishes, was composed by Elmer Bernstein.

Psycho (Varese Sarabande, 1960): Directed by Alfred Hitchcock and starring Anthony Perkins and Janet Leigh, *Psycho* introduced us to Norman Bates and the Bates Motel. Bernard Herrmann decided that the best way to score the movie was with strings, and his jagged, slashing use of violins helped turn the movie into an iconic classic.

To Kill a Mockingbird (Varese Sarabande, 1962): Harper Lee's classic American novel was made into one of the great American movies in 1962 by director Robert Mulligan. Gregory Peck starred as a Southern lawyer defending a black man against a trumped-up rape charge. Elmer Bernstein's evocative score is an intrical part of the storytelling.

How the West Was Won (Rhino, 1963): A history of Western settlement seen through the eyes of two families as they travel across the country from New York in search of a better life. Made by MGM to showcase the Cinerama widescreen technology, the film has a classic Western score by Alfred Newman to match the scale of the picture.

The Good, the Bad, and the Ugly (Capitol, 1966): Sergio Leone's classic 1966 spaghetti western starred Clint Eastwood and Lee Van Cleef, with an evocative original score by Italian composer Ennio Morricone.

Planet of the Apes (Varese Sarabande, 1968): This was a groundbreaking movie when it was released in 1968 as a result of its makeup and special effects and its biting social commentary about civil rights. Jerry Goldsmith's memorable score broke new ground in its avant-garde approach to the surreal material it complemented.

The Godfather (MCA, 1972): Francis Ford Coppola's adaptation of the Mario Puzo novel was scored by Italian composer Nino Rota, who creates a dark, chilling feeling when necessary, but also incorporates a sense of Sicilian melody for the film's lighter moments.

Chinatown (Varese Sarabande, 1974): Roman Polanski's 1974 movie about a tawdry tale of adultery linked to a land swindle plan starred Jack Nicholson, Faye Dunaway, and John Huston. The movie is enhanced by a classic film noir score from Jerry Goldsmith.

Taxi Driver (Arista, 1976): Directed by Martin Scorsese and starring Robert De Niro and Cybill Shepherd with then-thirteen-year-old Jodie Foster, the film is a brutal story about a nighttime New York taxi driver losing his grip on reality. Bernard Herrmann's last movie score featured two themes: a smokey sax jazz theme that fits nicely with the city's seedy nightlife, and a dark, dissonant orchestral mix that captures the approaching deranged madness of DeNiro's character.

Chariots of Fire (Polygram, 1981): This film follows the story of two young British track runners, played by Nigel Havers and Ben Cross, who compete for glory in the 1924 Olympics. Appropriately, Greek composer Vangelis provided music for the film, with a piano- and synthesizer-based score that perfectly captures the sweeping drama of the track races.

The Last Temptation of Christ (Geffen, 1988): Martin Scorsese's 1988 movie is based on the novel of the same name by Nikos Kazantzakis about the last days of Jesus Christ. Peter Gabriel delivered a score of immense depth for this movie, bringing African and Middle Eastern instrumentation and vocals from artists such as Baaba Maal and Nusrat Fateh Ali Khan to a movie score for the first time. Without a doubt, this soundtrack changed the way that Hollywood looked at film music. (Please note: The soundtrack album is entitled simply **Passion**, as for legal reasons it could not share the title of the film or the novel; this soundtrack should also not be confused with the 2004 movie *The Passion of the Christ*.)

Run Lola Run (TVT, 1998): In this German movie the title character, played by Franka Potente, tries to come up with a large amount of money in twenty minutes to save her boyfriend's life. The music, an electronic/techno score, drives the action at an incredible pace and was composed by Reinhold Heil, Johnny Klimek, and the movie's director, Tom Tykwer.

American Beauty (DreamWorks, 2000): British theater director Sam Mendes's movie debut told an offbeat tale of Lester Burnham (played by Kevin Spacey), who is lost in his life and decides to rebel against his job and his family. Thomas Newman's simple yet groundbreaking ethereal, rhythmic score features an array of instruments, including tablas, ukelele, and banjo.

THE MOTOWN SOUND

The history of Tamla Motown has been well documented in many books; here I give a brief overview and recommend some suggested albums by the essential artists who recorded for the label.

In late 1950s Detroit, Berry Gordy—who had owned a jazz specialty record store that had gone broke—was working on the assembly line at Ford's Lincoln plant. On the side, he began writing songs with his sister Gwen. When Jackie Wilson recorded some of their tunes and had a hit with **Lonely Teardrops**, Berry spotted a way out of the factory and began managing several groups, beginning with the Matadors (who later became Smokey Robinson and the Miracles).

In the early 1960s Gordy put together an impressive team of producers, songwriters, and musicians, and created one of the most unique and successful record labels ever. Initially called Tamla Records and focused on R&B, the new label was founded on a simple premise: Find talented artists and write and produce songs for them with a group of staff musicians and a rhythm section, the Funk Brothers, who supplied the unique percussive sound Motown would become famous for. In fact, the idea was to take care of everything in-house, including management, publishing, and even grooming. The Motown sound and image was to prove all-important, and Gordy had learned something invaluable during his time at Ford: the production-line technique. Based out of a house that became known over the course of the next decade as Hitsville, USA, and with the songwriting team of Lamont Dozier, with brothers Brian and Eddie Holland, Motown turned out a succession of young black singing groups and artists who dominated the singles charts.

The seventies saw Gordy move the label to Los Angeles, but, cut off from its roots, Motown's glory days were soon in the rearview mirror as artists like the Temptations, Michael Jackson, and Gladys Knight and the Pips left for other labels. Nonetheless, the label was still remarkably successful with artists such as Stevie Wonder, Diana Ross, Marvin Gaye, and the Commodores racking up huge sales. However, by the 1980s, amidst complaints about royalty payments to several of the writers and musicians, Motown's fortunes were in decline. In 1988 the label was sold and is now a part of the Universal group, but the catalog lives on, as does the music that defined a generation of African-Americans.

Though **THE MARVELETTES** went through a number of different lineups through the years, they scored many hits in the first half of the sixties, including Motown's first No. 1, **Please Mr. Postman**, in 1961. Their best album was **The Marvelettes**, released in 1967.

When he signed with Berry Gordy, **LITTLE STEVIE WONDER**, as he was then known, was just ten years old. He released his first recording at age twelve and by the mid-seventies had become one of the most important innovators R&B music has ever seen. Pretty much everything Stevie released in the seventies is regarded as a classic, but 1972's **Talking Book** stands out for its mix of songs that tackle his emerging political beliefs, as well as love.

GLADYS KNIGHT is a true soul singer, meaning that her background is rooted in gospel music. Her early career yielded a couple of moderately successful singles, but it wasn't until she joined Motown in 1966 that things really took off. She was actually only with the label for seven years, but they were some of the most important years of her career; together with the Pips, she was a regular on the charts for the next decade. **All I Need Is Time**, from 1973, was the last album they recorded for Motown and without a doubt is their best.

THE TEMPTATIONS have been through more than their fair share of tragedy, with only one of the original five-member lineup still surviving. In fact, at last count there have been at least fourteen different singers in the group. There's no denying, though, the classic music they recorded in the mid-sixties. As the decade closed, they decided to depart from the trademark Motown sound by getting all funky with the 1969 album **Cloud Nine**. It was a turning point not just for them but the label as well.

One of Motown's biggest acts and the most successful girl group ever, **THE SUPREMES** featured three singers: Diana Ross, Florence Ballard, and Mary Wilson. Although it took a few years for things to happen, when their break came, it was huge. The Supremes had a string of No. 1 singles and were the first black artists to be truly accepted by mainstream America. However, all was not well within the Motown camp, as Gordy increasingly seemed to favor Ross above the other Supremes and the other female artists on the label. When Florence Ballard left and was replaced by Cindy Birdsong, the group became known as Diana Ross and the Supremes, which was how it stayed until Diana left for her solo career in 1970. The 1966 release **I Hear a Symphony** finds the original lineup at its peak.

Founded in 1954 while the members were in high school and still performing together to this day, **THE FOUR TOPS** have avoided the pitfalls of so many of their peers. Not until 1997, when Lawrence Payton passed away, did the lineup change. A little known fact is that they were supposed to be on Pan Am Flight 103, which exploded over Lockerbie, Scotland, in 1988 as a result of terrorism, but their boarding was delayed by a TV taping in the UK. Their most consistent album release was **The Four Tops' Second Album**, released in 1965.

MARVIN GAYE began his career as an R&B singer and evolved through several incarnations with Motown, including a series of successful duet releases with Mary Wells and Tammi Terrell before becoming arguably the most influential and important black artist of his generation. He had grown progressively more tired and bored with the Motown formula, and as the Civil Rights movement began to address inequality and social injustice, so did Marvin's writing. His 1971 album **What's Going On** is his masterpiece and one of the most important soul albums ever recorded.

It was Smokey Robinson who encouraged his manager Berry Gordy to borrow the $800 it took to start the Motown label, and as a producer Robinson also played a key part in its early success. Of course, recording a string of hits—first with his group **SMOKEY ROBINSON & THE MIRACLES** and later as a solo artist—didn't hurt either. The group's 1971 album **One Dozen Roses** is a fine collection of songs with a number of hit singles, including **The Tears of a Clown**.

The five Jackson brothers (Jackie, Tito, Jermaine, Marlon, and Michael) recorded for Motown at a crucial point in the label's history. The hit groups from the sixties had peaked, and the solo artists that would keep the label successful in the seventies were only just beginning to make their mark. **THE JACKSON 5** put a pop spin on R&B that was infectious, and as a result they dominated the pop charts for the first few years of the decade. 1970's **ABC** catches them at their best, before the distractions of Michael's solo career.

MICHAEL JACKSON was still singing with his four older brothers when he had his first solo hit, and along with the Jackson 5 he left Motown for Epic Records in 1976. It was around this time that he decided to focus exclusively on his solo career, and he went on to become one of the biggest pop stars the world has ever seen. His final Motown record was the 1975 release **Forever Michael**.

After becoming the focus of the Supremes and getting involved in a personal relationship with Berry Gordy, **DIANA ROSS** broke out on her own and went on to become a worldwide superstar. Her first solo album, **Diana Ross**, from 1970, is regarded by many critics as her best. The album was later retitled **Ain't No Mountain High Enough**, after the hit single of the same name.

The saxophone-playing **JUNIOR WALKER** was an anomaly in the Motown system, an artist who, along with his band the All Stars, recorded mostly instrumental but highly danceable R&B tunes. His 1965 debut, **Shotgun**, features the man himself on vocals on several tracks.

MARY WELLS was one of Motown's earliest and brightest young stars. Producer Smokey Robinson helped cultivate her big voice and find a sexy subtlety that brought her several hit singles, including the No. 1 smash in 1964, **My Guy**. At the height of her Motown fame, though, she left to record for the 20th Century Fox record label (followed by stints at several other labels) but never achieved the same type of success. The album highlight of her Motown years and career was **Mary Wells Sings My Guy**, released in 1964.

Martha Vandella started at Motown as a secretary and occasionally was asked to do backing vocals for a variety of other artists. Finally she was given a shot on her own and had a string of hit singles with her group **MARTHA & THE VANDELLAS**. The 1965 release **Dance Party** was a collection that included several of the group's biggest hits, including **Dancing in the Street**.

One of Motown's earliest signings, **THE CONTOURS** were regarded as a high-energy live act. They had one of the label's first hits with **Do You Love Me?** in 1962, but they never quite fit in with the smooth presentation and sound that Motown became famous for. Although they regularly hit the R&B charts, the group became largely marginalized as Berry Gordy focused his attention on his other stars, and by 1967 the original lineup went their separate ways. The 1999 compilation **The Very Best of the Contours** collects their best tracks.

Famous for her series of duets with Marvin Gaye, **TAMMI TERRELL** might have had a huge career; no one will ever know, though, as she died as a result of a brain tumor in 1970 at just twenty-four years of age. Marvin himself was so upset at the loss of his partner that he went into seclusion for a year before emerging with his classic release, **What's Going On**. Terrell's 1968 album **Irresistible** showcases her voice on its own with a collection of good songs.

MUM, CAN I WEAR YOUR MASCARA?

In the early 1970s, rock music took a new commercial turn with the advent of glam rock. The bands and artists who became identified with the music came from a variety of backgrounds. Some of them transcended the short-lived moment and went on to enjoy long and diverse careers; others peaked quickly and never made it beyond those heady days of sequins and platform boots. But for a whole generation of teenage boys and girls, the androgynous look that went along with the music opened up a whole new world.

Marc Bolan had been kicking around various groups in the late sixties with his meandering, folk-inspired hippie songs. In 1968, he formed a duo with Steve Peregrine Took called Tyrannosaurus

Rex. After three albums and moderate underground success, Took left and was replaced by Mickey Finn, and the band name was shortened to **T. REX**. In 1970 the single **Ride a White Swan** (my favorite single of all time) began a rapid rise up the charts and sparked a string of hit singles in the UK that culminated in Marc enlarging T. Rex to a full band. By the time they recorded the album **Electric Warrior** (Reprise, 1971), T. Rex mania was sweeping Britain. Considered probably the definitive glam album, it included the U.S. hit **Bang a Gong (Get It On)**. Bolan and T. Rex went on to record another couple of fine albums in the next few years, but his star had faded by mid-decade. Unfortunately, Marc Bolan never had the opportunity to witness his musical influence, as he was killed in a car crash in 1977.

DAVID BOWIE has gone through so many incarnations that he's widely considered the master chameleon of rock music. In the early seventies, he was right there with Bolan wearing eyeliner and recording a classic glam album, **The Rise & Fall of Ziggy Stardust and the Spiders from Mars** (Virgin, 1972). Marvel as Bowie takes the abstract idea of an androgynous rock star from outer space named Ziggy Stardust and, with the help of guitarist Mick Ronson, pulls together a visionary, melodramatic album.

When **THE NEW YORK DOLLS** began playing around Manhattan in 1971 they were considered outrageous, not just because of their cross-dressing but also because they were downright obnoxious. As a result they created quite a loyal live following. However, although their early albums were well reviewed, they didn't sell, and after a brief stint with new manager Malcolm McLaren in 1975, it was pretty much over. McLaren went on to infamy as manager of the Sex Pistols and used the Dolls' attitude as his inspiration, thus giving them the unique distinction of being both a glam and a punk band! The band's first album **The New York**

Dolls (Mercury, 1973) was produced by Todd Rundgren and catches them at their trashy, noisy, rocking zenith.

SLADE jumped on the bandwagon when they hired former Animals bass player (and the man who discovered Jimi Hendrix) Chas Chandler as their manager. They then adopted a skinhead look and had a hit with a real foot-stomper (well, they were wearing Doc Martens), **Get Down and Get With It**. By 1971 the boys grew their hair, pulled on the metallic platform boots, and morphed into one of the most successful singles bands of the decade. They continued throughout the eighties and nineties and scored more hits during that time but never cracked the States, though their single **Cum on Feel the Noize** would later become a huge hit for Quiet Riot. Slade's good-time pub rock, with its huge hooks and pop sensibility, is best reviewed through a compilation, of which there are many. Try a more recent one, **Get Yur Boots On: The Best of Slade** (Shout Factory, 2004). It takes you chronologically through all the hits.

SWEET were originally a working-class rock band, but then began to experiment with more commercial pop and started to wear eyeliner, satin jackets, and stacked-heel shoes, a grab for chart success was clearly underway. By hooking up with the hit songwriters of the day, Nicky Chinn and Mike Chapman, they scored an impressive list of hit singles in the mid-seventies. The band's B-sides were radically different from their pop singles, though, and eventually the band decided to take control of their own destiny and started writing their own songs. The hits didn't come as fast, but they did continue throughout the decade to chart on both sides of the Atlantic. The early albums are intriguing for their mix of pop songs and harder rock tracks, but the album that probably sums it up best is a greatest-hits collection, **The Best of Sweet** (Capitol, 1992).

The now-disgraced **GARY GLITTER** (he was arrested several years ago for possession of child pornography) had a couple of major hits at the beginning of the glam era with songs like **Rock and Roll** and **Do You Wanna Touch Me**. The former song has been a staple at football and sporting events in the United States for many years. Out of all the glam performers of the early seventies, Gary Glitter was perhaps the most outlandish. He had the boldest outfits and the highest platform boots. As a 14-year-old kid, the first rock concert I went to alone was one of his shows at Birmingham Town Hall, and I remember him changing outfits three times! There are a number of compilations available, including **Rock and Roll: Gary Glitter's Greatest Hits** (Rhino, 1998).

NATIVE AMERICAN MUSICIANS AND SINGERS

Traditional Native American music featured voice-based chants with very little instrumentation apart from percussion and different types of wooden wind instruments (essentially flutes), and was performed at powwows (get-togethers). Most early recordings focused on drum groups who performed in unison for dances that would be accompanied by chants and traditional songs about harvests, weather, celebrations, and even war. As with most musical forms, when a guitar is added to the mix things begin to change. Several performers of Native American descent have become household names in the pop world—Cher, Shania Twain, and Wayne Newton, just to mention a few. The artists and albums listed below mix elements of both the ancient and modern musical worlds.

Born in Saskatchewan, Canada, **BUFFY SAINTE-MARIE** is a Cree Indian. In the 1960s she played the folk circuit and gained a reputation as an activist and one of the few performers to address Native American issues. Her biggest commercial success came when Donovan covered her song **Universal Soldier**, and the critics lauded her 1969 album **Illuminations**, on Vanguard, for both the eclectic choice of material and its recording techniques. By the mid-seventies she pretty much retired from recording, although she did collaborate with her husband, famed producer Jack Nitzsche, on movie soundtracks and returned with a couple of releases in the second half of the 1990s.

A Sioux Indian from South Dakota, **JOHN TRUDELL** is first and foremost an activist and poet who began reciting his work initially without any musical accompaniment. When he teamed up with guitarist Jesse Ed Davis in 1986, they recorded an album called **A.K.A. Grafitti Man** that they initially sold on cassette. Sadly, Davis died from a drug overdose prior to Trudell signing with Rykodisc and rereleasing the album on CD in 1992. Trudell continues to record and release records that address his heritage and the issues that Native Americans face.

As a member of Bob Dylan's backing group the Band, **ROBBIE ROBERTSON** achieved just about everything any working musician could want: seminal and critically acclaimed hit records, money, fame, and everything that goes along with it. It wasn't until after the Band called it quits, though, that he began to explore his maternal heritage as a Mohawk Indian. His 1998 album on Capitol, **Contact from the Underworld of Redboy**, is a flavorful mix of ambient blues, rock, and Native American sounds, and includes a track with a spoken word piece from Native American activist Leonard Peltier, who is in jail on murder charges that are believed by many to be false. For the album, Peltier's voice was recorded by telephone from prison.

JOANNE SHENANDOAH is a Wolf Clan member of the Iroquois Confederacy–Oneida Nation. The majority of her recordings are more traditional in style than the other artists on this list. She is a multi-instrumentalist; however, her voice is her true instrument. She teamed with pianist Peter Kater in 1995 for an album of traditional Iroquois songs called **Lifeblood** for SilverWave Records, a label devoted to releasing the music of Native American artists.

NAUGHTY GIRLS

Rock and roll is supposed to be scary, and there have been plenty of male rockers who scared the hell out of many a young teenager's parents. But what about the girls? There was a time when just the thought of a young woman picking up a guitar or singing in a rock band was considered risqué. Even before rock music there were women singers who ignored the "rules" and expectations placed on women. As rock (and society) has evolved, women are a much more accepted part of the music scene. Nonetheless, sexism continues to exist, and as long as women are sexualized by the media there's still a long way to go. Here's a sample of female artists who, for a variety of reasons, have been deemed "naughty."

BILLIE HOLIDAY was a true original. One of the most important American singers ever to record, she sang jazz with the intensity of a blues singer who had lived with the pain and tragedy she sang about. Her personal life was a soap opera of bad relationships and self-abuse, no doubt in response to her upbringing, which was largely without parental guidance and included rape at the age of ten and part-time prostitution as a teenager. But the *voice*, oh that voice! Billie Holiday stands right up there with the giants of the twentieth century, alongside the likes of Ella Fitzgerald and Frank Sinatra.

Benny Goodman gave Holiday her first real break in 1933, and through the next few years she sang with the likes of Duke Ellington, Count Basie, and Artie Shaw. Shaw's band, though, was all-white, and racism reared its ugly head when promoters started to object to her performing with them. She left the band and headed back to the clubs and to a new venue, Café Society, where an interracial audience immediately accepted her on her own terms. It was here that she met Lewis Allen, who gave her the song **Strange Fruit**, a composition addressing racist lynchings that through its popularity was to change and define her career.

Billie Holiday recorded throughout the 1940s and 1950s with a variety of bands and ensembles, and wrote her own material as well, most notably the single **God Bless the Child**. However, her drug abuse, which had progressed to opium and heroin, inevitably caught up with her, and she passed away in 1959. With an artist of this stature, I can only recommend that you immerse yourself in her work. She recorded for several labels during her career, and the Columbia Records years are available on the 1991 nine-CD box set called **The Quintessential Billie Holiday: 1933–1942**.

JUDY GARLAND makes it onto both the nice *and* the naughty girls lists. When she was younger, she certainly fit the girl-next-door image of how a young woman should be. But after years of prescription drug abuse (uppers and downers fed to her by her mother and the studio) and a string of failed relationships, her life started to unravel and her behavior became unpredictable, leading to her being fired from a couple of movies. She found herself with very little money and returned to her first love, singing, in the early 1950s, with live concert performances in order to support herself and her children (Liza Minelli, and Joey and Lorna Luft).

Her life and career did look up for a while. She hosted "The Judy Garland Show" on NBC in 1963 and 1964, but after another failed marriage, she was left broke once again and had to head out on concert tours to Europe and across the States to pay the bills. She died of an overdose of barbiturates in 1969. **Judy at Carnegie Hall**, recorded in 1961, was recently given a complete restoration and re-mastering treatment by Capitol Records to celebrate the fortieth anniversary of its release; it catches Judy on her first comeback and at her very best as she breezes through her musical legacy in fine style.

JOAN JETT wore leather; do we really need to delve into her credentials as a naughty girl any further? In the 1980s, as MTV was rapidly becoming the equivalent of a national radio station, image was everything, and a chick dressed in leather playing simple, loud rock and roll was a winner. It didn't hurt that she loaded the songs with hooks as well. Coming out of the punky, all-girl LA group the Runaways, Joan moved to New York to kick-start her solo career; after one independent release she formed the Blackhearts and recorded the debut album **I Love Rock 'n' Roll** (1981, Blackheart), which featured the now-classic single of the same name. Joan is credited with inspiring a whole generation of female rockers.

LIZ PHAIR paved the way for a new generation of female artists. Her 1993 debut, **Exile in Guyville**, on Matador Records was a play on words and a somewhat-answer to the Rolling Stones classic *Exile on Main Street*. It featured songs refined from previous demo cassettes that she had been selling around her hometown of Chicago for a couple of years. The album's subject matter spoke to young women of her generation in the way it addressed relationships with guys from a place of hard-won confidence. And it attracted a significant male audience as well. Liz has had mixed success in the years since, but once again it's worth mentioning that her breakthrough opened the doors that a lot of female artists have since walked through.

ALANIS MORRISETTE picked up the Liz Phair lyrical torch and added the pop hooks necessary to achieve mainstream success. She actually started her career as a child actor back in her homeland of Canada and recorded a couple of albums of pretty forgettable pop fluff. Her breakthrough album **Jagged Little Pill** (Maverick Records, 1995) took a more provocative direction with the help of her collaborator and producer Glen Ballard. On the back of the single **You Oughta Know**, which proved that guys would respond to a naughty lyric and that girls could relate, the album took off into the stratosphere and ended up selling several million copies, making her one of the biggest-selling alternative rock artists of the decade. She has continued to maintain a successful career and her records have all sold well.

NICE GIRLS

For every yin, there's a yang! So after checking out some naughty girls, it's time to dial it back and take a look at some female artists considered to be the "Girl Next Door" or "America's Sweetheart." These are women groomed to be easily digested by the public as nice girls.

Best remembered for her movies, **DORIS DAY** is in fact a multitalented actress, comedienne, and singer. She grew up around music; her father was involved in the local church and played the organ, and was also a music teacher. She had originally wanted to be a dancer but after badly injuring her foot in a car accident, she turned to singing and received her first break as a featured vocalist on radio broadcasts in her hometown of Cincinnati. She went on to work with some of the finest jazz and swing band musicians of the 1940s, most notably Les Brown, before becoming an actress. Whether singing in musicals or the goofy comedies she's best remembered for, Doris Day always delivered a solid performance and showcased her varied vocal skills throughout her career. The soundtrack to the 1955 movie **Love Me or Leave Me** (Columbia), based on the life of actress/singer Ruth Etting, who had been a popular recording star in the 1920s and 1930s, gave Day the opportunity to record some of the songs that Etting was known for. It's a side of Doris Day that deserves another listen, and was reissued in 1993.

Before **JUDY GARLAND** succumbed to decades of self-abuse and doomed relationships that led her to be known as difficult and troubled, she began her career in vaudeville, singing with her two sisters. When she got her break in movies as a contract player at MGM, the studio groomed her for musicals; of course, her star-making performance came as Dorothy in *The Wizard Of Oz*, which was followed by a string of successful films costarring Mickey Rooney, in which she played the sweet-voiced innocent girl. Before branching out into more adult roles, Judy was indeed considered a nice girl and "America's Sweetheart." Her first record was **Judy Garland Souvenir Album** released on the heels of her *Wizard Of Oz* fame, originally as three 78s in 1940 on Decca Records. It captures the seventeen-year-old Judy at her sweetest and most childlike, and collects together her early singles, including **You Made Me Love You**. At the time of writing, this collection was not available on CD. You could also pick up the classic soundtrack to **The Wizard of Oz** (Decca, 1940).

Generally thought of as Australian, **OLIVIA NEWTON-JOHN** was actually born in the United Kingdom. After spending her childhood and teens in Australia, she returned to the UK, where she began her career in the music business. After a short-lived stint in an all-girl band, she was given her first real break by Cliff Richard, one of Britain's biggest pop stars, when he invited her to become a regular on his early 1970s TV variety show, "It's Cliff."

As a prepubescent boy, I first saw her on that show; that's when I experienced my first crush on a singer! She had a Top-10 hit in the UK in 1971 with a cover of Bob Dylan's **If Not for You**, which also charted in the United States.

Olivia quit the UK scene a couple of years later and crossed the Atlantic to try her luck in America, where things happened very quickly for her, and she experienced major success as a country artist. Her 1974 release **If You Love Me, Let Me Know**, on MCA, is a slice of country pop at its best, with Olivia in fine voice. Toward the end of the decade, she attempted to cross over as a more mainstream artist, a transition that was completed with her role opposite John Travolta in the movie musical *Grease*. Her pop career continued into the eighties with a number of successful albums like **Physical** (MCA, 1981), until music trends began shifting in the middle of the decade. Realizing that it was time to make way for a new generation of stars, Olivia pretty much retreated from the music business to concentrate on her family and other interests.

When I first arrived in the United States in the late 1980s, **DEBBIE GIBSON** was the reigning princess of pop. She released a series of hit dance pop singles and two hugely successful albums toward the end of the "Me" decade. While she was competing with the likes of Madonna and a whole host of other teenage singers for chart honors, there was one big difference: Debbie Gibson wrote and arranged all of her own material. She was unable, however, to transcend the teen idol label, so, as she and her fans moved into their twenties, Debbie's career faded pretty quickly, and she stepped back from the fray. Her first album, released by Atlantic Records in 1987, was called **Out of the Blue**, and true to its name, four of the album's ten tracks hit the Top 5, making her an instant star. She has in subsequent years appeared on Broadway and released a couple of other albums under the name Deborah Gibson.

O, CANADA

In many ways the United States and Canada share a cultural heritage. A Canadian guy I traveled through Europe with in the eighties said it best: "We're like Americans, but without the guns!" Canada has produced some amazingly talented musicians, bands, and songwriters; here's a few that prove there's more to Canada than Celine Dion and maple syrup.

BARENAKED LADIES have become one of the most popular Canadian bands to ever cross over to U.S. and international audiences. Formed in Toronto at the end of the eighties, BNL set out to make people laugh. Their first full album did just that, with silly songs about Yoko Ono, Brian Wilson, and their breakthrough single, **If I Had $1,000,000**. That album, **Gordon**, was released in 1992 on Reprise Records and the group hasn't looked back since.

BLUE RODEO are one of the most talented Canadian bands of the last twenty years. With a rootsy mix of country, folk, and rock, their albums consistently go platinum (100,000 copies) in their homeland. The group is led by Jim Cuddy and Greg Keelor, who both write songs, play guitar, and sing. They played together in several other bands before forming Blue Rodeo. One of their best albums is **Lost Together** (1992) on Discovery Records.

THE GUESS WHO were Canada's answer to the British Invasion, recording a string of singles in the second half of the 1960s. They had an early hit in both Canada and the United States in 1965 with the song **Shakin' All Over**, originally recorded by Johnny Kidd and the Pirates. But they are best known for their single **American Woman**, which proved to be a huge hit for them. 1969's **Canned Wheat** on Buddha Records is a great collection of songs that reveals them to be a top-notch rock-and-roll band. The group underwent a few lineup changes but continued recording into the mid-seventies before breaking up. Trivia note: The group's original guitarist, Randy Bachman, went on to fame with his own group **BACHMAN-TURNER OVERDRIVE**, who had a major international hit in 1974 with the single **You Ain't Seen Nothin' Yet** from the album **Not Fragile** on Mercury.

Born in Alberta, **K.D. LANG**'s first musical hero was Patsy Cline, so it was natural that she would begin her career as a country artist. After several well-regarded independent Canadian releases in the early eighties, she was courted by major labels in the United States, signing with Sire and making an immediate impact with her first two releases, 1986's **Angel With A Lariat** and the 1988 follow-up **Shadowland**. She has since moved away from country and become one of the best interpreters of other people's music. In 2004 she released an album on Nonesuch Records called **Hymns of the 49th Parallel**, on which she covers material by other Canadian artists, including Neil Young, Joni Mitchell, and Leonard Cohen.

GORDON LIGHTFOOT was known as a songwriter for other artists before finding fame as a performer himself. In the early 1970s he recorded a number of folk-based albums that sold well and spawned several hit singles featuring personal, intimate lyrics. His 1970 release **Sit Down Young Stranger** on Reprise Records kick-started a run of successes that lasted for most of the decade. The album was later renamed **If You Could Read My Mind**, after the track of the same name became a hit single.

SARAH MCLACHLAN hails from Halifax, Nova Scotia, where as a child she was classically trained on both piano and guitar. After a short spell singing in a post-punk band, she set out on her own and landed a record deal with Vancouver-based indie label Nettwerk Records. Her third full-length album, **Fumbling Towards Ecstasy**, was released on Arista in 1993. The album made her an international star. She's also well known as the founder of Lilith

Fair, a traveling music festival featuring women artists that traversed the United States and Canada for several summers in the latter part of the 1990s.

MEN WITHOUT HATS get an honorable mention for having one of the biggest New Wave hits of the eighties with their single **The Safety Dance**. Taken from their debut, **Rhythm of Youth**, released on MCA in 1982, it has since guaranteed them a lifetime of VH1 '80s flashbacks.

MOXY FRÜVOUS are probably one of the more bizarre rock bands to come out of North America. The various members started out as street performers busking in their hometown of Toronto before scoring a record deal. Their albums have been wildly eclectic musically, with vocals ranging from a cappella harmonies to rapping. Their 1997 album, **You Will Go to the Moon**, is full of songs that take a smart, satirical look at U.S. culture, and is available on Bottom Line Records.

You can't write about Canadian bands without mentioning Toronto's **RUSH**. Simply put, they are the most famous rock band to come out of that country. Often disregarded by critics, the band is defined by singer Geddy Lee's distinctive voice. They have shown an amazing resilience and adapted accordingly as the musical landscape has shifted. Throughout their 30–plus–year history they've recorded a clutch of multiplatinum records of mainstream rock music, including the 1980 release, **Permanent Waves**, on Mercury Records.

JANE SIBERRY was classically trained on the piano as a young child in her hometown of Toronto. She went on to become a highly regarded, if somewhat eccentric, performer. Her work through the years has ranged from minimal self-released albums to more structured commercial releases on a major label. She's also recorded collections of traditional Celtic and American music on her own Sheeba record label. Her 1989 release for Reprise, **Bound By the Beauty**, is probably her most accessible album.

STEPPENWOLF were led by Toronto-based German immigrant John Kay, who in 1967 moved to California and created one of the greatest rock anthems ever recorded. **Born To Be Wild** was used in the Dennis Hopper cult road movie *Easy Rider*, which also starred Peter Fonda and Jack Nicholson. The song was originally on the album **Steppenwolf**, released on MCA in 1968. On a side note, a lyric in "Born to Be Wild" refers to "heavy metal thunder," which some music historians believe gave birth to the term heavy metal, used to describe hard rock in the 1970s and beyond.

Formed in Kingston, Ontario, in 1983, **THE TRAGICALLY HIP** have been consistently popular in their homeland with a mix of roots rock and pop melodies. For a short while in the mid-1990s they crossed the border and found a U.S. audience as well. Their 1993 album **Fully Completely** on MCA included the single **Courage**, which received generous college and alternative radio airplay, is deemed by many critics to be their best.

SHANIA TWAIN became one of the most popular country artists of the late 1990s by crafting slick production techniques onto good country pop songs. It all sounds so simple, although her early adult life was far from easy. She'd been singing as a kid and performing in bars as a teenager, but at the age of 21, her parents were killed in a car crash, and she had to take care of her four younger brothers, which she did by singing show tunes in resort hotels. She began incorporating some country tunes into her set and by the time her brothers were old enough to take care of themselves, she was ready to try her hand as a country singer.

After landing a record deal with Mercury Nashville and releasing her first album, Shania met producer "Mutt" Lange, who had made his name working with rock acts such as Foreigner and the Cars, and they began collaborating. (They also fell in love and married soon thereafter.) Her second album, **The Woman in Me**, was released on Mercury in 1995 and established her as a major star; it also marked a huge shift in country music as it was primarily marketed through stylish, sexy videos that appealed to a larger, more mainstream pop audience.

ONE HUNDRED ESSENTIAL ALBUMS FROM THE LAST HALF OF THE TWENTIETH CENTURY

When the first phonographic 10- and 12-inch 78s went on sale at the end of the nineteenth century, the majority of records featured recordings of opera singers. It wasn't until records began to feature the popular singers of the 1920s that sales of recorded music began to increase. However, since neither record-playing equipment nor the records themselves were affordable for most of the working and middle classes, it was only in the 1950s, when mass-produced electronic goods began to appear, that record sales really started to take off. After World War II, American teenagers began to challenge the status quo, and Western pop culture was born. From the midfifties until the early seventies, recorded music became synonymous with rebellion and cultural change, so many artists found audiences receptive to their visions.

Beginning in the eighties, however, the music business began eating itself, and by the nineties, as a result of mergers and acquisitions, multinational corporations took control of many of the most significant record labels. Consolidation was the name of the game throughout most of the entertainment industry, and as ownership of the majority of radio stations fell under the control of just a handful of corporations, artistic creativity was stifled. By the turn of the century, however, the rise of the Internet as an alternative distribution and marketing tool began to take control away from the corporations, so, in my opinion, we are at the beginning of a renaissance in the world of rock and pop music.

Putting together album "best of" lists is a daunting prospect; it's a wholly subjective task. I'm sure that some will look at the following pages and exclaim, "How could he not put [enter your favorite record here] in that list?" So, here's my disclaimer: The following lists feature twenty essential albums from each decade of the last half of the twentieth century. They are albums that I personally think are important to the history of recorded music, albums that I like, and albums that I like to recommend. Albums are listed not by order of preference but chronologically by year of release. Also, for diversity's sake, in each decade's list I have chosen only one album per artist.

The Fifties

The 1950s began with singers like Frank Sinatra topping the charts, but by the middle of the decade black rhythm and blues (R&B) had been co-opted by white artists, and Western pop culture and the world were changed forever. In the first half of the decade, the world was a little like the 1998 movie *Pleasantville*, black-and-white with a few shades of gray thrown in, but things were set to change when Bill Haley set the rock-and-roll ball rolling and became its first star. However, it wasn't until Elvis Presley shook his hips and sang **That's Alright Mama** in 1954 that the twentieth century suddenly exploded in Technicolor. The fifties was also a decade of rapid-fire jazz improvisation and saw a slew of memorable releases. Here's a list of albums from the 1950s that includes some of these classic jazz records, as well as albums by the early rock-and-roll giants:

STAN KENTON: *Innovations in Modern Music* (Capitol, 1950; reissued with additional material as *The Innovations Orchestra*, Blue Note, 1997)

BILL HALEY: *Shake, Rattle & Roll* (Drive Archive, 1955)

FRANK SINATRA: *Songs for Swinging Lovers* (Capitol, 1955)

ELVIS PRESLEY: *Elvis Presley* (RCA, 1956)

JOHNNY CASH: *Johnny Cash with His Hot and Blue Guitar* (Varese Sarabande, 1957)

RAY CHARLES: *Ray Charles* (Atlantic, 1957)

ELLA FITZGERALD & LOUIS ARMSTRONG: *Ella & Louis* (Universal, 1957)

BUDDY HOLLY & THE CRICKETS: *The "Chirping" Crickets* (MCA, 1957)

LITTLE RICHARD: *Here's Little Richard* (P-Vine, 1957)

CARL PERKINS: *Dance Album* (Varese Sarabande, 1957)

TITO PUENTE: *Top Percussion* (RCA, 1957)

JERRY LEE LEWIS: *Jerry Lee Lewis* (Rhino, 1957)

FATS DOMINO: *Fabulous Mr. D* (Collectables, 1958)

THE BIG BOPPER: *Chantilly Lace* (Polygram, 1958)

ART BLAKEY & THE JAZZ MESSENGERS: *Moanin'* (Blue Note, 1958)

CHUCK BERRY: *Chuck Berry Is on Top* (MCA, 1959)

DAVE BRUBECK: *Time Out* (Columbia, 1959)

MILES DAVIS: *Kind of Blue* (Columbia, 1959)

CHARLES MINGUS: *Mingus Ah Um* (Columbia, 1959)

RITCHIE VALENS: *Ritchie Valens* (Rhino, 1959)

The Sixties

The 1960s was when my own musical journey began. When I was a young kid, my dad worked in television and used to bring home the promotional 7-inch singles that the station would get by bands that were making waves, like Gerry & the Pacemakers and the Beatles. It was a good time to begin a love of melody and pop. The first album I ever owned was **Help!** by The Beatles, bought for me by my mum in 1966; I was eight years old.

MILES DAVIS: *Sketches of Spain* (Columbia, 1960)

SAM COOKE: *Night Beat* (RCA, 1963)

JOHN COLTRANE: *A Love Supreme* (Impulse, 1965)

THE WHO: *Sings My Generation* (MCA,1965)

THE BEATLES: *Rubber Soul* (Capitol, 1965)

THE BEACH BOYS: *Pet Sounds* (Capitol, 1966)

DONOVAN: *Sunshine Superman* (Epic, 1966)

BOB DYLAN: *Blonde on Blonde* (Columbia, 1966)

THE DOORS: *Strange Days* (Elektra, 1967)

THE JIMI HENDRIX EXPERIENCE: *Are You Experienced?*
    (MCA, 1967)

JEFFERSON AIRPLANE: *Surrealistic Pillow* (RCA, 1967)

LOVE: *Forever Changes* (Elektra, 1968)

PINK FLOYD: *The Piper at the Gates of Dawn* (Capitol, 1967)

THE VELVET UNDERGROUND: *The Velvet Underground &*
    Nico (Verve, 1967)

THE BYRDS: *Sweetheart of the Rodeo* (Columbia, 1968)

VAN MORRISON: *Astral Weeks* (Warner Brothers, 1968)

THE ROLLING STONES: *Beggars Banquet* (ABKCO, 1968)

THE SMALL FACES: *Ogden's Nut Gone Flake* (Columbia, 1968)

DUSTY SPRINGFIELD: *Dusty in Memphis* (Rhino, 1969)

LED ZEPPELIN: *Led Zeppelin* (Atlantic, 1969)

The Seventies

As the clock struck midnight on December 31, 1969, music's first great decade gave way to what was to become the era of glam, disco, and overindulged rock stars. It was also one of the most fertile decades in music history, with new genres springing up and the cross-pollination of others. The 1970s might have brought us long sideburns and polyester suits, but it also spawned a rich vein of artistic creativity; it was a golden decade for music, and it all eventually made way for punk rock.

MILES DAVIS: *Bitches Brew* (Columbia, 1970)

NEIL YOUNG: *After the Gold Rush* (Reprise, 1970)

JONI MITCHELL: *Blue* (Reprise, 1971)

MARVIN GAYE: *What's Going On* (Motown, 1971)

T. REX: *Electric Warrior* (Rhino, 1971)

THE ROLLING STONES: *Exile on Main Street* (Virgin, 1972)

PINK FLOYD: *Dark Side of the Moon* (Capitol, 1973)

ROXY MUSIC: *For Your Pleasure* (Virgin, 1973)

BRUCE SPRINGSTEEN: *The Wild, the Innocent, and the E Street Shuffle* (Columbia, 1973)

QUEEN: *Queen II* (Hollywood, 1974)

DAVID BOWIE: *Low* (Virgin, 1977)

FLEETWOOD MAC: *Rumours* (Reprise, 1977)

THE SEX PISTOLS: *Never Mind the Bollocks Here's the Sex Pistols* (Virgin, 1977)

BLONDIE: *Parallel Lines* (Capitol, 1978)

THE POLICE: *Outlandos d'Amour* (A&M, 1978)

STEVE REICH: *Music for 18 Musicians* (ECM, 1978)

THE CLASH: *London Calling* (Epic, 1979)

GANG OF FOUR: *Entertainment!* (EMI, 1979)

JOY DIVISION: *Unknown Pleasures* (Warner Brothers, 1979)

TALKING HEADS: *Fear of Music* (Sire, 1979)

The Eighties

As the seventies gave way to the eighties punk was pretty much out of fuel, and the New Romantic period was just beginning with bands like Duran Duran and Spandau Ballet. MTV was about to introduce a whole slew of photogenic stars, and the decade of greed, as it was to become known, gave us a wealth of instantly disposable pop music. The 1980s was also the heyday of synthesizers and drum machines, and it saw the beginnings of a new genre, hip-hop, that was to take the world by surprise, as well as some classic pop music by artists like Michael Jackson. Although much of the music recorded and released during the eighties fails to stand up in the cold, hard light of the new millennium, there were a number of artists who came of age during this period and many albums that prove it wasn't all satin clothes and funny hairstyles.

DAVID BOWIE: *Scary Monsters* (Virgin, 1980)

TALKING HEADS: *Remain in Light* (Sire, 1980)

THE SOUND: *From the Lion's Mouth* (Renascent, 1981)

ELVIS COSTELLO: *Imperial Bedroom* (Rykodisc, 1982)

MICHAEL JACKSON: *Thriller* (Epic, 1982)

THE BLUE NILE: *A Walk Across the Rooftops* (A&M, 1983)

NEW ORDER: *Power, Corruption, & Lies* (Warner Brothers, 1983)

R.E.M.: *Murmur* (IRS, 1983)

VIOLENT FEMMES: *Violent Femmes* (Rhino, 1983)

KATE BUSH: *Hounds of Love* (EMI, 1984)

FRANKIE GOES TO HOLLYWOOD: *Welcome to the Pleasuredome* (Island, 1984)

PETER GABRIEL: *So* (Geffen, 1986)

RUN-D.M.C.: *Raising Hell* (Arista, 1986)

THE SMITHS: *The Queen Is Dead* (Sire, 1986)

GUNS N' ROSES: *Appetite for Destruction* (Geffen, 1987)

MIDNIGHT OIL: *Diesel and Dust* (Columbia, 1987)

PRINCE: *Sign 'O' the Times* (Paisley Park, 1987)

U2: *The Joshua Tree* (Island, 1987)

PUBLIC ENEMY: *It Takes a Nation of Millions to Hold Us Back* (Def Jam, 1988)

THE STONE ROSES: *The Stone Roses* (Jive, 1989)

The Nineties

For a brief moment in the 1990s, at least a part of the music business returned to basics. When Nirvana broke through in 1993 an explosion of alternative rock followed, and for a short while the punk ethic was back. Of course, it wasn't long before the major labels co-opted the movement, and it was beaten to death pretty quickly. But the nineties are memorable for a number of breakthrough releases by new and emerging songwriters and groups. It will also be remembered as the decade that saw hip-hop come of age, and for several classic albums by established artists.

PUBLIC ENEMY: *Fear of a Black Planet* (Def Jam, 1990)

MASSIVE ATTACK: *Blue Lines* (Virgin, 1991)

NIRVANA: *Nevermind* (Geffen, 1991)

TALK TALK: *Laughing Stock* (Polydor, 1991)

U2: *Achtung Baby* (Island, 1991)

MY BLOODY VALENTINE: *Loveless* (Warner Brothers, 1991)

R.E.M.: *Automatic for the People* (Warner Brothers, 1992)

PJ HARVEY: *Rid of Me* (Island, 1993)

JEFF BUCKLEY: *Grace* (Columbia, 1994)

LIZ PHAIR: *Exile in Guyville* (Matador, 1993)

BJÖRK: *Post* (Elektra, 1995)

ALANIS MORISSETTE: *Jagged Little Pill* (Maverick, 1995)

PULP: *Different Class* (Island, 1995)

BECK: *Odelay* (DGC, 1996)

BELLE & SEBASTIAN: *If You're Feeling Sinister* (Matador, 1996)

RADIOHEAD: *OK Computer* (Capitol, 1997)

ELLIOTT SMITH: *Either/Or* (Kill Rock Stars, 1997)

AIR: *Moon Safari* (Astralwerks, 1998)

MERCURY REV: *Deserter's Songs* (V2, 1998)

THE FLAMING LIPS: *The Soft Bulletin* (Warner Brothers, 1999)

ORGAN GRINDERS

After the guitar, the Hammond B3 organ is perhaps the most important jazz and blues instrument. It was invented in 1935 by clockmaker Laurens Hammond and was the first electric instrument to be widely used. It is also very heavy—about 400 pounds to be precise—plus it comes with the also-hefty Leslie speaker, named after its inventor, Don Leslie. Having moved one or two of these beasts around myself over the years, I can testify to the back pain that goes along with being a roadie for a B3 player! But when you hear the unique sound this instrument makes, you understand why players would rather drag one of these organs out on tour with them instead of a modern keyboard that emulates the sound: There's just no comparison.

In the fifties and sixties, **JIMMY SMITH** became one of the most influential exponents of the B3, showcasing the versatility of the instrument by playing gospel, blues, and jazz arrangements and reinventing the way the instrument was played by subsequent artists. His Blue Note recordings are legendary, and he collaborated with a number of highly regarded musicians during this time, including Art Blakey, Kenny Burrell, Lou Donaldson, Stanley Turrentine, and Ike Quebec. **The Sermon!**, from 1958 on Blue Note, showcases Jimmy at his best; the CD reissue in 2000 includes bonus tracks. After dropping out of the business a couple of times in the seventies and nineties, Jimmy returned to music, working on an album with fellow organist Joey DeFrancesco (see entry later in this essay) before his death in February 2005.

REUBEN WILSON emerged in the late 1960s, primarily as a player of what was then called soul-jazz. The albums he recorded for Blue Note during this time featured musicians like Grant Green and Lee Morgan, but outside of a small fan base they went largely unnoticed. He carried on into the seventies doing session work, but pretty much quit by the eighties, until he experienced something of a renaissance during the nineties as a new generation of musicians and samplers began to "borrow" from him. Suddenly, his work was showing up on songs by jazz/hip-hop acts like A Tribe Called Quest. Consequently, his music found a new audience and his old, out-of-print records became highly collectable. **Blue Mode**, from Blue Note in 1969, mixed soul-jazz, blues, and funk to create a laid-back record.

TRUDY PITTS emerged out of Philadelphia, as had Jimmy Smith, and although she played with perhaps a little more of a pop sound than some of her contemporaries, there's no doubt that she's been largely unrecognized. Not only was she a classically trained pianist, but she could also sing. When she left college, drummer Bill Carney asked her to audition for his combo (a job previously held by Shirley Scott), and though she didn't get the job, he was taken with her personally and suggested that she play more jazz, which she did. After falling in love and marrying, they began to play together in a group called Trudy Pitts and Mr. C. She made a number of albums under her own name in the 1960s for the Prestige record label, most of which featured covers of pop hits, but they were played in a soul-jazz groove. **Introducing the Fabulous Trudy Pitts**, on Prestige from 1967, features her husband on drums as well as guitarist Pat Martino. The album includes some Bill Carney originals and covers of popular songs like **Matchmaker, Matchmaker** and **The Spanish Flea**. In 1998 it was combined with another of her albums, **These Blues of Mine**, and reissued by Prestige as **Trudy Pitts with Pat Martino: Legends of Acid Jazz**. These days Trudy Pitts still lives in Philadephia and teaches privately.

LONNIE SMITH, who later in his career became Dr. Lonnie Smith (because he liked the way it sounded), earned his reputation as a member of George Benson's mid-sixties quartet. He went on to collaborate extensively with alto sax player Lou Donaldson and brought his funk grooves to whomever he played with. His 1968 Blue Note release **Think!** showed him as a bandleader and playing a little more R&B than his later work.

JOEY DEFRANCESCO is one of the key players in a recent revival in the B3's fortunes. Another Philly-raised organ player and a third-generation musician, he is the son of organist Papa John DeFrancesco. Joey has explored many different styles of music on the instrument. In 1989 at age 17 he released his debut album, **All of Me**, on Columbia Records; it is an album that announced the arrival of an important young musician.

Another young player who has picked up the torch is **JOHN MEDESKI**. Although he began as a classical piano player, he switched to jazz as a teenager and admired the likes of Oscar

Peterson and Bud Powell. Medeski has delved into musical theory and studied world music, and he plays a number of different keyboards, such as the clavinet and mellotron. Once he discovered the B3, though, he began to explore its possibilities, and with his trio Medeski, Martin & Wood, he fused avant-garde jazz and rock into a unique mix. **Combustication**, from 1998 on Blue Note, shows off the band's multifaceted improvisations.

A compilation worth picking up that features performances by some of the original organists as well as younger players is **Organized: An All-Star Tribute to the Hammond B3 Organ** by various artists on Windham Hill (2000).

POETRY IN MOTION

Poetry has been an art form since humans first used language to communicate. No one quite knows who the first poets were, but one thing's for sure, it was inevitable that music and poetry would find a way to complement each other.

LEONARD COHEN was a seasoned writer and poet long before he began recording and performing his work. He had, however, been playing guitar since he was a teenager back in his hometown of Montreal, Canada. His first published work was a book of poems called *Let Us Compare Mythologies* in 1956, published when he was twenty-two. He continued writing poetry, as well as a couple of novels, and by now he was in New York City and the sixties were redefining popular culture. When folksinger Judy Collins recorded his song **Suzanne**, Leonard Cohen began performing his own songs on stage. His first album for Columbia in 1968, **The Songs of Leonard Cohen**, a collection of bleak, barren songs about life's losers, immediately established him as a rare voice with a solitary point of view. He has continued to write, record, and, for the most part, stay relevant. Although he's never really been accepted as a singer, he's nonetheless considered one of the most important songwriters of his generation.

Often described as punk rock's poet laureate, **PATTI SMITH** is without a doubt one of the most significant female rock performers ever. Although born in Chicago, she grew up in Philadelphia and Woodbury, New Jersey. A lonely child, she discovered poetry as a solace in her teens, especially the work of the Beats such as Allen Ginsberg. She moved across the Hudson River to Manhattan when she was twenty-one and began connecting with writers and artists such as photographer Robert Mapplethorpe. She also became involved in fringe theater and met guitarist Lenny Kaye, who took along his guitar and played with her at some of her poetry readings.

Within a few years, the two had put together a band, the Patti Smith Group, that became part of the first punk explosion centered around CBGB's, the club on the Bowery that became synonymous with the New York rock scene. Her 1975 debut album on Arista, **Horses**, was produced by the Velvet Underground's John Cale and captures Patti as she learns to structure her poetry within the context of a song. It's raw and direct in both its music and lyrics. After another couple of albums that were a little more accessible and yielded a couple of radio hits including **Because The Night**, a song she co-wrote with Bruce Springsteen, Patti largely dropped out of sight in the eighties. She married Fred "Sonic" Smith from the band MC5 and moved to Detroit to raise her two children. Both Patti's brother and Fred died of heart attacks in 1994, and Patti was spurred back to writing, recording, and performing. Her 2004 release **Trampin'** on Columbia Records restates her authenticity as an artist as she takes on the realities of a post-9/11 world.

JIM CARROLL is perhaps best known to a younger audience as the guy Leonardo DiCaprio played in the 1995 movie based on Carroll's memoir, *The Basketball Diaries*. The movie followed Jim's downward spiral into drug addiction, and because it was set in contemporary times, featured a soundtrack of mid-nineties alternative rock bands; however, Jim's own peers were the punks of mid-seventies New York City. Jim was a poet in his own right, first published at just sixteen years of age. Like his pal Patti Smith, he began writing songs as well, and the Jim Carroll Band's debut release in 1980, **Catholic Boy**, on Atco Records, is widely regarded as one of the finest examples of a poet crossing over into the rock world and pulling it off. The songs are full of edgy, painful verses that reflect the life he was leading in New York during some of that city's darker days. He made another couple of records in the eighties and nineties, and since recovering from his addictions continues to dabble as both a songwriter and musician.

POLYESTER SUITS AND WRAPAROUND DRESSES

No book on music would be complete without at least some reference to disco. Today's dance music traces its ancestry back to the early seventies, when the disco movement was born out of the funk music being played in the discotheques of New York City. As those records began selling, labels smelled a buck and began signing producers and artists who could deliver songs that were shorter, had pop hooks, and could be played on the radio. By the time John Travolta pulled on that white polyester suit in the 1977 movie *Saturday Night Fever* with the Bee Gees providing the soundtrack, the world was about to be introduced to some of the most innovative music of the decade and some of the biggest misjudgments in fashion history! As future generations look back, they may well forgive the suits and even the winged hairdos the women wore, but the huge gold medallions that slammed into men's exposed chests in discos around the world will perhaps always be a mystery.

My own experience was nowhere near as glamorous. As a teenager in England in the mid-seventies, my disco days were basically about going to youth-center gatherings of other self-conscious adolescent boys and standing around the edge of the dance floor watching groups of two or three girls dancing around their handbags as the lights bounced off the mirrored ball. But let's go ahead and spin that ball right now, and take a look at some of the records that defined the disco daze:

GLORIA GAYNOR: *Never Can Say Goodbye* (MGM, 1975)

THE ISLEY BROTHERS: *The Heat Is On* (Sony, 1975)

KC & THE SUNSHINE BAND: *KC & the Sunshine Band* (Rhino, 1975)

DONNA SUMMER: *Love to Love You Baby* (Universal, 1975)

VAN MCCOY: *The Hustle and the Best of Van McCoy* (Amherst, 1976)

ABBA: *Arrival* (Polygram, 1977)

THE BEE GEES AND OTHERS: *Saturday Night Fever* (Polygram, 1977)

VILLAGE PEOPLE: *Village People* (Casablanca, 1977)

CHIC: *C'est Chic* (Atlantic, 1978)

SISTER SLEDGE: *We Are Family* (Musicrama, 1979)

LIPPS INC.: *Mouth to Mouth* (Casablanca, 1980)

Please note that at time of this writing the above-mentioned Gloria Gaynor album is out of print. If you can't find a copy, I recommend instead her **Greatest Hits** (Polygram, 1982).

QUEENS OF PUNK

If today's manufactured pop princesses were to step back and review the history of women in rock, one of the stops they should be forced to make is at the feet of the women listed below, who defied the conservative roles that women had been told were their only options and jumped into the noisy, rambunctious rebellion of punk rock.

SIOUXSIE SIOUX's credentials are about as good as it gets. She was right there at the birth of the London punk rock movement. The original lineup of her band, **SIOUXSIE & THE BANSHEES**, even included Sid Vicious on drums before he joined the Sex Pistols. (And, at one time, Cure front man Robert Smith did double duty as a guitar player in both bands.) Siouxsie is considered a pioneer inasmuch as she charted her own course, taking elements of both punk and goth music to create her own sound and look, which was that of a detached, unattainable punk goddess.

As the band continued recording through the eighties and nineties, they incorporated various world rhythms into their sound. Although she and drummer/husband Budgie now seem to devote themselves to their once-side-project the Creatures, the Banshees could still have another shout or two left. The band's dark and dramatic debut release, 1978's **The Scream** on Geffen Records, set the tone right out of the gate. The album was recorded by future U2 and Dave Matthews Band producer Steve Lillywhite, apparently within just a week, and features the classic single **Hong Kong Garden.**

By the time **DEBBIE HARRY** became the beautiful blonde front woman for **BLONDIE**, she had already been a folk singer and a Playboy bunny. It was, however, as a waitress at New York's famous Max's Kansas City club that she began to mix with the artists and musicians who would eventually, along with herself, redefine the New York music scene. After spending some time in an all-girl band named the Stilettos, she and boyfriend/collaborator Chris Stein formed Blondie. Within just a few years the group had moved beyond punk rock and established itself as the biggest New Wave band in the world, and Debbie became an international sex symbol.

The band spent the best part of a decade touring the world and conquering both singles and album charts wherever they went. Debbie went solo in the early eighties and although she had some success, she was ready to add another string to her bow with acting, appearing in a number of independent movies, including *Hairspray* for John Waters. Blondie eventually regrouped at the end of the nineties and have made something of a comeback, but the album that catches Debbie at her peak and the band at their tightest is probably their third, **Parallel Lines**, released in 1978 on Chrysalis.

Hailing from Akron, Ohio, **CHRISSIE HYNDE** had already been playing music influenced by bands like the Rolling Stones and the Stooges when she took herself to England in the mid-seventies to check out the scene. She found herself in the middle of the punk rock explosion and, not surprisingly, decided to form a band. **THE PRETENDERS**' original lineup included Pete Farndon on bass, James Honeyman-Scott on guitar, and Martin Chambers on drums. While the band came together with a punk rock, DIY ethic, their musical knowledge and skills were far from rudimentary. The band's debut album **Pretenders**, issued in 1980 on Sire, followed quickly by **Pretenders II** (also on Sire) the following year, were both packed with bluesy rock and roll with punk attitude and a pop sensibility.

The band experienced a couple of early tragedies with the deaths of both Farndon and Honeyman-Scott from drug overdoses. But through the years, Chrissie has resurrected the band several times and continued to tour and record. What was it (indeed, still is) about Chrissie Hynde that made her stand out from the pack right from the start? Well, the mop-top bangs hanging over her eyes and the tight black clothes have something to do with it, but the truth is that she was always so much more than a sex symbol. She and the Pretenders wrote and recorded some great rock songs, and at the end of the day, it's the work that stands out.

When punk rock came to Australia, the local music scene coughed up a handful of stellar acts like the Saints, but **THE DIVINYLS** were probably the most explosive band to come out of the early 1980s Sydney scene, largely due to **CHRISTINA AMPHLETT**, who teamed up with guitarist Mark McEntee. Christina's outfit—a schoolgirl uniform with torn fishnet stockings—created the sleazy sex-kitten image, and the band's music often rocks with accompanying sordid lyrics. In a later incarnation the group had an international hit with the single **I Touch Myself** from their 1991 album, **Divinyls**, on Virgin Records.

THE RAT PACK

When future generations pore over the history of show business in the twentieth century, they will certainly have some intriguing questions: for example, "What was the deal with that guy Elvis Presley?" (Who knows, in another five hundred years he'll most likely have been deified and be considered a prophet.) Or, "What was so interesting about watching television shows with people doing gross things for money or pretending to be trapped on an island?"

Another question that will no doubt be raised is, "What on earth was the Rat Pack?" In the faint hope that a copy or two of this book might survive the oncoming global warming and whatever follows, and in the interest of suggesting more music you should listen to, let me briefly explain the Rat Pack and its significance.

The Holmby Hills Rat Pack was originally a name given to a bunch of drinking buddies who would party at the home of Humphrey Bogart and his wife Lauren Bacall in the late 1940s. Frank Sinatra attended the parties quite regularly, and as the 1950s turned into the 1960s, the torch was passed on to Frank and four of his closest friends; they became became known as "the Rat Pack," and they epitomized the cool hipster lifestyle of the successful male entertainer. Dressed in tuxedoes, the gang—led by Sinatra and including Dean ("Dino") Martin, Sammy Davis Jr.

Peter Lawford, and Joey Bishop—ruled over Las Vegas at its most hedonistic. They hung out, boozed, womanized, made movies together, and played live cabaret shows during which they sang and joked around. Together, they pretty much put Las Vegas on the map as an adult playground.

The times were a lot simpler then; nobody was too worried about political correctness, and, in fact, some of the Rat Pack's antics were downright childish, even obnoxious. But what helped them carry it off was that they weren't trying to be cool or posturing for credibility—they were cool just being themselves, and they backed it up with shovelfuls of talent, especially Frank, Dino, and Sammy. In these days of manufactured stars, to look back at the careers of these three men is to look at three giants of entertainment.

Born in 1915, in Hoboken, New Jersey, just across the Hudson River from New York City, **FRANK SINATRA** became probably the greatest all-around entertainer of the twentieth century. From his earliest days as a singing waiter, Sinatra knew he wanted to be a star, and after being given some early breaks by bandleaders Harry James and Tommy Dorsey, he went on to become the most popular singer of his generation. By the mid-1940s, his singing career was in full swing and he had his own radio show. He began a parallel career acting in movies, including the classic musical *Anchors Aweigh* with Gene Kelly.

In the fifties Sinatra moved into television with his own show and began making regular trips to the Sands Casino in Vegas, as well as continuing to make movies and showcase his acting chops in several serious roles, most notably in *From Here to Eternity* (1953), for which he won an Oscar for Best Supporting Actor. His singing career was at its peak in the fifties; working with arrangers Nelson Riddle and Billy May, he made several classic records including **In The Wee Small Hours** (with Riddle, 1954) and **Come Fly With Me** (with May, 1957), both for Capitol Records.

He successfully transitioned into the sixties and the era of rock and roll by continuing to record and make movies, for the most part musicals and comedies.

He retired for the first time in 1971 but resurfaced just a few years later and continued to perform until he was eighty years old. He even recorded a couple of duet albums for Capital Records (**Duets**, 1993, and **Duets II**, 1994) toward the end of his life with a variety of other singers, including Tony Bennett, Lena Horne, and U2's Bono; they became two of his best-selling releases ever, although they were far from his best material. Frank Sinatra died in 1998 at the age of eighty-two but left behind a breathtaking legacy of recorded work. It's tough, then, to single out just one album to recommend, but for me the ultimate Sinatra album is his 1955 Capitol release **Songs for Swinging Lovers**. This recording finds "Old Blue Eyes" reinterpreting classic American pop standards with arrangements by Nelson Riddle, and is without a doubt one of the best albums ever released by any artist.

DEAN MARTIN, or "Dino" as he was known to his friends (and which was also his real first name), like Sinatra enjoyed huge success in everything he tried his hand at: stage, film, radio, television, and, of course, his singing career. Born in Ohio of Italian immigrant parents, after a spell as a boxer in his teenage years, he determined that showbiz would be kinder to his looks. Martin started out as a crooner and did moderately well on the New York club circuit. When he met comedian Jerry Lewis in 1946 the pair teamed up, with Dino playing the straight man to Lewis's manic-clown antics. They became huge stars very quickly, and it wasn't long before they replicated their club success in Hollywood with a string of hit comedies in the first half of the fifties. Their personal relationship began to deteriorate, though, and by 1956 they stopped working together. Martin had always been the junior member of the team, and freed from the shackles of being Lewis's sidekick, he began to rekindle his singing career, racking up several hits including **Volare**.

Again, like Sinatra, Martin took on a couple of dramatic film roles that proved he was more than just a cool party guy, although he continued to play that role as host of his own NBC television show. When he hit Vegas at the end of the fifties for a series of successful performances at the Sands, he teamed up with his pal Sinatra and the other members of the Rat Pack, and over the next few years they made three movies together: *Ocean's Eleven*, *Sergeant's 3*, and *Robin and the Seven Hoods*. The guys would act in the movies during the day and then reconvene on stage at the Sands in the evening for an anything-goes song-and-comedy routine.

So began an illustrious period of time during which the Rat Pack ruled over the hippest, if somewhat self-indulgent, showbiz party ever thrown. The party couldn't last forever, though, and after the assassination of President John F. Kennedy (who had partied with the boys before becoming president), America changed. The Civil Rights movement was beginning to assert itself, the Beatles arrived, and the Vietnam War was just beginning. All of a sudden a bunch of wiseass, cool drunk guys didn't seem that important anymore.

Dean Martin's career, though, survived the changes. He continued to make movies and records, he hosted a weekly television variety show on NBC for a number of years, and he continued to perform. His years of partying were catching up with him, though, and he largely retreated from the public eye in the eighties. Dean Martin passed away in 1995 at the age of seventy-eight. His 1960 Capitol album recorded with Nelson Riddle, **This Time I'm Swingin'!**, is probably his best record and catches him at his peak as a vocalist.

SAMMY DAVIS JR. shared a number of talents with Sinatra and Martin—singing, acting, comedy—but he had something else that separated him from the rest of the pack: He could dance. Sammy's career started in Harlem, performing with his father when he was just a young boy in a vaudeville act called the Mastin Gang. When they did a show in 1941 with Tommy Dorsey's orchestra, whose featured vocalist at that time was Frank Sinatra, the two met and became fast friends. After being drafted and spending the last two years of World War II in the military, Sammy returned to civilian life and began his recording career.

The fifties were to bring him into the spotlight for a number of reasons. In 1954 he lost his left eye in an auto accident while driving from Los Angeles to Las Vegas, and while recovering, he converted to Judaism. These were times of much racial intolerance, and Sammy's romance with several white actresses and his marriage to one of them, May Britt, caused a lot of controversy, but he persisted with his career. Some of his hits from the time include **Something's Gotta Give** and **That Old Black Magic**. Supported by his pal Sinatra, Sammy broke through in Vegas and in the movies as part of the Rat Pack. He also was hugely successful on Broadway in several musicals, including *Mr. Wonderful* and *Golden Boy*, and success continued as he then hosted his own television variety show.

In the seventies, he continued to make movies and record songs that hit the charts, including the song he is usually most identified with, **The Candy Man**. By the eighties, however, his career was on the wane, though he did perform again in 1988 with Sinatra and Martin on a reunion tour that was cut short after Martin fell ill. Sammy's last movie was 1989's *Tap*, where he gave a highly praised performance alongside Gregory Hines. Sammy was the first of the main Rat Pack trio to pass away. In 1990 his four-pack-a-day smoking habit caught up with him, and he died of lung cancer. The 1960 album **I Got a Right to Swing**, reissued recently on Universal, finds Sammy singing his way through his best studio album with a collection of swing and (unusual for him) several R&B numbers.

As for the Rat Pack on record, in 2001 Capitol released **The Rat Pack Live at the Sands**, a recording of a performance at the famed Sands Casino in Las Vegas from September 1963 that had been sitting unreleased in the vaults for almost forty years. The songs are reasonable enough for a live club performance, but the real treat is the jokes and the banter between the guys. It's a glimpse into a golden era of show business.

ROCK EN ESPAÑOL/LATIN ALTERNATIVE

When I first moved to Los Angeles I was struck very early on by the diversity of its population, particularly the Latino culture that has played such an important role in the city's history. People who describe themselves as Latino are now the major ethnic group in LA. I don't speak Spanish, although I've picked up a few words over the years and now know that the letter *J* is pronounced as an *H*. I've also become very fond of Mexican food, but the Latino influence in LA is not just Mexican. The city is home to a whole array of people who've moved here from countries like Brazil, Argentina, Guatemala, Peru, Chile, and Nicaragua.

What I've noticed most about the Latino influence here is the music. I'm fortunate that the producer of my radio show, Ariana, is of Argentinean heritage, and she was able to guide me in my early explorations of the music that is now known as Latin alternative. I'm proud to say that my show and the station have led the way in exposing talented Latino artists to our audience. It's a sad commentary on the radio industry that the mainstream Spanish-language radio stations operate in exactly the same way as the mainstream Anglo stations in that they won't open up their playlists to exciting new music.

There's also been something of a revival in Latino cinema in the last few years with spectacular Mexican movies such as *Amores Perros* and *Y Tu Mamá También* that use music to such great effect, as well as the films of Spanish director Pedro Almodóvar. As the American demographic landscape shifts, we are beginning to see a new generation of young artists who are being influenced by the music and culture of their parents' homelands. Here's a list of some of my favorite Latin alternative artists, their home countries, and recommended albums:

JULIETA VENEGAS: *Bueninvento* (BMG, 2000): Venegas is a singer/songwriter from Mexico who also plays accordion.

NORTEC COLLECTIVE: *The Tijuana Sessions, Vol. 1* (Palm Pictures, 2001): The Collective are a group of DJs from Tijuana, Mexico, mixing traditional Norteno sounds with electronic beats.

OZOMATLI: *Embrace the Chaos* (Interscope, 2001): Ozomatli are the quintessential Los Angeles band, with members of Latin, white, black, and Asian heritage.

SI*SÉ: *Si*Sé* (Luaka Bop, 2001): Si*Sé are the New York City duo of Cliff Cristafaro and Dominican-descended vocalist Carol C. They mix Latin rhythms with drum and bass.

ATERCIOPELADOS: *Evolucion* (BMG, 2002): Aterciopelados from Colombia fuse traditional Latin sounds with pop style.

CONTROL MACHETE: *Solo Para Fanaticos* (Universal, 2002): Control Machete are a Mexican Latin rap group.

KINKY: *Kinky* (Nettwerk, 2002): Kinky are from Monterey, Mexico; they mix traditional Mexican sounds with alternative rock and dance music.

RADIO ZUMBIDO: *Los Ultimos Dias del Am* (Palm Pictures, 2002): Radio Zumbido is a project by Guatemalan artist Juan Carlos Barrios. He takes found sounds and short-wave radio broadcasts and pastes them together with electronic music and various Latin sounds.

EL GRAN SILENCIO: *Super Riddim Internacional, Vol. 1* (EMI, 2003): This band from Monterey, Mexico, combine Latin rap with rock music.

JUANA MOLINA: *Segundo* (Domino, 2003): Molina is an Argentinean songwriter who began her career as a television actress. Her albums are darkly atmospheric.

ROCK ROYALTY

What's in a name? Most bands usually spend hours on end discussing what to call themselves. It's important to think about the message that a name can send out; e.g., if you're a hard rock band then something like "Flowers" probably isn't going to cut it. Choosing a stage name that sounds royal sends a particular message, even if it's your real name (as is the case with Prince). The following list features several artists who picked their regal names and a couple who inherited them.

Breaking out of the latter part of the UK glam movement, the band **QUEEN**, led by the flamboyant Freddie Mercury, created a huge sound of layered guitars and vocals. Taking the grandiose excesses of progressive and hard rock and adding a twist of kitsch,

Queen were one of the supergroups of the seventies and eighties. Freddie Mercury's sex appeal was a big part of Queen's theatrical live productions, making it ironic that his homosexuality was largely hidden from the public until his death from AIDS in 1992. Their fourth album, **A Night at the Opera** (Elektra, 1975), which includes the single **Bohemian Rhapsody**, was the album where everything came together and the band broke through worldwide.

During the 1980s, there was no bigger star than **PRINCE**. He melded pop, funk, R&B, and rock into a hedonistic mix that oozed sex. Always experimenting in the studio with new instrumentation and equipment, Prince has put out a body of work that has revealed remarkable diversity. His third album, **Dirty Mind** (Warner Brothers, 1980), was recorded in his home studio with Prince playing pretty much all the instruments. It was sexually explicit, with its tales of ménage à trois and other nocturnal activities, and musically broke just about all the rules of how a funk and soul record should sound.

QUEEN LATIFAH is the only female rapper (to date) to convert early notoriety into a multifaceted career, adding "producer" and "actor" to her résumé and gaining an Oscar nomination for her role in the film adaptation of *Chicago*. Her 1989 release **All Hail the Queen** (Tommy Boy) includes the usual bragging songs that many rappers felt necessary to record at the time, but also addresses serious social issues plaguing African-American communities.

B.B. KING is probably the most important electric guitarist to ever play the blues, and he can sing them pretty darn good, too. Born on a plantation in Itta Bene, Mississippi, he worked the fields and sang in church as a child, so the blues were engrained at an early age. When he moved to Memphis as a young man, his cousin Bukka White taught him to play blues guitar, and the rest is history. King has been performing for nearly sixty years and has had too many hits to mention here. He is something of a road warrior, and his live shows have always been a big part of the legend that he has become. **Live at the Regal**, recorded in Chicago in 1965 on MCA, catches him at his best as an entertainer.

QUEENS OF THE STONE AGE are led by Josh Homme, who put the group together after his previous band Kyuss called it quits. The idea for the new group was to take the stoner guitar rock of his previous group and crank things up a couple of notches, while keeping the essence of a simple hard-rock groove. The band achieved notoriety pretty quickly and attracted a number of well-known guests for recording and touring, including Dave Grohl (from Foo Fighters) and Mark Lanegan (from the Screaming Trees). The group's third album, **Songs For The Deaf** (Interscope, 2002), is a full-on rock assault from one of the best new rock bands of the last decade.

KING CRIMSON has been the main musical vehicle for guitarist Robert Fripp for more than thirty-five years. One of the original progressive rock bands to come out of England at the end of the sixties, the group's early releases mixed extended improvised jazz rhythms and classical music with anything but pop. Through the years, various incarnations of the group—Fripp and his numerous collaborators—have taken a trip down just about every musical avenue there is. Much of their work has been a little less than accessible and some of it downright pretentious, but Fripp's purpose has never been to make a hit record. He's more like a science professor experimenting with ingredients to see if they can be combined in different ways to make something new. **Larks' Tongues In Aspic** (Caroline, 1973) is one of their best.

CAROLE KING's output as a songwriter is daunting. Working initially in New York's famed Brill Building (which housed more than 150 music-related businesses), King, together with her writing partner Gerry Goffin, is responsible for some of the most famous songs of the second half of the twentieth century. **Will You Love Me Tomorrow**, **The Locomotion**, and **(You Make Me Feel Like a) Natural Woman** are just a few. As a solo recording artist she had a major hit with **Tapestry**, released in 1971 on Epic Records. It was one of the biggest selling albums of the decade. A beautiful collection of songs about love and longing, it became the soundtrack for many young women.

ROLLING STONES TOP 10

As anyone who grew up discovering music in the sixties will tell you, at some point one was asked the inevitable question, "Who do you like more, the Stones or the Beatles?" After the initial flush of pop stardom for both bands, the Rolling Stones cultivated their image as the bad boys you wouldn't let your daughter hang out with. The Beatles, of course, were no saints either; they just didn't let the naughty stuff get into the papers. However, there's no doubt the Stones lived more dangerously than the Fab Four, and their music reflects it. Although their live shows are still one of the biggest events on the concert calendar, their recorded output hasn't been that exciting in recent years. But in the first half of their career they recorded some of the most exciting and important records ever released. Here's a list of ten essential Rolling Stones albums in order of preference, with my favorite first:

Aftermath (ABKCO, 1966): The band is firing on all cylinders on this, their first collection of all original compositions. With tracks like **Under My Thumb** and **Paint It, Black**, the Stones were entering the golden age of their songwriting.

Beggars Banquet (ABKCO, 1968): This was a major turning point for the band as they began to get dark and dirty. Songs like **Sympathy for the Devil** and **Street Fighting Man** catch the Stones at their swaggering, ballsy best.

Exile on Main Street (Virgin, 1972): Mick Taylor and Keith Richards finally hit a groove as collaborative guitarists on this double album, rated by many critics as the group's finest. The re-mastered CD features all eighteen original tracks, including **Rocks Off**, **Tumbling Dice**, **Sweet Virginia**, and **Let It Loose**.

Let It Bleed (ABKCO, 1969): This was their first album with Mick Taylor on lead guitar replacing Brian Jones, who had been fired from the band earlier in the year and was found drowned in his swimming pool shortly thereafter. Worth the price of admission just for songs like **Gimme Shelter**, **Midnight Rambler**, and **You Can't Always Get What You Want**.

Sticky Fingers (Virgin, 1971): This one initially received as much attention for the zipper on the original cardboard cover as it did for the music. The drug references in many of the songs also gained a little attention; songs like **Sister Morphine** and **Dead Flowers** hint at the group's self-indulgent lifestyle. In a different vein, **Wild Horses** is probably one of the greatest country songs ever written.

Their Satanic Majesties Request (ABKCO, 1967): The Stones' answer to the Beatles' *Sgt. Pepper* was released in the same summer and finds the band mining similar psychedelic grooves. One of my favorite albums, it includes the trippy **She's a Rainbow** and **2000 Light Years from Home**.

Out of Our Heads (ABKCO, 1965): It took the Stones a few years to find their songwriting chops; this is the album where it all came together. There are still some great covers, but they're alongside such classic Stones songs as **(I Can't Get No) Satisfaction** and **The Last Time**.

Some Girls (Virgin, 1978): The mid-seventies had been a little difficult for the Stones: Mick Taylor left the group, new guitarist Ron Wood joined, Keith Richards got arrested in both the UK and Canada on drug charges, and, for a while, it seemed that the music had become secondary to the soap opera unfolding around it. With gems like **Miss You, Shattered**, and **Beast of Burden**, this was a return to form.

Tattoo You (Virgin, 1981): As the band entered the eighties, they had one last great album left in them. A mix of big rock songs and more subtle ballads, the album includes the classic **Start Me Up** and **Waiting on a Friend**.

12 X 5 (ABKCO, 1964): The band's second U.S. release includes a number of original songs, but like the Beatles, the Stones began by covering old blues songs. The best tracks here are the covers, including the classic singles **Time is on My Side** and **It's All Over Now**.

SCOTLAND: HIGH LAND HARD RAIN

I have some Scottish ancestry on my grandmother Rita's side and although I've never been there, some of my favorite bands over the last thirty years have come from that beautiful, yet sometimes harsh, country. Whether it be the rock and glam sounds of the Sensational Alex Harvey Band, the chiming guitar-based soul-pop of Orange Juice, the anthemic rock of Simple Minds, or the beautifully crafted songs of Travis, Scotland has given the world a plethora of talented artists and groups. Here's a list of twenty essential albums:

STONE THE CROWS: *Teenage Licks* (Phantom, 1971)

THE SENSATIONAL ALEX HARVEY BAND: *Next* (Polygram, 1974)

SIMPLE MINDS: *Reel to Real Cacophony* (Virgin, 1979)

ALTERED IMAGES: *Happy Birthday* (Sony, 1981)

JOSEF K: *The Only Fun in Town* (Phantom, 1981)

ASSOCIATES: *Sulk* (V2, 1982)

ORANGE JUICE: *Rip It Up* (Phantom, 1982)

AZTEC CAMERA: *High Land Hard Rain* (Warner Brothers, 1983)

BIG COUNTRY: *The Crossing* (Polygram, 1983)

THE BLUE NILE: *A Walk Across the Rooftops* (Virgin, 1984)

THE JESUS AND MARY CHAIN: *Psychocandy* (Warner Brothers, 1985)

THE PASTELS: *Sittin' Pretty* (Homestead, 1989)

WET WET WET: *Holding Back the River* (Phantom, 1989)

COCTEAU TWINS: *Heaven or Las Vegas* (Capitol, 1990)

THE TRASH CAN SINATRAS: *Cake* (London, 1990)

PRIMAL SCREAM: *Screamadelica* (Warner Brothers, 1991)

TEENAGE FAN CLUB: *Bandwagonesque* (Geffen, 1991)

BELLE & SEBASTIAN: *If You're Feeling Sinister* (Matador, 1996)

TRAVIS: *The Man Who* (Epic, 1999)

FRANZ FERDINAND: *Franz Ferdinand* (Epic, 2004)

SEE NO EVIL

It is said that the deprivation of one sense can heighten others and inspire some of us to greatness. The musicians listed below are all blind but have overcome their inability to see through their eyes by creating music that looks out from the soul and connects universally.

RAY CHARLES was probably one of the most eclectic musicians to ever record consistently through a career that spanned six decades. After losing his sight as a six-year-old child, he attended a music school for the blind in Florida and began performing as a musician in his teens. His original style was based on Nat King Cole's, and he achieved a certain amount of early success before beginning to develop his own style and voice.

By the mid-1950s Charles was recording for Atlantic Records, with a string of R&B hits like **I Got a Woman** and **The Right Time**. By 1960 he had jumped labels to ABC, who had promised him more artistic freedom, and it immediately showed as he began recording songs like **Hit the Road, Jack** that crossed over to the pop charts. What he did next turned the music world on its ear, as he began recording country music. His 1962 release **Modern**

Sounds in Country and Western Music for ABC is, in effect, a collection of country classics recorded by a soul singer who was able to inhabit the material and make it his own. It features three Hank Williams songs, including **Hey, Good Lookin'**, and the Don Gibson classic **I Can't Stop Loving You**. A second volume was released later that year.

The rest of the sixties saw Charles moving more in a pop direction, and he recorded consistently into the seventies. Although he never really repeated the creative achievements of his early career, he did become a huge influence on many soul and rock artists alike. His concert and touring schedule was always busy, and I'm happy to say that I had the chance to see him myself a few years ago on a double bill with Willie Nelson. Ray Charles passed away on June 10, 2004. Later that year, Universal released a movie biography, *Ray*, starring Jamie Foxx, which explored Charles's personal life and music career. In 2005, Foxx went on to win a Golden Globe and an Oscar for best actor for his uncanny depiction of the man.

STEVIE WONDER was a boy wonder. He sang like a pro as a toddler, mastered harmonica and drums, and began recording on the Tamla Motown label in his hometown of Detroit at age twelve. Motown marketed him as "Little Stevie Wonder," the boy genius. He soon dropped the "little," and his talent spoke for itself. In 1963, his single **Fingertips, Part 2**, hit No. 1 on the charts and established the thirteen-year-old musician as a commercial success. Brilliant hit singles recorded by Wonder in the 1960s include Bob Dylan's **Blowin' in the Wind**, Ron Miller's **A Place in the Sun**, and songs of his own like **Uptight, Castles in the Sand**, and **My Cherie Amour**.

When his Motown contract expired in 1971, Wonder made two albums on his own, playing most of the instruments himself. Motown lured him back with a contract, giving him artistic control over his work, and those now-classic albums produced by the multitalented Wonder took soul, rock, gospel, pop, and even funk music in new directions. He was an early exponent of the synthesizer in black music. His lyrics, meanwhile, addressed social and racial issues, not with anger but with eloquence. Hit singles that emerged included **You Are the Sunshine of My Life**, **Superstition**, **Living for the City**, **Higher Ground**, and **Sir Duke**, a tribute to Duke Ellington. Later Wonder hits include **Ebony and Ivory**, a somewhat sappy duet with Paul McCartney, and **I Just Called to Say I Love You**, from his soundtrack for the movie *The Woman in Red*.

Although blind almost since birth, Wonder has always been an irrepressible optimist and a tireless activist. He has fought world hunger, opposed drunk driving, advocated stiffer gun-control laws, and lobbied effectively for the establishment of a Martin Luther King, Jr., national holiday. As one of his hit songs describes it, **That's What Friends Are For**. Stevie's 1976 release for Motown, **Songs in the Key of Life**, is a two-album set that finds him at his most spiritual and socially conscious.

One of the most impressive things about **BLIND WILLIE MCTELL**, apart from his guitar playing, was that he recorded under a whole host of different names so that he could do separate deals with different record labels who didn't know they were hiring a guy who was already recording for someone else. Hailing from Georgia and growing up in a musical performance family, he played accordion and harmonica as well as the guitar. Unusual for a blues player, he settled on a 12-string as his instrument of choice, and by the time he began recording in the late 1920s he had developed a picking style rather than the traditional rhythmic method of playing the blues. He was hugely popular in Atlanta and the South and performed and recorded throughout the thirties and forties. Not too many of his early recordings have survived or been issued on CD, but in 1949 he recorded an album of fifteen tracks for Atlantic Records, which is available on CD as **Atlanta Twelve String**. His career continued sporadically through the fifties, and he became a church pastor just prior to his death in 1959.

THE BLIND BOYS OF ALABAMA found fame in the 1990s recording a couple of Grammy Award–winning albums for Peter Gabriel's Real World label. The original lineup (known as the Five Blind Boys of Alabama), however, formed in Alabama at the Talladega Institute for the Deaf and Blind in 1937 and began recording their unique gospel harmonies in the late 1940s. Their career has now spanned seven decades and many recordings. The 1987 collection **The Five Blind Boys of Alabama** from the Gospel Heritage label is an excellent anthology of some of their work from the seventies and eighties.

JOSÉ FELICIANO was born in Puerto Rico but grew up in New York City. He learned how to play both accordion and guitar at an early age. After releasing a number of flamenco and Spanish-language albums in the first half of the sixties, he broke through into the mainstream in 1968 with a cover of the Doors' **Light My Fire**. That track came from the album **Feliciano!**, released on RCA, which also includes recordings of three Lennon and McCartney compositions and a cover of the Mamas and the Papas song **California Dreamin'**.

ANDREA BOCELLI, who lost his sight as a young boy, has made a huge name for himself in recent years as an impassioned classical pop vocalist. Born in Tuscany, Italy, he completed law school before training as a tenor. He then pursued his singing career throughout Europe in the early nineties, recording several albums of operatic and traditional material from his homeland that received great acclaim, including the 1997 release **Viaggio Italiano** on Polydor. Bocelli was, however, largely unknown outside his homeland until he recorded a duet with Celine Dion in 1999. The song was **The Prayer** and it became a worldwide hit, turning Bocelli into an international star.

SISTER, SISTER

I don't think I'm going to shock you with the statement that the music industry is dominated by men. It's a fact that on the business end of things, managers, booking agents, producers, engineers, and record label executives have by tradition been men. Not to mention that, despite many talented and successful female musicians, the majority of performers are also men. It's tough being a woman in any business—there's still a glass ceiling, and women have to constantly prove themselves, in many cases more so than men. What better way to feel supported as a musician than to make music with your sister? Here are a few examples of sisters who've done it for themselves.

THE ANDREWS SISTERS—LaVerne, Maxene, and Patty—began singing together as young girls in their hometown of Minneapolis. They first hit the pop charts in 1938 and between then and 1951 achieved more than chart 100 singles. They were popular for their well-practiced harmonies, but also for the songs that entertained America during World War II, such as **Boogie Woogie Bugle Boy**. They were regulars on overseas trips made by U.S. entertainers to visit the troops. They also backed Bing Crosby on a number of big hits and appeared in many movies. There are several compilations available, but **Their All-Time Greatest Hits** from MCA (1994) is a wonderful two-CD collection that covers their recordings for Decca between 1939 and 1950.

THE CORRS are an Irish group comprised of three extremely attractive sisters—Andrea, Sharon, and Caroline—and their brother Jim. Mixing traditional Irish sounds with pop, in the mid-

1990s they were just about the biggest-selling Irish band in Ireland and the UK, with perhaps the exception of U2. The group never quite broke in the United States, although they did gain a loyal fan base, especially in the East Coast cities of Boston and New York. Their 1998 album **Talk on Corners** was released in the UK on East West and reissued in the States in 1999 on Atlantic as a special-edition CD with remixed tracks.

HEART were originally named the Army and formed in the mid-1960s in Vancouver, B.C., by brothers Mike and Roger Fisher. It wasn't until Seattle-based sisters **NANCY AND ANN WILSON** joined the band in 1974 that things really began to happen. They experienced fame twice over, first in the mid-seventies and then again in the second half of the eighties when they achieved stardom on a large scale, playing to huge arena crowds. The earlier part of their career is well represented by the 1977 album **Little Queen** on Portrait, which was a mix of both hard rock and more acoustic songs and includes one of their best-known hits, **Barracuda**. Their 1985 Capitol release **Heart** was a comeback album of sorts and shows the band headed towards the album-oriented rock and power-ballad territory that they are perhaps best known for today. In the nineties, the group recorded sporadically, so Nancy and Ann took time out on several occasions with a side project, **THE LOVEMONGERS**. The Lovemongers recorded a "grunge" cover of Led Zeppelin's **The Battle Of Evermore** for the movie *Singles* (directed by Nancy's husband Cameron Crowe), as well as a couple of albums and EPs.

KATE & ANNA MCGARRIGLE are part of a musical dynasty that includes Kate's ex-husband Loudon Wainwright III and two Wainwright offspring, son Rufus and daughter Martha. But when they first started out, it was just the two sisters from Montreal, Canada, writing and singing their songs. Their debut release, **Kate & Anna McGarrigle**, was recorded by Nick Drake's producer Joe

Boyd, originally for Warner Brothers in 1975, and is probably one of the finest examples on record of folk rock. It's available now on CD from Boyd's Hannibal Records.

From Oakland, California, came **THE POINTER SISTERS**— Ruth, Anita, June, and Bonnie—and in the mid-1970s they were regular fixtures on the R&B charts. Bonnie set off on a solo career in 1978 leaving the group as a trio, but in the first half of the eighties they enjoyed crossover pop success with a number of singles like **He's So Shy** and **Jump (for My Love)**. Their earlier work is well represented on the 1975 Blue Thumb Records release **Steppin'**.

SMELLS LIKE TEEN SPIRIT: THE SEATTLE SOUND

When Kurt Cobain sang "here we are now, entertain us" in the song **Smells Like Teen Spirit** in 1991, not only did alternative rock explode out of independent record stores and into the mainstream, but Seattle, the city that had been home to the band, also found itself the center of the music industry's attention for the next few years, as record label representatives rushed to the Pacific Northwest with checkbooks in hand, signing just about every band in town. The year 1992 became the year of the Seattle, or grunge, music scene. Here's a list of the ten best bands (and representative works) from that time and place, some of whom became household names, some of whom didn't:

> **MUDHONEY**: *Every Good Boy Deserves Fudge* (Sub Pop, 1991)
> **PEARL JAM**: *Ten* (Epic, 1991)
> **THE GITS**: *Frenching the Bully* (Broken Rekids, 1992)
> **SCREAMING TREES**: *Sweet Oblivion* (Epic, 1992)
> **NIRVANA**: *In Utero* (DGC, 1993)
> **THE POSIES**: *Frosting on the Beater* (DGC, 1993)
> **ALICE IN CHAINS**: *Jar of Flies* (Columbia, 1994)
> **SOUNDGARDEN**: *Superunknown* (A&M, 1994)
> **SUNNY DAY REAL ESTATE**: *Diary* (Sub Pop, 1994)
> **PRESIDENTS OF THE UNITED STATES OF AMERICA**:
> *Presidents of the United States of America* (Columbia, 1995)

SONIC YOUTH

There have been child stars since the days of traveling minstrels. In vaudeville, families often introduced children to the act as soon as they could walk, to add a lighthearted dimension to their performance. Child actors from Shirley Temple to Macaulay Culkin have charmed and entertained all-age audiences in their film work for decades. What is it about kids who can perform that attracts us? There's a certain novelty involved, of course. In fact, some of these kiddie acts are pure theater in the way they pull at adults' emotions and appeal to the kid in all of us. But there are also children who are clearly gifted in ways that no one can explain. Here are a few who fall into both categories.

Much has been said and written about **MICHAEL JACKSON** through the years, especially in regard to his private life: Allegations of child abuse have dogged him since the mid-1990s. Ironic then, that Michael was a child star. He was just five years old when he joined four of his brothers in the family group that became known as the Jackson 5. As the band's lead singer Michael became a pop star at just eleven years old, and the group churned out a string of hits for the Tamla Motown record label in the early seventies. This inevitably led to Michael striking out on a solo career. His early singles, such as **Got to Be There** and **Rockin' Robin**, all charted, and then he hit No. 1 with **Ben**. Michael was a pop star in his own right at just thirteen. When the Jacksons, as they were now known without their former lead singer, and soloist Michael both left Motown in the mid-seventies to sign with Epic Records, both careers faltered. But in 1979 the album **Off the Wall**, produced by Quincy Jones, took him from child pop star to adult superstar. Three years later, his next album, **Thriller**, changed pop music—with Michael's innovative use of dance and stylized videos, *Thriller* became the biggest album of all time, selling more than 50 million copies.

DONNY OSMOND's story was similar in some ways to Michael Jackson's. He was the youngest brother in the family group the Osmonds, and he was also the band's lead singer and focal point. In the first half of the seventies, the Osmonds gave America a seemingly endless stream of bubblegum hits that were to define the pop charts for several years. Donny made his first solo record in 1971 at age twelve, and in many ways he competed with Michael Jackson both on the charts and for the hearts of young girls in America and Britain for much of the early seventies. Donny also recorded several albums of pop ballads with his sister, but unlike Michael Jackson, Donny never had breakout success as an adult. In fact, he didn't release an album as an adult until his early thirties, when in 1989 he resurfaced with a surprisingly good record of pop-rock songs, called **Donny Osmond**, on Capitol Records. Donny joined with his sister Marie to host "Donny and Marie," a TV variety show in the mid-seventies, and he has also done theater, most notably the lead role in *Joseph and the Amazing Technicolor Dreamcoat* on Broadway for five years in the mid-nineties. He reteamed with sister Marie at the end of that decade for a short-lived daytime TV talk show.

Taking a leaf out of the Jackson 5's playbook, the three **HANSON** brothers—Zac, Taylor, and Isaac—appeared in 1997 with a pop sensibility that defied their years. They were respectively eleven, thirteen, and sixteen when their first major-label album, **Middle of Nowhere**, which included the smash hit single **MMMBop**, was released on Mercury Records. As a result of clever, thoughtful marketing, as well as the fact that with the help of their producers and co-writers they had put together an album of quality pop songs, Hanson became huge teenage stars. Although their follow-up material failed to deliver the same success, there's little doubt that they ushered in an era of young stars such as Britney Spears and Christina Aguilera, and boy bands such as *NSYNC and the Backstreet Boys. Hanson have continued writing and recording, and the last page of their story is yet to be written.

From the Pacific Northwest comes **SMOOSH**. The group is two preteen sisters, Aysa, who plays keyboards and sings, and Chloe, who plays drums. They play indie rock, and the Seattle music community has embraced them to such an extent that they've already opened for Death Cab for Cutie, Sleater-Kinney, and even Pearl Jam! Their debut album **She Like Electric** was released on Pattern 25 in 2004.

SWEDISH MADE

Sweden is the land of Volvos, Saabs, IKEA, Absolut vodka, and numerous tennis players like John McEnroe's old nemesis Bjorn Borg. Unlikely as it might seem, it's also a hotbed of pop music. Not only is there a rich history of jazz and pop music being made by homegrown artists, but the country is also home to some of the world's best recording studios, as well as producers and songwriters who work with some of today's biggest stars.

ABBA were the band that brought Swedish pop to the rest of the world, and at the height of their fame they were the second-largest earner of foreign income (after Volvo) for the Swedish economy. When they won the Eurovision song contest in 1974 with a song called **Waterloo**, few could've predicted that they would dominate the world's pop charts for the rest of the decade and in so doing define for many the way the seventies will be remembered.

Bjorn Ulvaeus and Benny Andersson first teamed up to write songs together in 1966, and when they brought their girlfriends, Agnetha Faltskog and Anni-Frid Lyngstad (Frida), together in the early seventies, pop music history was about to be made. Over the course of the next seven years the band had a string of hits like **S.O.S.**, **Mamma Mia**, and **Dancing Queen**. By now Bjorn had married Agnetha and Benny and Frida had also tied the knot. The group's success had exceeded anything they could've imagined or wished for, but the strains of work and career took a toll on their personal lives, and by 1980 both couples had separated. It's tough for most couples who work together to manage to keep a working relationship going after a breakup, but in this case there were two couples in business together, and not surprisingly they called it quits by 1982.

Benny and Bjorn have continued working together and moved into the world of musicals, writing *Chess* (with Tim Rice) and the

ABBA story *Mamma Mia*. Frida and Agnetha have both done solo work but largely retreated from the public eye. But thanks to movies like *Muriel's Wedding* and various greatest-hits collections through the years, ABBA have never really gone away. The group's 1977 release **Arrival** on Universal Records includes a handful of their biggest hits and some pretty good tracks in between—seventies pop at its brightest and best.

ACE OF BASE were the nineties version of ABBA: Jonas Berggren and his sisters Jenny and Linn were joined by Ulf Ekberg. With a hot producer and songwriter working with them, they attempted to replicate the supergroup's success. They started well with a huge international hit, **All That She Wants**, which preceded the album **Happy Nation**. It was reworked with additional songs and renamed **The Sign** for its 1993 U.S. distribution on Arista. It was both a pop and a dance record and dominated the singles and album charts throughout Europe in 1994. While their follow-up release **The Bridge** (Arista, 1995) also went platinum, the band were not to see the longevity of ABBA.

ROXETTE were a band that found their moment in pop history at the end of the eighties. The duo, comprised of Per Gessle and Marie Fredriksson, had been making music together since 1986. Their career highlight was 1988's **Look Sharp!** on Capitol Records, which gave them four international hits, including **The Look**.

THE CARDIGANS began their career with couple of pop hits early on, including **Lovefool** from their 1996 album **First Band on the Moon** on Mercury. Because of blonde singer Nina Persson's bright, sunny vocals, they've been wrongly cast as a simple pop group; in fact, most of their albums have revealed a darker side if you listen past the hooks. The 2003 album **Long Gone Before Daylight**, released in the United States in 2004 on Koch, was actually recorded after the band took three years away from each other before deciding whether or not they could work together again. It's a stripped-down-to-the-basics affair that finds Nina (now with black hair) contemplating the darker side of love.

THE SOUNDTRACK OF OUR LIVES formed from the ashes of the seminal Swedish rock band Union Carbide Productions. Led by larger-than-life bearded vocalist Ebbot Lundberg, they mix sixties psychedelic pop influences like the Doors with raw blues. Their third album, the 2001 release **Behind the Music** on Hidden Agenda, will take you on a ride that stops off at pick-up points from bands like the Rolling Stones, the Stooges, and Love, but ultimately it's their own trip.

KOOP is the brainchild of Magnus Zingmark and Oscar Simonsson, whose work combines their jazz background with club culture and hip-hop. They met in a jazz club in the university town of Uppsala before relocating to Stockholm and beginning work largely as a studio project. Their second album **Waltz for Koop**, released in 2001 on Palm Pictures, took things to their logical next step and added real musicians and singers to the mix; it walks a delicate line between cool hipster jazz and a sensibility that knows its moment transcends its influences.

TAKE FIVE: THE GIANTS OF JAZZ

The first truly American musical art form was jazz, and its influences are still felt almost one hundred years after it developed out of a potpourri of other musical styles. At the turn of the twentieth century the port city of New Orleans, home to many immigrants and a large black population, played a key role in the early evolution of both blues and jazz. Whether it was played on a drum or a box, percussion had always been an important part of African-American music, and brass bands played a key part in celebrations such as weddings and funerals. When horn and clarinet players began experimenting with the blues, a different musical style began to take shape.

When the players and their music moved north to Chicago and then east to New York City, jazz began to find its way into clubs and started to incorporate other instruments and styles such as piano and ragtime. In New York City, the first swing bands, or big bands, began to form, and black and white musicians started to play together at a time when racism was still an ugly blight on the American cultural landscape. It's hard to believe now, but in the twenties and thirties jazz music was disdained by many uptight whites in the same way that hip-hop is today.

Earlier in this book, the essay "Livin' Large: The Big Band Boom!" covers some of the most important big bands from their heyday in the 1940s. The forties also saw the advent of bebop, wherein the soloists dispensed with melody and focused on the chords. During the fifties both swing and bop evolved and headed toward the sixties, when innovative young players began to push the boundaries of the traditional jazz ensemble. In the seventies a rise of blues funk and a not-always-successful fusion of jazz and pop occurred, while in the eighties Afro-Cuban jazz emerged. Perhaps more than any other musical form, jazz draws from the creative, spiritual, and emotional side of the human condition. The following recommendations shine a spotlight on some of the most important players, whatever their instruments, who have helped to both define jazz music and help it evolve.

Born in 1901 in New Orleans, **LOUIS ARMSTRONG** is recognized as one of the founding fathers of jazz. From humble beginnings he became both a virtuoso cornet player and a distinctive vocalist. In fact, it's fair to say that his imaginatively improvisational style of playing has endeared him to each successive generation of jazz musicians, and his outgoing personality won over generations of fans.

At age twenty-one Louis followed his early mentor Joe "King" Oliver to Chicago and shortly afterwards spent a few years in New York City before heading back to the Windy City to form his own group, the Louis Armstrong Hot Five. By the end of the twenties he was once again in Manhattan and had established himself as a top player and bandleader. He spent the next five years touring Europe and the States solidifying his reputation. His next step was the movies, and over the course of a film career that spanned some thirty years, he appeared in more than thirty features, including *Pennies from Heaven, Atlantic City, The Glen Miller Story,* and *High Society.*

During his career Satchmo, as he became known (shortened from Satchel mouth), recorded with just about everyone of any note, including singers like the Mills Brothers, Ella Fitzgerald, and Billie Holiday, and bandleaders like Benny Goodman and Duke Ellington. His contributions to jazz are immeasurable and his recorded output is not only huge but covers a lot of time and musical ground. So it's difficult then to single out one album for recommended listening; nonetheless **Louis Armstrong Plays W. C. Handy**, released in 1954 on Columbia Records, finds him with his All Stars playing eleven songs written by one of the most important exponents of blues songwriting. After several years of ill health, Louis Armstrong passed away in 1971.

One of jazz's early innovators and composers, **JELLY ROLL MORTON** was born in New Orleans in 1890. He became well known for his travels, playing piano and gambling through much of the American South and along the way melding blues, ragtime, and minstrel-show songs to create his own style. He moved west to Los Angeles, where he achieved a certain notoriety as a performer, and then as jazz began to take off he headed to Chicago where he put together his band, the Red Hot Peppers, and made his first recordings in what became known as the "New Orleans style."

He found himself in New York at the end of the 1920s just as the swing movement was beginning, but, ironically, Morton didn't take to orchestral jazz even though several of his songs were appropriated by various big bands. He pretty much fell off the radar screen as swing began to dominate popular music and passed away in relative obscurity in 1941. The only way to begin to explore his music is with a compilation. **His Best Recordings 1926–39** on Jazz Masters (released in 1996) is as good a place as any to start.

A classically trained pianist and composer, **DAVE BRUBECK** had the biggest-selling jazz single ever in 1960 with **Take Five**. Chances are you've most likely heard it even if you don't know it, as it's become one of the most ubiquitous jazz compositions ever recorded. Brubeck studied music at the College of the Pacific in

California at the beginning of the 1940s, after which he spent the last couple of years of World War II in Europe leading an army band. When he returned to the States he formed his first group, a trio that eventually expanded to a quartet with the addition of alto sax player Paul Desmond, who wrote "Take Five."

Throughout the 1950s the band made a good living by playing the college circuit, and with the success of "Take Five." they spent a good part of the 1960s traveling the world. Although the original quartet broke up in the late sixties, Brubeck has continued to record and perform with a variety of musicians, including his sons. The album **Time Out**, which included "Take Five," was released by Columbia in 1959 and found him experimenting for the first time with different time signatures, a brave and innovative move that paid off with the single and album's huge commercial success.

Regarded by most aficionados as the best and most important saxophone player in the history of jazz, **CHARLIE PARKER** was an extremely intuitive and fast musician who was a key figure in the development of bebop. He was born in 1920 and grew up in Kansas City, Missouri, where he first picked up a baritone sax at school before switching to alto. He decided at age fifteen that he wanted to become a professional musician and by seventeen he was already playing with a number of bands. He went to New York City in 1939 and worked with several groups including Jay McShann's orchestra and later with Earl Hines and Billy Eckstine. He became good friends with Dizzy Gillespie; the two of them had much in common, including the speed at which they played, and together they took their new style of jazz and headed west to Hollywood.

Gillespie returned to New York after they'd completed their Los Angeles engagement but Parker stayed, mainly to indulge his heroin habit and alcoholism. After suffering a nervous breakdown in 1947 he did finally make it back to Manhattan and cleaned up enough to resume his career; for the remainder of the decade he recorded and performed in the United States and Europe with his own quintet (which featured a young Miles Davis). However, his drug addiction was always nearby and in the early fifties it took hold of him again. Like so many others he was unable to conquer it and died in 1955 at age thirty-four.

Parker's legacy is one of an early innovator who burned brightly for too short a time, but there's no doubt he influenced the way jazz has sounded during the last fifty years. The live album **Jazz at Massey Hall**, recorded in 1953 and reissued on CD by the Original Jazz Classics label, features Parker's favorite band lineup: Dizzy Gillespie, Bud Powell, Max Roach, and Charles Mingus. It's essential Parker listening.

His career was short, as he died in 1967 at the age of just forty, but **JOHN COLTRANE** left a huge imprint on the world of jazz. While Charlie Parker is widely regarded as the most innovative sax player to ever blow a tune, Coltrane was surely the most prolific and experimental. He played both alto and tenor at various times early on in his career and later picked up the soprano saxophone as well. He worked with a number of bandleaders from the mid-forties through the mid-fifties, including King Kolax and Dizzy Gillespie, but his reputation and future were secured when he joined Miles Davis's quintet in 1955.

Coltrane had, however, begun using heroin in the early part of the decade and around the time he joined Davis's group, his addiction began to take its toll on his physical and emotional state. Davis, who had by then beaten his own addiction some years earlier, fired Coltrane several times. When Coltrane finally kicked his habit with the help of a spiritual awakening, he began his solo career while continuing as a sideman to numerous bandleaders such as Thelonius Monk and did a few more stints with Davis. In

1964 he recorded **A Love Supreme** for Impulse Records, celebrating his spiritual rebirth in four parts with his classic quartet, featuring McCoy Tyner, Elvin Jones, and Jimmy Garrison. The album captures Coltrane at his most emotionally centered and technical best.

DIZZY GILLESPIE was probably best known for his trademark bulbous cheeks when he played, but his contributions to jazz are immeasurable. He started off as a trombone player before switching to trumpet. After playing in a number of bands he landed a well-paying gig in Cab Calloway's orchestra in New York City, and later was a featured player in a whole slew of bands, including those led by Ella Fitzgerald and Duke Ellington. When he teamed up with Charlie Parker in 1941, they played and recorded together in a number of bands, but what Dizzy really wanted to do was lead his own orchestra. He did so several times but was never able to sustain it for long due to the financial constraints, so most of his recordings with his own bands are with smaller groups. He was also one of the first American jazz composers and performers to start incorporating Afro-Cuban rhythms into his music. **Ken Burns' Jazz Collection: Dizzy Gillespie**, released on Verve in 2000 to coincide with Burns's landmark PBS series of the same name, is an admirable compilation that covers all the key periods of Dizzy's career.

No essay on jazz greats could be complete without mention of **MILES DAVIS** or **COUNT BASIE**. Both men's contributions to jazz are monumental, and detailed discussion and album recommendations can be found in other essays in this book (see "Miles Davis: Icon" and "Livin' Large: The Big Band Boom!"). In addition, there are far too many jazz artists to cover within the scope of this book. However, some other key artists, their musical specialties, and recommended albums are:

ART BLAKEY (drummer): *Moanin'* (Blue Note, 1958)

ORNETTE COLEMAN (alto saxophonist): *Science Fiction* (Columbia, 1971)

JACK DEJOHNETTE (drummer): *Special Edition* (ECM, 1979)

BILL EVANS (pianist): *Conversations with Myself* (Verve, 1963)

STAN GETZ (tenor saxophonist): *Getz/Gilberto* (Verve, 1964)

DEXTER GORDON (tenor saxophonist): *Go!* (Blue Note, 1962)

CHARLIE HADEN (bass player): *Liberation Music Orchestra* (Impulse, 1969)

LIONEL HAMPTON (drummer and vibraphonist): *Hamp and Getz* (Verve, 1955)

HERBIE HANCOCK (pianist): *Empyrean Isles* (Blue Note, 1964)

KEITH JARRETT (pianist): *The Survivor's Suite* (ECM, 1976)

CHARLES MINGUS (bass player and pianist): *Pithecanthropus Erectus* (Atlantic, 1956)

THELONIUS MONK (pianist): *Genius of Modern Music, Vol. 1* (Blue Note, 1947)

OSCAR PETERSON (pianist): *On the Town* (Verve, 1958)

DJANGO REINHARDT (guitarist): *The Best of Django Reinhardt* (Capitol, 1996)

HORACE SILVER (pianist): *Horace Silver & The Jazz Messengers* (Blue Note, 1955)

FATS WALLER (pianist and vocalist): *The Very Best of Fats Waller* (Collectors Choice, 2000)

TEN ALBUMS YOU MISSED

The following are ten albums that you've probably never heard of, but are so good that you should seek them out and add them to your collection.

AZURE RAY: Azure Ray (Warm, 2001): Orenda Fink and Maria Taylor formed Azure Ray in 2001. Their self-titled debut from the same year features a collection of eleven fragile confessional songs dripping with dark melancholy and beautiful harmonies.

THE BLUE NILE: A Walk Across the Rooftops (A&M, 1984): There's a certain mystique about the Blue Nile, who hail from Scotland, probably because they record so infrequently and rarely tour. In fact, they've only released four records in their twenty five-year career. I first heard *A Walk Across the Rooftops*, their first release from 1984, on a road trip from Woodstock in upstate New York to JFK Airport in the fall of 1988. I was catching a plane to London; when I got off at Heathrow, the first thing I did was go to a record store to purchase a copy.

THE COMSAT ANGELS: Waiting for a Miracle (Polydor, 1980): Known in the United States as the **CS ANGELS**, the Comsats, as their fans call them, hailed from Sheffield in England and were contemporaries of Joy Division, U2, and Echo & The Bunnymen. *Waiting for a Miracle* was their debut release from 1980 and is arguably the best debut of the post-punk movement.

The album features swirling keyboards and chiming guitars, and Stephen Fellows's dry, insighful lyrics.

JACK FROST: **Jack Frost** (Arista, 1991): Jack Frost was a side project from Steve Kilbey of the Church and Grant McLennan of the Go-Betweens. Released in 1991, *Jack Frost* is a collection of understated songs featuring acoustic guitars and woodwind instruments, plus drumbeats and synthesizers, with both singers sharing vocal duties.

THE LIBERTY HORSES: **Joyland** (Gramavision, 1993): Brothers Neil and Calum MacColl fronted this band that recorded just this one album in 1993. Their late sister Kirsty as well as Eddie Reader provided additional vocals, creating a collection of sparkling, upbeat folk-influenced pop pieces. But listen to the lyrics: The real genius of *Joyland* is that it's a little darker underneath than at first glance, making this a lost gem.

PATTI SMITH: **Gone Again** (Arista, 1996): When Patti Smith returned with this album in 1996 it had been almost ten years since her last release. In the intervening time she had lost both her husband (Fred "Sonic" Smith of MC5) and her brother, as well as one of her best friends, Robert Mapplethorpe. The album reflects her grief, but not in a maudlin, self-absorbed sense. This is a collection of poems/songs that reflect on loss and look ahead at the same time.

THE SOUND: **From The Lion's Mouth** (Korova, 1981; reissued on Renascent, 2002): I first heard of this band when sitting up late one night in 1982 watching the brilliant BBC television program "The Old Grey Whistle Test," known for its championing of new bands with live in-studio performances. I was enraptured by the power of the songs and the intensity of the lyrics sung by front man Adrian Borland. I was a little drunk that night, so it was with some trepidation that I headed to the record store the next day to pick up a copy of the album. I needn't have worried.

It's one of the most explosive albums I've ever heard, and this band should've been huge.

SPOON: **Girls Can Tell** (Merge, 2001): Britt Daniel and Jim Eno have been making music together as Spoon in Austin, Texas, since 1994. Maturing from their early punk roots, by the time *Girls Can Tell* was released in 2001 Spoon had become a tight indie pop band. This album shows off their Nirvana and Pixies influences and hints at a pop sensibility that would become even clearer on subsequent releases.

TALK TALK: **Laughing Stock** (Polydor, 1991): By the time Talk Talk recorded this, their final album, they had been through the New Wave pop-star phase and fallen out with their previous label EMI as they began to experiment with deeper, less commercial work. Their new label Polydor gave them the budget to attempt different methods of making rock music, and they took the form to new heights as the music moves through guitar feedback and ambient loose-form, jazz-influenced sounds with minimal lyrics. Listen in a darkened room . . . alone.

SCOTT WALKER: **Tilt** (Drag City, 1995): As a member of the Walker Brothers, Scott Engel (originally from Ohio) achieved pop-star status in the UK in the mid-sixties with a succession of chart hits. He followed it up with a number of highly regarded solo albums toward the end of the decade. The seventies and eighties saw sporadic releases, then in 1995 came this album. Walker's crooning voice moves through aria-like moments and grim, powerful songs. The music is dense and threatening, inhabited by unknown creatures that are surely out to get you.

THIS IS REGGAE MUSIC

The Caribbean island of Jamaica gave birth to reggae music in the 1970s after a gradual progression of other musical styles that had evolved through the previous thirty years. The original folk music of Jamaica is a calypsolike style known as mento; in the early 1950s, as young Jamaicans began hearing R&B from radio stations in the American South, the island's musicians incorporated those influences. By adding horns and offbeat rhythms, the original ska music was born, the Skatalites being its best-known exponents.

By the 1960s ska had evolved into a more sophisticated style that became known as rocksteady, in which the music was slowed down, the drums and horns took more of a backseat, and bass guitar drove the rhythm, allowing for vocals to play a larger role in the music. At this time, a band called Tommy McCook & the Supersonics led the way. It's widely agreed that a 1968 single by Toots & the Maytals called **Do the Reggay** took the music forward to its next step. That release was the defining moment for the genre that became known around the world as reggae. It was, however, Bob Marley who made reggae an international phenomenon. Marley (along with the Wailers at first) took the music and added a protest element to the lyrics that connected with people the world over. The fact that he smoked a ton of pot might have made him a few fans as well!

Dub plates were the next evolution, as producer King Tubby discovered that leaving off a vocal track on the b-side of a single opened the music up and the instrumental pieces could be reinterpreted by DJs "toasting" (rapping) over the music. Toasting was in turn an early precursor to rap and hip-hop. Other offshoots in recent years have included dancehall and ragga. I've put together a list of twenty of the most important artists in Jamaica's music history and their recommended albums:

THE SKATALITES: *Ska Authentic* (Musicrama, 1967)

THE ETHIOPIANS: *Engine '54: Let's Ska and Rock Steady* (Jamaican Gold, 1968)

JACKIE MITTOO: *Evening Time* (Musicrama, 1968)

DESMOND DEKKER & THE ACES: *Israelites* (UNI, 1969)

JIMMY CLIFF: *Wonderful World, Beautiful People* (A&M, 1970)

THE HEPTONES: *On Top* (Musicrama, 1970)

BOB MARLEY & THE WAILERS: *Catch a Fire* (Tuff Gong, 1973)

TOOTS & THE MAYTALS: *Funky Kingston* (Mango, 1973)

KEN BOOTHE: *Everything I Own* (Trojan, 1974)

KING TUBBY: *Dub from the Roots* (Jetset, 1974)

U-ROY: *Dread in a Babylon* (Caroline, 1975)

BIG YOUTH: *Natty Cultural Dread* (Trojan, 1976)

LEE "SCRATCH" PERRY: *Super Ape* (Island, 1976)

LINVAL THOMPSON: *Starlight* (Mango, 1976)

ERNEST RANGLIN: *Ranglin Roots* (Tropic, 1977)

GREGORY ISAACS: *Cool Ruler* (Caroline, 1978)

PRINCE BUSTER: *Fabulous Greatest Hits* (Sequel, 1980)

PETER TOSH: *Mama Africa* (Capitol, 1983)

SLY & ROBBIE: *Taxi Fare* (Heartbeat, 1986)

TOMMY McCOOK & THE SUPERSONICS: *Down on Bond Street* (compilation album; Trojan, 1997)

THIS LAND IS YOUR LAND: PROTEST SINGERS/PROTEST SONGS

No one knows for sure who the first protest singer was. I imagine minstrels roaming the European countryside in medieval times singing about how some lord or landowner was putting one over on the serfs. However, the first U.S. singer/songwriter we know for sure who left behind a body of work and laid down the blueprint for others was Woody Guthrie. Woody took the folk music of his youth and fused it with lyrics that reflected his left-wing political beliefs, and he also told stories of folks he met along the way. Some of the artists who followed in his footsteps were contemporaries who shared his convictions, while others have used their music to make their own political statements, such as Chumbawamba, Rage Against the Machine (their name pretty much says it all), and Ani DiFranco, whose songs often address feminist issues. A note on Britain's Chumbawamba: Although best known in the United States as a one-hit wonder for their 1997 single **Tubthumping**, they are in fact an extremely anti-establishment outfit.

> **WOODY GUTHRIE**: *This Land Is Your Land: The Asch Recordings, Vol. 1* (Smithsonian Folkways, 1997)
> **BOB DYLAN**: *The Times They Are A-Changin'* (Columbia, 1964)

JOAN BAEZ: *Joan Baez 5* (Vanguard, 1964)

PHIL OCHS: *I Ain't Marching Anymore* (Hannibal, 1965)

PETE SEEGER: *A Link in the Chain* (Columbia, 1966)

GANG OF FOUR: *Entertainment!* (EMI, 1979)

BILLY BRAGG: *Talking with the Taxman about Poetry* (Elektra, 1986)

RAGE AGAINST THE MACHINE: *Rage Against the Machine* (Epic, 1992)

ANI DIFRANCO: *Not a Pretty Girl* (Righteous Babe, 1995)

CHUMBAWAMBA: *English Rebel Songs 1381–1984* (Mutt, 1998)

TIE ME KANGAROO DOWN: AUSSIE ROCK

The history of Australian rock begins somewhere in the 1950s, with homegrown singers copying the styles of their American and British heroes. At that time the country was still very much tied to the motherland of Great Britain and was experiencing what came to be known as the "cultural cringe," a turning away from all locally produced art, music, and theater. By the 1980s things were changing, and Australia has through the years produced some fine musical artists. (And, I might add, designers, artists, actors, and movie directors. Oh, and don't forget the wine!) Here's a must-have collection of albums and artists from Down Under.

THE EASYBEATS were the first Australian band to break internationally, in 1967 with an album called **Friday on My Mind** (reissued in 1992 on Repertoire records). The record featured the title cut as a hit single and a whole album's worth of mainly self-penned gems that reflect the time and the band's place in it.

The irony is that although the band came together in Sydney, its members were immigrants from England, Scotland, and Holland. The main songwriters, Harry Vanda and George Young, went on to write and produce for AC/DC, a band fronted by Young's younger brothers Angus and Malcolm.

Speaking of **AC/DC**, check out the essay "Headbangers Ball" for more details on the band and their history, but let me state here that **Back in Black**, released in 1980 on Epic, is probably the best heavy metal record ever released.

MEN AT WORK were the first Australian rock band to achieve true international stardom. The group rode out of Melbourne and onto the world's charts at the end of 1982 with their fun take on New Wave, and at the height of their fame held the unique distinction of simultaneously having the No. 1 single, **Down Under**, and album in both Britain and the U.S. The album was **Business as Usual** and is available on Columbia records.

MIDNIGHT OIL formed in Sydney in the mid 1970s and was the first Australian band to mix blistering guitar rock with outspoken and passionate lyrics. Over the course of the band's career singer Peter Garrett took on subjects such as exploitation of the environment and the abuse of Australia's indigenous aboriginal peoples, and with his band mates crafted lyrically and musically powerful songs. Their 1987 release on Columbia Records, **Diesel and Dust**, tackled the aboriginal issue head on; it catches the band pulling back a little from their blunt rock approach and exploring melodies while retaining a lyrical directness uncommon in mainstream music. The album was the band's most successful, achieving a breakthrough in the United States that saw it achieve platinum status.

In the second half of the seventies, **LITTLE RIVER BAND** was Australia's top musical export with a sound that could've come straight out of California. In fact, the group's musical style was very similar to the West Coast's own Eagles. The band's singer, Glenn Shorrock, had a voice that was as smooth as they come, and the group's songs were made for the AM radio middle-of-the-road format. **Sleeper Catcher**, the band's fourth album, was released on Capitol in 1978, and with the help of the singles **Reminiscing** and **Lady** became the first Australian record to achieve platinum status in the United States. The album is now available on the Collectables label, packaged with the 1981 album **Time Exposure** as a double CD.

INXS were Australia's first true international rock stars. The band was started by three brothers, Andrew, Tim, and Jon Farriss, who with Kirk Pengilly, Garry Beers, and Michael Hutchence formed the group in 1977 in Perth, Western Australia. They all moved to Sydney in 1980 and began playing pubs up and down the east coast. The band began to mix a New Wave sensibility with their straight ahead blues rock approach and honed their style over the course of five albums until in 1987 their album **Kick** (Atlantic) did just that. The band added a dance/funk feeling to their solid rock foundation and created the perfect pop/rock album of its time, in the process kicking down the doors to international stardom. When Hutchence mysteriously passed away in a Sydney hotel room in the fall of 1997, the INXS story came to a grinding halt. The surviving members, however, have since performed with guest vocalists at a number of high-profile concerts, such as the opening ceremonies of the Sydney Olympics in 2000. In 2005, INXS took part in a reality TV show to find a new lead singer.

NICK CAVE first grabbed attention as the leader of punk/goth band the **BIRTHDAY PARTY**. In their brief career (1977-83), they moved from Melbourne to London and then on to Berlin, achieving near-legendary status for their stage show, which saw Cave throwing himself around howling like a demented puppet shorn of its strings. (I saw him down a bottle of Greek tequila during just such a performance in Athens in 1982 as guitarist Rowland Howard's blistering feedback assaulted the audience.) Their 1981 album **Prayers on Fire**, reissued on the Buddha label, is about as dark and merciless a record as you will ever hear. With his next band, **NICK CAVE & THE BAD SEEDS**, he found the ideal canvas on which to paint his dark, gloomy tales of love, murder, and, yes, redemption. His dark, distinct vocals are more likely today to grace a piano ballad, but he can still rock and his diverse catalog is well worth exploring. My favorite album is the 1996 Mute release **Murder Ballads**, a somewhat humorous collection where every song is about some type of macabre, untimely death! The album includes duets with PJ Harvey and Australia's pop princess Kylie Minogue.

THE SAINTS, led by Ed Kuepper and Chris Bailey, were the first Australian punk band to achieve significant recognition. Their initial success came in England, where their 1977 single, **(I'm) Stranded**, became a big hit. As the seventies ended, Kuepper left the group, and with Bailey running the show the music matured into more melodic blue-collar pop. The eighties saw the band achieve international recognition with the 1987 release **All Fools Day** on TVT.

THE GO-BETWEENS formed in 1978 in the same town as the Saints, Brisbane. After relocating to London, they spent the better part of the eighties making beautiful, lush pop music. Centered around songwriters Robert Forster and Grant McLennan, the group recorded six albums before calling it a day after the release of their final and probably best album, 1988's **16 Lovers Lane**, on Jetset Records. Both Forster and McLennan went on to modest solo careers before reuniting in 2000 for another Go-Betweens album, **The Friends of Rachel Worth**, also on Jetset.

THE WARUMPI BAND were the first aboriginal band to break through on a commercial level, in large part due to the support of Midnight Oil, who in 1986 had them open on a tour of outback aboriginal settlements (an equivalent to Native American reservations). Although the group tours Australia regularly, they record infrequently. However, their 1987 album **Go Bush**, on Festival records, showcases their unique mix of country, blues, and rock. I saw the Warumpi Band open for Midnight Oil in the legendary Coolangatta club The Patch, and it ranks as one of my most memorable concert experiences.

The following is a list of other classic Oz rock albums:

SKYHOOKS: *Ego Is Not a Dirty Word* (Mushroom, 1975)

COLD CHISEL: *East* (WEA International, 1980)

THE MASTER'S APPRENTICES: *Hands of Time* (Raven, 1980)

MENTAL AS ANYTHING: *Creatures of Leisure* (Mushroom, 1983)

HOODOO GURUS: *Mars Needs Guitars* (Elektra, 1985)

HUNTERS AND COLLECTORS: *Human Frailty* (Liberation, 1986)

MONDO ROCK: *Boom Baby Boom* (Columbia, 1986)

ICEHOUSE: *Man of Colours* (WEA International, 1987)

THE DIVINYLS: *Divinyls* (Virgin, 1991)

PAUL KELLY: *Comedy* (Dr. Dream, 1992)

YOTHU YINDI: *Tribal Voice* (Hollywood, 1992)

JET: *Get Born* (Elektra, 2003)

TO THE BEAT OF THEIR OWN DRUM

Drummers are the backbone of any band. A good drummer can create a mood that makes you want to throw your body around the dance floor in abandon or, alternately, slip into a groove that sets your toes tapping and your mind thinking about after-hours activities. Through the years there have been several drummers who've transcended their roles at the back of the stage and led their own bands. Here's a few of the key cats.

When **GENE KRUPA** moved from Chicago to New York at the end of 1934, he hooked up with the legendary Benny Goodman and played with him in a couple of different band incarnations, earning a reputation for his drum solos. After falling out with Goodman, Krupa began his own orchestra and by the early 1940s the band really started to cook with the help of some fine players and vocalists. He had a couple of film roles during this time as well, including a major part (as a bandleader) in the comedy *Ball of Fire*. He got himself into a bit of trouble around the same time as a result of his drug use, and the band broke up as a result. He returned to Goodman for a while before starting up another big band of his own, and continued working into and through the fifties with a number of different combos. There is a 1993 compilation of his early hits called **Best of Big Bands: Drum Boogie** on Columbia featuring the vocalists Irene Day and Anita O'Day, and several trumpeters, including the thrilling Roy Eldridge. Thanks to my dad for turning me on to Gene Krupa.

While I was too young to see Gene Krupa perform, when I was a teenager I saw **BUDDY RICH** and his big band a couple of times, thanks to my mum, who, after hearing me talk about Cream and Ginger Baker, insisted that I had to go and see a "real" drummer. It certainly opened my eyes to music beyond pop and rock. Buddy Rich was self-taught and began his career as a young kid in vaudeville. (He also sang and tap-danced.) From the mid 1940s through the 1950s he played with greats like Charlie Parker, Lionel Hampton, Tommy Dorsey, and Harry James. In 1966 he started his own big band and toured the world for the next twenty years. Unfortunately he also became infamous, at least in the music business, as a nitpicking perfectionist. He had a reputation for treating his musicians poorly, but as a drummer he's remembered as probably the greatest. **Mercy Mercy**, from 1968 on Blue Note, is a live recording that catches Rich at his most essential.

In the 1960s **GINGER BAKER** made his name as the drummer and percussionist with rock supergroup Cream. Interestingly, he started as a jazz drummer and then got into R&B and led the band the Graham Bond Organisation, which included Jack Bruce on bass. Together, they joined with Eric Clapton to form Cream. Baker's playing with that band influenced a whole generation of rock drummers, and not just because of his own style. He also spoke in interviews about his own musical heroes, and in doing so turned a lot of young players on to Krupa and Rich. After Cream he was in the short-lived Blind Faith with Clapton and Steve Winwood, and then formed his own band, Ginger Baker's Air Force, whose self-titled first album was recorded live at London's Royal Albert Hall in 1970 (reissued on Polygram) and covers a lot of ground, displaying Baker's many influences. Baker has continued to record through the years and has put out a number of albums exploring percussion sounds from around the world.

PHIL COLLINS's first career was as a child actor. His roles included the Artful Dodger in *Oliver!* when it originally ran in London's West End in the early sixties, and a small part in The Beatles' *A Hard Day's Night*. As a drummer, in 1970 he joined the band Genesis, which was then fronted by Peter Gabriel. Over the course of the next five years the band achieved a modest level of success and a certain cult status with several theatrical and progressive rock records. When Gabriel left in 1975 to pursue a solo career, Genesis almost folded, but after the group auditioned hundreds of singers, Collins stepped from behind the kit to become the band's unlikely new vocalist. Genesis went on to become one of the biggest bands of the late seventies and early eighties. The group's success allowed Collins to step out on his own and find solo fame. **Face Value** from 1981 (Atlantic) is his best effort and includes the hits **In The Air Tonight** and **I Missed Again**. In the late nineties, as his pop career stalled, he got back behind the drums and formed the Phil Collins Big Band, a sporadic project that released a live album in 1999 called **A Hot Night in Paris**, also available on Atlantic records.

TOO GOOD FOR WORDS

Sometimes I don't want to hear lyrics. All I need is a good instrumental album. By this, I don't mean jazz or lounge-y background music, though; I'm talking about music that can both sit on your shoulder and make you want tap your feet. Music that can simultaneously chill you out and make you imagine other worlds. And just when you think you have its measure, it turns around and completely surprises you. Here are my ten favorite (mostly) instrumental albums, in order of preference:

RY COODER & V. M. BHATT: *A Meeting by the River* (Waterlily Acoustics, 1993)

MIKE OLDFIELD: *Tubular Bells* (Virgin, 1973)

STEVE REICH: *Music for 18 Musicians* (ECM, 1978)

TANGERINE DREAM: *Phaedra* (Virgin, 1974)

JAPANCAKES: *If I Could See Dallas* (Kindercore, 1999)

THE MERCURY PROGRAM: *A Data Learn the Language* (Tiger Style, 2002)

RYUICHI SAKAMOTO: *BTTB* (Warner Brothers, 1999)

BRIAN ENO: *Apollo: Atmospheres & Soundtracks* (EG, 1983)

NORTEC COLLECTIVE: *The Tijuana Sessions, Vol. 1* (Palm Pictures, 2001)

JEAN MICHEL JARRE: *Oxygène* (Dreyfus, 1977)

TRAINS, PLANES, AND AUTOMOBILES

This essay takes a look at albums by groups whose names were inspired by some of my favorite forms of transportation, not to mention one of my favorite films.

THE B-52'S were one of the first acts to break out of Athens, Georgia, in the 1970s. Their unique brand of humor and kitschy image, mixed with an innate sense of danceable pop music, made them seem like refugees from *The Jetsons*. They went on to major success at the end of the eighties with **Cosmic Thing** (Warner Brothers, 1989); however, my favorite album of theirs (and I still have it on a cassette somewhere) is the 1980 release **Wild Planet** on Warner Brothers.

Coming out of Harlem in the mid-1950s, **THE CADILLACS** were one of the early pioneering R&B vocal groups and one of the first to introduce dance steps into their stage act. They deliberately chose their moniker for its association with the quality car of the same name. Most of their recordings are out of print, but if you're a flea-market shopper, look out for **The Fabulous Cadillacs** on Jubilee Records from 1957.

THE CARS were, along with Blondie, one of America's most successful New Wave groups. Although primarily thought of as a singles band, they also released a couple of stellar albums. Their first release, **The Cars**, from 1978 on Elektra is chock-full of familiar pop songs.

Guitarist Jimmie Vaughan formed the **FABULOUS THUNDER-BIRDS** with vocalist Kim Wilson in Austin, Texas, in 1974. By the mid-1980s they were the most popular roadhouse blues band in the country, opening up on major tours for artists like the Rolling Stones. Their second album, **What's the Word**, reissued in 2000 on Benchmark with live bonus tracks, features some of their best work.

FICTION PLANE are a band fronted by Joe Sumner, the son of Gordon Sumner (who is better known as Police front man Sting). Their music falls somewhere between Nirvana and U2, with just a hint of the Police. I reckon Joe has a better voice and rocks in a way his dad hasn't for a long time. They released a much-overlooked album on MCA in 2003 called **Everything Will Never Be OK**.

Named after a Ford car, **GALAXIE 500**, a short-lived (1986–90) Boston-based band, are cited by a whole slew of alternative and indie pop bands as an influence. Their second album, **On Fire**, originally released in 1989 on Rough Trade, was reissued on CD by Rykodisc (as was all their catalog) in 1997. When the band split, vocalist Dean Wareham went on to form the group Luna.

JEFFERSON AIRPLANE were one of the first bands to break out of the San Francisco psychedelic rock scene centered in Haight Ashbury. Their 1967 album on RCA, **Surrealistic Pillow**, was groundbreaking in that it was the first album of its genre to scale the heights of the pop charts. The band later morphed into Jefferson Starship, but seeing as how that's a fictional mode of transportation, we'll leave it at that.

U2 named themselves after the American high-altitude spy planes that spent the best part of the Cold War taking photographs of the Soviet Union's nuclear and military installations. My favorite U2 album is their third, **War**, from 1983, released on Island Records.

WIRE TRAIN were a band from San Francisco that had some moderate success in modern rock radio in the late 1980s. Their first album, **In a Chamber**, from Columbia in 1983, is well worth the ride.

TROPICALIA

As the Beatles kicked the musical doors open to the fast-approaching counterculture in the United States in 1964, the rest of the world was also beginning to shift from black and white into color. In Brazil, a new musical movement emerged that was largely driven by a political ideology opposed to the military coup and dictatorship that had imposed itself that same year on the country's population. The movement became known as Tropicalia, and it took all forms of musical styles, from traditional Brazilian bossa nova and samba, to jazz, blues, folk, and psychedelic rock. In fact, the various artists who became identified with the movement had very diverse backgrounds and musical styles. The threads that tied them together were their lyrics, which scorned the political climate, and their willingness to experiment. Here are some of the most important Tropicalia artists and recommended listening.

CAETANO VELOSO is arguably Brazil's greatest contemporary songwriter. His career has now spanned five decades, and he is revered in his homeland. It wasn't always the case; in fact, as the Tropicalia movement began to threaten the military dictatorship running Brazil in the second part of the sixties, both he and his friend Gilberto Gil were imprisoned. Through the years he has written and recorded songs in just about every musical style imaginable, and he is regarded as one of the finest songwriters of the Portugese language. His Tropicalia high point was his first solo album, **Caetano Veloso**, released in 1968 and available on CD as an import from Universal. In 2004 he released an English-language album of covers of songs written by American artists for Nonesuch called **A Foreign Sound**. The choice of material is astounding, from Jerome Kern's **Smoke Gets in Your Eyes** to Cole Porter's **Love for Sale**, Stevie Wonder's **If It's Magic**, and Nirvana's **Come As You Are**.

MARIA BETHÂNIA is Caetano Veloso's sister, and although she played a major part in the movement's early days by performing in shows that Caetano was putting together, she is interestingly enough more of a traditional vocalist, with a distinctive torchy singing style. Her first two albums are now available on one CD: **Maria Bethânia/Maria Ao Vivo**, a 2003 EMI import release.

A psychedelic rock band formed by three brothers (Arnaldo, Sérgio, and Cláudio Baptista) with vocalist Rita Lee, **OS MUTANTES** worked for a while as the backing band for Caetano Veloso and recorded songs by other major figures in the movement. Their 1968 debut **Os Mutantes** finds them mixing up a bagful of influences and psychedelic sounds with gleeful abandon. This album was released domestically on Omplatten Records, but if you can't find it, David Byrne's Luaka Bop label released a rather good compilation in 1999 called **Everything Is Possible: The Best of Os Mutantes**.

TOM ZÉ was a largely overlooked figure until recently and probably the most eccentric of the Tropicalia musicians. He studied at music college and early on in his career worked with Caetano Veloso, Gal Costa, and Gilberto Gil, among others, as well as writing songs for and performing in several musicals. His albums veered from playful pop to classic bossa nova to tape loops of found sounds such as music made by power tools. When I saw him perform in 1999 he included metal grinding tools as a part of the stage show; talk about making sparks fly! Tom Zé had pretty much called it a day until he was rediscovered by David Byrne in the early 1990s. Luaka Bop's 1990 release of a compilation of Zé's work, **Brazil Classics, Vol. 4: The Best of Tom Zé— Massive Hits**, is a great introduction to this true artist.

GILBERTO GIL is a multi-instrumentalist who, although best known as a guitarist, is no slouch on a whole host of other instruments, including the accordion and drums. His early success came as a result of bringing traditional Brazilian folk music together with bossa nova and jazz as a part of the Tropicalia movement. Like Veloso, he was imprisoned and then exiled for a number of years to England, where he worked consistently as a session musician with some of the leading bands of the day, including Pink Floyd. His second album, **Gilberto Gil**, released in 1968 and available on import from Polygram International, is probably his best and features musical backing from Os Mutantes.

GAL COSTA is one of Brazil's most highly regarded and respected pop singers. In the mid–1960s she was one of several female voices who sang the music of the Tropicalistas. Her early work was alongside Caetano Veloso, his sister Maria Bethânia, Gilberto Gil, and Tom Zé in a musical production *Nós, por Exemplo* (We, by Example) that ended up playing a number of different cities, and her career was thus launched. Her 1969 album **Gal Costa** is probably the most experimental and psychedelic release of any of the artists in the movement. It's available on import from Universal. (Costa actually released two self-titled albums in 1969; this is the second of the two, featuring the Caetano Veloso compositions **Cinema Olympia** and **The Empty Boat**.)

JORGE BEN was first known as a guitar-playing samba artist until he began to embrace a more eclectic approach to his songwriting and performing. His mother was African and his connection to that culture led him to include funk and soul in his Tropicalia musical grab bag. He wasn't controversial like some of his contemporaries, but was nonetheless a key player in the development of Brazilian music. In the 1970s he really explored his West African roots with a series of recordings culminating in the 1976 release **África Brasil**. The CD is available as an import on Universal and is widely regarded as introducing African beats to Brazilian popular music.

TURNING JAPANESE

The last forty years of Japanese popular culture have given us miniature electronic entertainment gadgets and smaller, more reliable automobiles, as well as Godzilla, anime, Pokémon, and Tamagotchi (electronic critters that live in a key chain). Their comics, music, and films are consumed in mass quantities, and in many cases the stories they tell are linked to the past and reinterpret classic Japanese themes. Japanese society places a huge emphasis on work ethic, so many Japanese find little time for leisure. Maybe that helps explain the quirky nature of much of their entertainment. Japanese people are hugely respectful of artists and musicians, and over the years many American jazz and pop artists have found more respect there than at home. Japan's own musicians have had mixed success outside of their country. Here are a few of my favorites and their work.

RYUICHI SAKAMOTO is probably the most talented and versatile musician Japan has ever produced and ranks with the world's best. He began playing piano at age three and through the years has performed jazz, classical, and electronic music. His first band was the Yellow Magic Orchestra, who became big stars in their homeland and had a cult following in Europe in the early eighties. After Yellow Magic Orchestra broke up, he began another chapter in his career, that of a film score composer, when he wrote the soundtrack for the movie *Merry Christmas Mr. Lawrence* (Milan,

1983), a film in which he also acted alongside David Bowie. Other film soundtrack work includes Bernardo Bertolucci's *The Last Emperor*, on which he collaborated with Talking Heads' David Byrne, and *Little Buddha*. Around this time he also set about pursuing his solo recording career. He has through the years collaborated with artists as diverse as David Sylvian, Iggy Pop, and Brian Wilson, and also recorded a collection of work by the Brazilian composer Antonio Carlos Jobim. A few years ago I had the honor of interviewing him and watching him do a solo piano performance. His album **Beauty**, released in 1990 on Virgin, catches him at his most eclectic, fusing various electronic and world music sounds together.

Anyone who takes his name from a character in *Planet of the Apes* is all right by me. Keigo Oyamada, aka **CORNELIUS**, did just that and makes music that mixes up a whole basketful of influences, skipping through pop, hip-hop, guitar rock, cartoon samples, and vocal harmonies. Also known as a producer and remixer, Cornelius's 1997 **Fantasma** on Matador showcases his myriad influences.

Coming out of the same Shibuya-kei (nineties Japanese New Wave pop that centered around the west Tokyo district of Shibuya) scene in Tokyo as Cornelius, **PIZZICATO 5** led the way with their mix of kitschy pop. They are hugely popular in their homeland and have managed to ride out a number of lineup changes along the way. Their 1995 release on Columbia, **Romantique 96**, was their homage to the French pop of the sixties and a play on words of Serge Gainsbourg's **69 Année Érotique**.

CIBO MATTO's Yuka Honda and Miho Hatori were Japanese-born but are based out of New York City. They had moved to the United States separately and first met up playing in another band, Leitoh Lychee, before forming Cibo Matto. Their music reflected the cultures of both Tokyo and Manhattan, with a potpourri of samples, pop, and hip-hop, and English and French vocals. When Yuka and Sean Lennon became involved in a relationship, he joined the band for a while as their touring bass player. Their name is Italian for "food madness," and many of their early songs were named after foods, like **Artichoke**, **Birthday Cake**, and **Beef Jerky**. Their first album **Viva! La Woman** from Warner Brothers in 1996 laid out their manifesto.

I saw **BOOM BOOM SATELLITES** by accident a couple of years ago as an opening act for Moby. Basically a duo, Masayuki Nakano and Michiyuki Kawashima create music that mixes big beat with rock, and it's not too far a stretch to describe them as a Japanese Chemical Brothers. **Out Loud** from 1999 on Sony showcased their incredibly smart production skills as well.

YOKO ONO will always be remembered as the woman who became John Lennon's second wife. Unfortunately for her, they got together at around the time the Beatles were imploding, and she was unfairly scapegoated by many as the reason the band broke up. Not only is this untrue, it has also overshadowed her own unique body of work as an avant-garde artist. A lot of people had a problem with her screaming vocal style, but they misread where Yoko was coming from. (By the way, both Yoko and John undertook primal scream therapy.) Her music, as with her art, challenged its audience to use their imagination; it was about concept, not structure. In 1971 she released **Fly**, a double album reissued in the late nineties on Rykodisc. This collection featured more formal songs and saw her accompanied by the Plastic Ono Band, which included John and Ringo.

Before she met John, Yoko's life was both traumatic and fascinating. The book *YES Yoko Ono* (Harry N Abrams, 2000) gives insight into her personal history, and features analysis of her art and music by various writers.

TWENTY BEST DOUBLE ALBUMS

With the advent of digital compact discs in the mid-1980s, the 12-inch vinyl album as we knew it slipped away into history, along with compact cassette tapes and 7-inch singles. They were merely following the path of 8-track tape cartridges and 10-inch 78s, all music-delivery formats whose time had come and gone. The golden era of 12-inch cardboard album sleeves also ended with the demise of vinyl. What had begun as simple album sleeves to protect the records inside evolved over the years to become a showcase for creative designs featuring artwork and photography that in many cases became synonymous with the albums themselves.

In 1966 Bob Dylan took things a stage further when he released **Blonde on Blonde** (Columbia), the first-ever double album. It had a foldout double sleeve that, when opened up, revealed a series of photographs of Dylan and friends. Back in the sixties and seventies, vinyl albums were restricted to approximately twenty-three minutes of music per side, so if an artist wanted to release more than forty-five minutes of music, the options were to stagger the release of two albums or put out a double release.

In the years between *Blonde on Blonde* and the arrival of CDs that could hold substantially more music, there were many double- and multi-album releases, most of which could probably have been edited down to single LPs. But there were also some classic releases that managed to hold a listener's interest through all four sides, in some cases because of the quality of songwriting and in others through conceptual storytelling. Here are my top-20 double-album recommendations, two of which were released in the Digital Age as double CDs. I've excluded triple sets, compilations, and live releases.

BOB DYLAN: *Blonde on Blonde* (Columbia, 1966)

FRANK ZAPPA AND THE MOTHERS OF INVENTION: *Freak Out!* (Rykodisc, 1966)

THE BEATLES: *The White Album* (Capitol, 1968)

THE JIMI HENDRIX EXPERIENCE: *Electric Ladyland* (MCA, 1968)

MILES DAVIS: *Bitches Brew* (Columbia, 1969)

THE WHO: *Tommy* (MCA, 1969)

THE ROLLING STONES: *Exile on Main Street* (Virgin, 1972)

THE WHO: *Quadrophenia* (MCA, 1973)

LED ZEPPELIN: *Physical Graffiti* (Atlantic, 1975)

STEVIE WONDER: *Songs in the Key of Life* (Motown, 1976)

MARVIN GAYE: *Here, My Dear* (Motown, 1978)

THE CLASH: *London Calling* (Epic, 1979)

PINK FLOYD: *The Wall* (Capitol, 1979)

BRUCE SPRINGSTEEN: *The River* (Columbia, 1980)

FRANKIE GOES TO HOLLYWOOD: *Welcome to the Pleasuredome* (Island, 1984)

THE MINUTEMEN: *Double Nickels on the Dime* (SST, 1984)

HÜSKER DÜ: *Zen Arcade* (SST, 1984)

PRINCE: *Sign 'O' the Times* (Paisley Park, 1987)

PREFAB SPROUT: *Jordan: The Comeback* (Epic, 1990)

OUTKAST: *Speakerboxxx/The Love Below* (La Face, 2003)

TWENTY ESSENTIAL ALBUMS OF THE TWENTY-FIRST CENTURY (SO FAR)

The new millennium is still young, but already we've seen a number of albums released that as time passes will stack up against the best from any decade. Here are my favorite twenty from the years 2000 to 2004:

BADLY DRAWN BOY: *The Hour of Bewilderbeast* (XL, 2000)

SHELBY LYNNE: *I Am Shelby Lynne* (Island, 2000)

RADIOHEAD: *Kid A* (Capitol, 2000)

JILL SCOTT: *Who Is Jill Scott? Words and Sounds, Vol. 1* (Hidden Beach, 2000)

TRAVIS: *The Man Who* (Epic, 2000)

RYAN ADAMS: *Gold* (Lost Highway, 2001)

THE AVALANCHES: *Since I Left You* (Modular, 2001)

COUSTEAU: *Cousteau* (Palm Pictures, 2001)

SIGUR RÓS: *Ágaetis Byrjun* (PIAS America, 2001)

ZERO 7: *Simple Things* (Palm Pictures, 2001)

BECK: *Sea Change* (DGC, 2002)

BRIGHT EYES: *Lifted, or The Story Is in the Soil, Keep Your Ear to the Ground* (Saddle Creek, 2002)

COLDPLAY: *A Rush of Blood to the Head* (Capitol, 2002)

NORAH JONES: *Come Away with Me* (Blue Note, 2002)

DAMIEN RICE: *O* (Vector, 2003)

MY MORNING JACKET: *It Still Moves* (ATO, 2003)

OUTKAST: *Speakerboxxx/The Love Below* (La Face, 2003)

FRANZ FERDINAND: *Franz Ferdinand* (Domino, 2004)

RILO KILEY: *More Adventurous* (Brute/Beaute, 2004)

THE ARCADE FIRE: *Funeral* (Merge, 2004)

TWO TURNTABLES AND A MICROPHONE: ESSENTIAL ELECTRONICA

Beginning in the UK in the late 1980s, the house music club scene started a new trend of club culture and gave rise to a new breed of DJs. No longer was a DJ someone you hired to play the hits or oldies at weddings. In the second half of the 1990s we saw the rise of the DJ as cultural icon. All of a sudden kids were buying turntable decks instead of guitars, and DJs became the new rock stars. Some of them went on to pioneer a fusion of DJ culture with electronic music, began hiring singers and musicians, and started making their own records. Here's a couple of the pioneers and the platters that matter.

THIEVERY CORPORATION are Rob Garza and Eric Hilton, who teamed up in Washington, D.C., in the mid-1990s to open a nightclub and form a record label, both called Eighteenth Street Lounge (ESL). After a couple of early albums, EPs, and remix compilations, they released **The Richest Man in Babylon** on ESL in 2002, in which they explored familiar areas of world music from Asia, the Caribbean, and Brazil, and enlisted several vocalists including Shinehead and Emiliana Torrini.

GROOVE ARMADA are another duo, this time from the UK. Tom Findlay and Andy Cato began working together as DJs in 1995, and it didn't take long for them to become highly sought after, so it was a natural progression for them to open their own club, which they named Groove Armada. They soon made the jump from DJ work to studio projects, and they released their first album **Northern Star** in 1998 on Tummy Touch records, mixing funk with ambient house. By their third full-length release, **Goodbye Country (Hello Nightclub)** (2001, Jive Records), they had expanded their musical palate and added vocal stylings that ranged from folk to rap, then put together an eight-piece touring band to perform their music on stage.

Tom Rowlands and Ed Simons are the **CHEMICAL BROTHERS**, who took electronica out of the clubs and into stadiums. They brought together rock, hip-hop, and dance music, and created what came to be known as big beat. Their albums were solidly beat- and percussion-driven, and they were able to cross electronic music over to rock fans for the first time. Their second album, **Dig Your Own Hole**, released in 1997 on Astralwerks, included Noel Gallagher's vocal contribution on the single **Setting Sun** and arrived in the United States just as the electronica movement was beginning to break, announcing them as the new genre's superstars.

DJ SHADOW is the handle for Josh Davis, a pioneer in instrumental hip-hop. While his friends were picking up guitars and other traditional rock instruments, he was drawn to the DIY ethos of hip-hop and the DJs who performed with the various groups he admired (like Public Enemy). His debut **Endtroducing**, released on Mo Wax in 1996, built an album entirely of samples layer by layer into a collection that is considered a milestone in DJ culture and electronic music.

Guitarist Rick Smith, singer Karl Hyde, and DJ Darren Emerson made up **UNDERWORLD**, one of the first electronic acts to take guitar-based rock music and back it with techno beats, creating a unique hybrid. They were largely ignored commercially until the single **Born Slippy** (from the cult movie *Trainspotting*) brought them to a wider audience and led to critical and commercial success as both a recording and touring outfit. The 1999 V2 Records album **Beaucoup Fish** was their last with Emerson, who left the band shortly after its release.

FATBOY SLIM is the name that former Housemartins member and Pizzaman (a recording project, not a part time job!) Norman Cook gave himself for his most successful musical incarnation. He had already established himself as a major remixer and producer when he decided to make his own records, and the singles **Rockefeller Skank** and **Praise You** were huge international hits. They're off the 1998 album **You've Come a Long Way Baby** on Astralwerks, which took big beat to the masses on both sides of the Atlantic.

UNKNOWN PLEASURES: GOTH MUSIC

When and where goth music got its start is debatable, but I'm going to go with the theory that it sprang up somewhere between the UK punk and New Romantic movements in the late 1970s with the band Joy Division, whose lead singer Ian Curtis sang songs so dark and bleak that it was not too big a surprise when he took his own life in 1980. (The band's remaining members later regrouped as New Order.) Goth music took punk's outward anger and turned it inward, with lyrics that often reflected a sense of trepidation. The addition of synthesizers and keyboards gave the music an often sweeping melodrama that added to the overall sense of foreboding.

Goth was, in fact, the logical next step after punk, and as the post-punk movement took hold, several punk bands evolved into goth bands. The clothing and "look" were equally as important as the music: lots of dark clothes, with a preference for long, flowing coats, religious symbols, and in some cases white pancake makeup with heavy black eyeliner. Goth's heyday was the mid-1980s, although it has since mutated and now includes bands that play goth pop, industrial, and alternative metal. If you have a penchant for rainy, dreary days and the game Dungeons & Dragons, here's a list of must-have goth albums:

JOY DIVISION: *Unknown Pleasures* (Qwest, 1979)

JOY DIVISION: *Closer* (Qwest, 1980)

BAUHAUS: *In the Flat Field* (4AD, 1980)

BAUHAUS: *Mask* (Beggars Banquet, 1981)

SIOUXSIE & THE BANSHEES: *Juju* (Geffen, 1981)

THE CURE: *Pornography* (Elektra, 1982)

CHRISTIAN DEATH: *Only Theater of Pain* (Frontier, 1982)

THE CURE: *The Head on the Door* (Elektra, 1985)

SISTERS OF MERCY: *First and Last and Always* (Elektra, 1985)

THE MISSION UK: *God's Own Medicine* (Mercury, 1986)

VOULEZ-VOUS COUCHER AVEC MOI?

The question I've been asked most often as I've been work-ing on this book is whether I was going to include a list of the perfect make-out music. The thing is, what's perfect for one person can be a total turnoff for another, and as with most situations in relationships, timing is everything. Let me give you an example: If you're a guy and you've just persuaded your date to come back to your place, starting off with something calm and smooth is probably a good bet. Indie rock or heavy metal is most likely not, unless you're both into indie rock or heavy metal, in which case you probably don't need this list. See what I mean? As for girls looking for something to get a guy going, in my experi-ence if a woman initiates a kiss, that usually does the trick. Pick the music you like; he's not going to be too worried. However, if you need further direction, here is a list of albums that I know have worked for others. But please, handle with care, and remember there are no guarantees in life except death and taxes.

AIR: *Moon Safari* (Astralwerks, 1998)

THE BLUE NILE: *A Walk Across the Rooftops* (A&M, 1984)

JOHN COLTRANE: *Ascension* (Impulse, 1965)

PETER GABRIEL: *Passion* (Geffen, 1989)

SERGE GAINSBOURG WITH JANE BIRKIN: *Jane Birkin et Serge Gainsbourg* (Universal France, 1969)

MARVIN GAYE: *Let's Get It On* (Motown, 1973)

AL GREEN: *The Supreme Al Green* (Hit Records, 1992)

MASSIVE ATTACK: *Blue Lines* (Virgin, 1991)

MOODSWINGS: *Moodfood* (Arista, 1992)

VAN MORRISON: *Poetic Champions Compose* (Mercury, 1987)

MAURICE RAVEL: *Bolero* (try the Montreal Symphony Orchestra recording conducted by Charles Dutoit; Decca, 1999)

THE ROLLING STONES: *Sticky Fingers* (Virgin, 1971)

ROXY MUSIC: *Avalon* (Virgin, 1982)

DONNA SUMMER: *Love to Love You Baby* (Universal, 1975)

THE VELVET UNDERGROUND: *VU* (Verve, 1985)

BARRY WHITE: Anything; seriously, anything . . .

ZERO 7: *Simple Things* (Palm, 2001)

WHAT WERE THEY THINKING? TEN ALBUMS THE WORLD COULD'VE LIVED WITHOUT

In any given year, several thousand records are released. It's always hard to predict if a new artist or group will hit, as the record-buying public's tastes can shift so quickly. As a result record labels rely heavily on their roster of already-successful artists to continue to produce the goods. But as anyone who has studied such things will tell you, there comes a time for most artists, whether they're painters, actors, or musicians, when the creative juices run dry. Here are ten examples of albums that prove that point.

When **LOU REED**'s record label RCA pushed him for new material in 1975, he delivered **Metal Machine Music** (reissued on Buddha), a double album with one single track of pretty much unlistenable guitar feedback on each of its four sides. Then again, there are others who consider this to be an avant-garde masterpiece.

When **PETER FRAMPTON** and **THE BEE GEES** were persuaded to make a movie based on the Beatles' **Sgt. Pepper's Lonely Hearts Club Band** in 1978, everybody involved must've been taking mind-altering substances. The soundtrack to the film (on Polydor) includes Beatles covers by Frampton and the Bee Gees as well as by Aerosmith and Earth, Wind & Fire. Generally regarded as one of the worst films ever made, the soundtrack is pretty much a disaster as well.

When Paul Kantner left Jefferson Starship in 1984, the remaining members were allowed to keep the last part of their name, and **STARSHIP** resurfaced with **Knee Deep in the Hoopla**, released in 1985 on RCA. The album was a big commercial success and includes the huge hit single **We Built This City**, but it's hard to believe that this band is the remnants of the once-mighty Jefferson Airplane.

There are several references in this book to **THE CLASH**. For my money they are one of the most important bands in the history of popular music. As the punk movement gave way to the eighties, they released several albums of vital, inspirational music and had the credibility to back it up. And let's face it—credibility in the music business is a rare commodity. So what to make of their final album, **Cut The Crap**, released in 1985 on Epic? Well, the fact is that this album was recorded by the remnants of the Clash. Mick Jones had been thrown out of the band and this album was a half-hearted collection of uninspired songs. It was a last hurrah from Joe Strummer and Paul Simonon, reflecting the sad truth that punk's glory days were long gone.

THE ROLLING STONES were truly one of the greatest and most important bands to play and record music in the twentieth century. Their body of recorded work includes several albums that you'll find on any critic's all-time greatest albums list. So what was going on when they released **Dirty Work** in 1986 (now on Virgin)? With the exception of the song **One Hit (to the Body)**, the album is full of substandard material and performances that reveal the tensions that were eating away at Mick Jagger and Keith Richards's relationship after Jagger's solo effort **She's the Boss** (which would also be at home in this category) the previous year.

In 1989 David Bowie decided to reinvent himself once more, this time as a member of a band, **TIN MACHINE**, that included Reeves Gabrels on guitar and Tony and Hunt Sales (the sons of comedian Soupy Sales) on bass and drums. The 1989 debut release **Tin Machine** (Virgin) was a hard-rocking guitar album that garnered a lot of press but yielded little music of any note. They released a second collection a few years later before Bowie realized his career had stalled and went back to his more idiosyncratic solo work.

Whatever you might think of **OZZY OSBOURNE**, and chances are it'll be colored by his reality TV show, he did front probably the most important heavy metal band of all time (Black Sabbath). His early solo career was also impressive, with a series of album releases that solidified his superstardom. How then to explain his 1995 Epic Records release **Ozzmosis**? Simply put, it was the moment when it became clear that Ozzy was going through the motions. With nothing to say, it was an album so overproduced not even the guitar heroics of Zakk Wylde could save it.

One of the greatest rock bands of the 1980s, **VAN HALEN** was never quite the same after singer David Lee Roth left in 1985. However, the group's success continued with his replacement, Sammy Hagar. When Hagar called it quits, Eddie Van Halen and the rest of the band thought about bringing Roth back but then changed their minds and hired former Extreme singer Gary Cherone instead.

Van Halen III followed in 1998 on Warner Brothers and found the band going through the motions, leaving fans wondering if they'd ever kiss and make up with Diamond Dave.

The biggest-selling country artist of the 1990s, **GARTH BROOKS** decided to do an entire album of more pop-oriented material in 1999, but instead of standing behind his artistic decision, he chose to shield himself with an alter ego. **In the Life of Chris Gaines**, released by Capitol, found him wearing a wig for the cover photo and performing a collection of middle-of-the-road pop. It wasn't so much that the album was bad, it was more the concept that sucked.

STEELY DAN, the kings of seventies sophisticated smooth pop (when it actually made some kind of sense), returned in the year 2000 after a twenty-year absence with the Giant Records release **Two Against Nature**, an album of . . . seventies-style sophisticated smooth pop! Amazingly, the National Academy of Recording Arts & Sciences decided to reward them with the Grammy that they should have received in 1975.

XENOPHILIA: MUSIC WITHOUT BORDERS

W*orld music* is a generic term coined in the 1980s to describe the ethnic music from various parts of the world that was beginning to be heard in Europe and the United States. World music had been trickling its way toward Western ears for many years, but in the 1980s, with major artists like Paul Simon and David Byrne making records with African and Brazilian musicians, respectively, and Peter Gabriel exploring the sounds of North Africa and the Middle East for his soundtrack to Martin Scorsese's *The Last Temptation of Christ* (and setting up the Real World record label to release CDs by world artists), the music found a wider audience. There are several essays in this book that discuss styles such as Afrobeat and Tropicalia in depth; here we explore music from other parts of the world.

AFRO CELT SOUND SYSTEM's name pretty much tells you what to expect, and then some. The band was formed in 1995 by a group of Irish and African musicians who brought with them various indigenous instruments from both cultures and then added modern production techniques. Their first album, **Volume 1: Sound Magic**, released in 1996, captures the pure joy of musicians from different backgrounds coming together and finding common ground. It is available on Peter Gabriel's Real World label.

VISHWA MOHAN "V. M." BHATT is an Indian musician who invented a guitarlike instrument with nineteen strings called the Mohan Veena, which sounds like a cross between the traditional Indian sitar and the Hawaiian slack key guitar. He has recorded many solo albums and participated in a number of fascinating collaborations. Sometimes gifts arrive when least expected· In 1993 my friend David Torn, an amazing guitar player and film composer, gave me a copy of the newly released **A Meeting by the River**, Bhatt's collaboration with Ry Cooder, recorded in one evening without rehearsal. It's available on Water Lily Acoustics and is one of the most prized recordings in my collection.

Cuban music is more popular and widely heard outside its borders than ever before, and a large part of its renaissance is as a result of the Wim Wenders–directed documentary movie and Ry Cooder–produced album, both called **Buena Vista Social Club** (the album was released in 1997 by Nonesuch). The film and CD document the gathering of the **BUENA VISTA SOCIAL CLUB**, a group of amazing septuagenarian musicians who had rarely been heard outside of Cuba since the 1959 revolution that brought Fidel

Castro to power. The album is a celebration of true talent and the human spirit. I highly recommend the DVD as well.

TOUMANI DIABATE and **BALLAKÉ SISSOKO** both come from Mali and play a stringed instrument called a kora that looks like a cross between a harp and a lute. They collaborated on a CD called **New Ancient Strings**, released on Hannibal in 1999.

Known as the "Barefoot Diva," **CESARIA EVORA** combines several musical styles, including Portuguese fados and West African percussion, and sings in a unique style called *Morna* that reflects a sense of nostalgia. She put the former Portuguese colony of Cape Verde on the international music map in 1992 with her album **Miss Perfumado**, available on several record labels, including Windham Hill.

The Pakistani master of Qawwali, a 700-year-old devotional singing style, **NUSRAT FATEH ALI KHAN** was a giant of world music. After collaborations with Eddie Vedder and Massive Attack, he was at the height of his fame when he passed away in 1997. His album **Mustt Mustt**, recorded with guitarist and producer Michael Brook, was released by Peter Gabriel's Real World label in 1990.

Born in Egypt, **UMM KULTHUM** was the Arab world's greatest singer, a heavy hash smoker, and opium addict who dressed as a boy when she was younger to evade religious authorities, and was a double agent during World War II. Intrigued? So was most of Egypt. When she died in 1975, more than 3 million people followed her casket through the streets of Cairo. More than thirty years later, radio stations in Egypt still honor her on the first Thursday of every month by playing her music. Even Israeli radio plays her music so as to entice Palestinians to their frequencies. **La Diva, Vol. 5**, released in 2001, is just one of many compilations of her work and is an import from EMI Arabia.

Tibetan artist **YUNGCHEN LHAMO** only began to sing professionally after escaping to India from her Chinese-occupied homeland and meeting the Dalai Lama, Tibet's exiled spiritual leader. He encouraged her to travel abroad and use her talents to help bring attention to the Tibetan people's adversities. Her 1998 album **Coming Home** on Real World Records showcases her unique voice on a collection of Tibetan folk songs with light acoustic instrumentation.

LATA MANGESHKAR and her younger sister, Asha Bhosle, are divas of the Indian film industry, Bollywood. Lata is perhaps a little more soulful in her style. **Rough Guide to Bollywood Legends: Lata Mangeshkar**, released by World Music Network in 2004, is a career retrospective with sixteen tracks spanning from 1949 to 1994. Rough Guide also released a similar compilation by her sister.

Better known as the Bulgarian Women's Choir, **LE MYSTÈRE DES VOIX BULGARES** has been recording since the 1960s, originally for Bulgaria's state-run Television & Radio System. Now independent of the state and financed by world tours, they continue to perform choral arrangements of traditional folk styles. Utterly unique, the first album widely available in the United States was titled **Le Mystere des Voix Bulgares** (The Mysterious Voices of Bulgaria) and was released on Nonesuch Records in 1990. I had them on my radio show in 1999, and one of the most amusing sights I've ever witnessed was this group of more than twenty-five women with such beautiful voices standing outside during a soundcheck break smoking cigarettes.

A leader of the Latin America's *Nueva Canción* (new song) movement—made up of artists who used their music to protest the various dictatorial regimes in place across that continent in the sixties and seventies—Argentinean **MERCEDES SOSA** is a big woman who prefers to sit rather than stand during her performances, which engenders a unique intimacy at her concerts. Her album **Live in Argentina**, released on Tropical Music in 1992, is a live recording that catches the excitement of the crowd as well as her wonderful performance.

Hailing from Mali in West Africa, **ALI FARKA TOURE** is called the "Bluesman of Africa" and is regarded as one of the finest guitar players in the world. **Talking Timbuktu**, his collaboration with another guitar great, Ry Cooder, was released in 1994 on Hannibal.

NEIL YOUNG: ICON

Neil Young is one of the most respected rock and folk guitarists of the past forty years. Originally from Toronto, he grew up in Winnipeg, where he began playing guitar as a young boy. Right from the start he played in two different styles: On the one hand, he played in a rock band called the Esquires, and on the other, he also played folk music at local coffeehouses. When he moved back to Toronto in the mid-sixties, he continued his dual musical life, playing with a lot of different people and forming a band called the Mynah Birds with Bruce Palmer and Rick James. (Yes, *the* Rick James of **Super Freak** fame!)

When things didn't go very far with that band, Neil and Bruce decided to head to California. When they met up with Stephen

Stills (with whom Neil had crossed paths before), Richie Furay, and Dewey Martin, they formed the band Buffalo Springfield, a group that found early success in 1967 with their hit single **For What It's Worth** and their debut album, **Buffalo Springfield**, on Atco Records, which brought them (along with the Byrds), recognition as leaders of the California folk rock scene. Neil left the band the following year, however, and set out as a solo performer whose career would take him back and forth through periods of folk and rock music (most notably with the band Crazy Horse), with detours into many other styles and on/off collaborations with David Crosby, Stephen Stills, and Graham Nash. When alternative rock exploded out of Seattle with the grunge movement, Young was cited as a major influence by bands like Nirvana and Pearl Jam. Here's a list of select CDs that span the many facets of Neil Young's prolific career:

> **NEIL YOUNG & CRAZY HORSE**: *Everybody Knows This Is Nowhere* (Reprise, 1969): The first album with the band who would become his long-time collaborators, and a rock record.
>
> **NEIL YOUNG**: *After the Gold Rush* (Reprise, 1970): His first classic album, a mix of beautiful acoustic folk and country songs.
>
> **CROSBY, STILLS, NASH & YOUNG**: *Déjà Vu* (Atlantic, 1970): CSN's second album topped their first, in large part because of the addition of Neil.
>
> **NEIL YOUNG**: *Harvest* (Reprise, 1972): Quite possibly his most eclectic release, with both acoustic and electric guitar–driven songs, as well as a couple with the London Symphony Orchestra.
>
> **NEIL YOUNG**: *Tonight's the Night* (Reprise, 1975): A turning point for Neil, with a collection of songs reflecting on

the loss of a couple of close friends and his disillusionment with fame.

NEIL YOUNG & CRAZY HORSE: *Zuma* (Reprise, 1975): This album finds Crazy Horse accompanying Neil as he hits his stride with a batch of songs that feel comfortably inhabited.

NEIL YOUNG: *Comes a Time* (Reprise, 1978): Back to an acoustic collection of folk and country. The *Harvest* fans love this one.

NEIL YOUNG & CRAZY HORSE: *Rust Never Sleeps* (Reprise, 1979): Includes the classic **My My, Hey Hey** and finds Neil lyrically looking at his art and how it fits within the context of the entertainment industry.

NEIL YOUNG & CRAZY HORSE: *Ragged Glory* (Reprise, 1990): The eighties were a little lean, but this album is a return to form. Neil relishes the role of lead guitarist and the songs find him tapping into a new awareness of the important things in his life.

NEIL YOUNG: *Unplugged* (Reprise, 1993): The MTV show gave Neil the opportunity to re-record and reinvent some of his best-loved songs in this collection that spans 25 years of material.

NEIL YOUNG & CRAZY HORSE: *Greendale* (Reprise, 2003): The soundtrack to Neil's concept movie of the same name. The songs tell the stories of a multi-generational cast of characters living in the fictional town of Greendale.

FRANK ZAPPA: ICON

Well, we're at the end of the book, and as we hit the letter Z, we come to a truly unique artist, Frank Zappa. We can't be sure, but Frank probably recorded and released more music than any other artist ever, with the bands the Soul Giants and the Mothers of Invention and later as a solo artist. Through his career he mixed pop, hard guitar rock, jazz, doo-wop, and orchestral music with satirical lyrics that poked fun at just about everything. He recorded for a number of major labels and also released his own material. He was also one of the finest guitar players of his generation. Toward the end of his life (he died of cancer in 1993 at the age of just fifty-two) he struck a deal with the Rykodisc label, which began reissuing his catalog. The list below highlights just a few of his many, many releases:

THE MOTHERS OF INVENTION: *Freak Out!* (Rykodisc, 1966): A double-album debut that shot out a multitude of musical directions. Taking traditional pop song structure and pulling things apart to see how they worked, it was a theme he would return to throughout his career.

FRANK ZAPPA: *Lumpy Gravy* (Rykodisc, 1967): A compilation of all sorts of experimental odds and ends, including some spoken word pieces (by people with their heads inside a piano) and orchestral recordings.

THE MOTHERS OF INVENTION: *We're Only in It for the Money* (Rykodisc, 1968): Zappa's lyrics were always observational and at a time of great social upheaval, he took on the authorities and their detractors, the hippies. An album that truly acknowledged its moment in time.

FRANK ZAPPA: *Hot Rats* (Rykodisc, 1969): Frank's releases without the band tended to be more experimental; this album finds him flirting with the fusion of jazz and rock music.

THE MOTHERS OF INVENTION: *Weasels Ripped My Flesh* (Rykodisc, 1970): A mix of live and studio recordings, this catches the band sailing through some pretty nifty instrumentals but also includes the by-now-expected experimental avant-garde noodlings.

FRANK ZAPPA: *The Grand Wazoo* (Rykodisc, 1973): Another album of jazz-rock (his third), but this time with a whole slew of musicians making up a mini-jazz orchestra.

FRANK ZAPPA: *Zappa in New York* (Rykodisc, 1978): Recorded live at the Palladium a couple of years before it was released, this album's reissue includes extra tracks left off by the label on its initial release.

FRANK ZAPPA: *You Are What You Is* (Rykodisc, 1981): Frank takes satirical aim at religion, disco, punk rock, and pretty much everything else making news as the "decade of greed" began.

FRANK ZAPPA: *Jazz from Hell* (Rykodisc, 1986): As Frank experimented with sounds beyond his guitar, he became fascinated with the Synclavier synthesizer. This instrumental album of jazz-rock was almost entirely recorded on the instrument and actually won Zappa a Grammy.

FRANK ZAPPA: *Civilization Phaze III* (Barking Pumpkin, 1995): This album took Zappa the best part of a decade to complete and includes his final recordings. It's a two-disc collection that features more of his Synclavier recordings, with some recycled spoken word pieces from *Lumpy Gravy*, as well as orchestral and piano compositions.

FRANK ZAPPA

INDEX

A

Entries in **boldface** denote albums; those in quotation marks denote singles.

B

F

K

O

P

X

Y

ABOUT THE AUTHOR

Since arriving at KCRW in the spring of 1998, Nic Harcourt has helped propel the careers of such artists as Norah Jones, Pete Yorn, David Gray, Dido, Sigur Rós, Starsailor, and Coldplay through live in-studio sessions during *Morning Becomes Eclectic*. Hosted by Nic, the station's signature music program can be heard weekday mornings from 9 AM to noon (PST) on public radio station 89.9 FM KCRW and worldwide—streaming live—at www.kcrw.com.

KCRW has long been regarded as a Los Angeles cultural institution, and Harcourt has raised the bar for the station by introducing such noteworthy events as station-sponsored "KCRW and KCRW.com Presents" concerts, the debut of the "Next Up!" concert series, and A Sounds Eclectic Evening, the first-ever KCRW-produced concert to benefit the station.

In 1999, Nic oversaw production of KCRW's fifth compact disc release of live in-studio performances, *Morning Becomes Eclectic* (Mammoth Records). Since then, he has also produced the sixth and seventh live CDs in the KCRW series, entitled *Sounds Eclectic* (Palm, 2001) and *Sounds Eclectic Too* (Palm, 2002).